Utilitarianism
and Its Critics

PHILOSOPHICAL TOPICS
PAUL EDWARDS, GENERAL EDITOR

Utilitarianism and Its Critics

Edited, with an Introduction, by

JONATHAN GLOVER

NEW COLLEGE, OXFORD UNIVERSITY

Macmillan Publishing Company
New York
Collier Macmillan Publishers
London

Editor: Helen McInnis
Production Supervisor: George Carr
Production Manager: Sandra Moore
Text and Cover Designer: Angela Foote
This book was set in Caledonia by Digitype, and printed and bound
by Quinn-Woodbine. The cover was printed by Phoenix Color Corp.

Macmillan Publishing Company
866 Third Avenue, New York, New York 10022

Collier Macmillan Canada, Inc.

Library of Congress Cataloging-in-Publication Data

Utilitarianism and its critics / edited with an introduction by Jonathan Glover.
    p.   cm. — (Philosophical topics)
  Bibliography: p.
  ISBN 0-02-344134-8
  1. Utilitarianism. I. Glover, Jonathan. II. Series:
Philosophical topics (New York, N.Y.)
B843.U843   1990   89-8279
171'.5 — dc20   CIP

Printing: 1 2 3 4 5 6 7   Year: 0 1 2 3 4 5 6

CONTENTS

PART THREE
PERSONS, JUSTICE, AND RIGHTS

PART FOUR
LIFE AND DEATH

PART FIVE
CONSEQUENCES AND CHARACTER

PART SIX
DIRECT AND OBLIQUE STRATEGIES

Utilitarianism
and Its Critics

INTRODUCTION

WE DO NOT reach adult life with open minds about right and wrong. Our ideas have been shaped by television, religion, books, and, probably most of all, by family and friends. The morality created in us by these influences may be a set of rules. They may forbid killing, lying, stealing, cruelty to animals, taking certain drugs, perhaps swearing, and perhaps certain sexual acts.

Part of growing up is noticing that the rules vary. To be brought up in a different place or a different historical period would be to absorb a set of rules only partly overlapping our own. And even within a single society, there are fundamental disagreements. Does the rule against killing rule out abortion, or capital punishment, or killing in war? Is sex outside marriage wrong? Is it always wrong for a doctor to lie to a dying patient? Is it right to use animal experiments to further medical research? Is it wrong for some people to be rich when others are desperately poor?

Part of becoming independent is to stand back from the rules we have absorbed. Are they better than the alternative moral beliefs other people hold? On what basis is the list of rules drawn up? How should we decide whether to add new ones or to give up some of them?

The Appeal of Utilitarianism

Part of the attraction of utilitarianism is that it claims to replace arbitrary-seeming rules by a morality with a single coherent basis. Acts should be judged as right or wrong according to their consequences.

1

Happiness is the only thing that is good in itself. Unhappiness is the only thing that is bad in itself. Everything else is only good or bad according to its tendency to produce happiness or unhappiness.

The conventional moral rules can seem to have a special authority. They are sometimes thought to have a religious basis. Even where religion is not invoked, they are often presented as a kind of ghostly legal system, commanding obedience despite some obscurity as to how these moral "laws" were enacted. For those who find this unsatisfactory, utilitarianism may be attractive. It sees morality as a human creation, serving human ends. Morality, like such unmystical activities as agriculture or house-building, has the function of serving people's happiness. The myth of commands and prohibitions is to be replaced by rational calculation of the consequences of different courses of action.

Utilitarianism appeals to the value many of us place on conscious experience. Some of us think that, in a universe without consciousness, it would not matter what happened. Unseen sunsets, however beautiful, are of no value at all. Things only matter because of their place in the lives of conscious beings. If you feel some indignation at the thought of some of the greatest paintings being bought as an investment and locked away unseen in bank vaults, you have something of this outlook.

For the utilitarian, the existence of consciousness is a necessary condition of things having value, but not a sufficient one. The beings who are conscious have to have some preferences, some likes and dislikes. Evolution might have thrown up nothing more than a species with "mere" consciousness: with sight, hearing, or some other sense, but whose members never minded what happened. Utilitarians think that, in such a world with no other species and with no possibility of that one evolving further, nothing would be good or bad.

Utilitarianism is rooted in the psychological response, found in some of us, that it does not matter what happens to a being with "mere" consciousness, but that it matters a lot whether, for instance, suffering occurs. Jeremy Bentham, the first systematically utilitarian philosopher, writing about the moral claims of animals, said, "The question is not, can they *reason?* nor can they *talk?* but can they *suffer?*"

Another part of the appeal of utilitarianism is its emphasis on the future rather than the past. Sometimes an old quarrel between individuals or between groups or nations is largely rooted in the past. "He broke his promise." "But she lied to me before that." "They are occupying our territory." "But it was ours before it was theirs." In cases like these, anyone who thinks "Forget the past. Let us look for ways of getting on together now" has something of the utilitarian spirit. Capital punishment is sometimes debated in terms of whether murderers deserve to die, or whether the state has the right to take life. There is the alternative view that the main thing is the effects of capital punishment. Perhaps the misery and horror of death row would be justified if a lot of murders were prevented, but not without such extra deterrent effect. To think this way is again to have something of the utilitarian outlook.

Another central feature of utilitarianism is its emphasis on equality. In evaluating consequences of different policies or courses of action, each person's interests are to be weighed equally: everyone is to count for one and no one for more than one. This gave a radical edge to Bentham's comments on existing society. He quotes Alexander Wedderburn ("at that time Attorney or Solicitor General, and afterwards successively Chief Justice of the Common Pleas, and Chancellor of England, under the successive titles of Lord Loughborough and Earl of Rosslyn") who said of utilitarianism, "This principle is a dangerous one." Bentham agreed that it *was* a danger to some: "In a government which had for its end in view the greatest happiness of the greatest number, Alexander Wedderburn might have been Attorney General and then Chancellor: but he would not have been Attorney General with £15,000 a year, nor Chancellor, with a peerage with a veto upon all justice, with £25,000 a year, and with 500 sinecures at his disposal, under the name of Ecclesiastical Benefices, besides *et caeteras*."

Bentham developed his utilitarian philosophy mainly in the context of thinking about the legal system. It is not a coincidence that utilitarianism was partly a reaction to the barbarous eighteenth-century penal system. The punishments imposed on offenders had some notable features that would affront anyone of utilitarian disposition. The principles cited in their justification often looked to the past, appealing to retribution rather than reform. There was no coherent way in which the principles were related to each other. And, most of all, it was much more clear that the penal system created misery than that it effectively prevented it.

Objections to Utilitarianism

Some of the objections to utilitarianism are practical. It is said to be unworkable. We can predict only some of the consequences of our actions. We have no way of measuring happiness. We cannot say, for instance, that the birth of a child gives the parents three hundred and seven times the happiness they would get from a holiday in France. There are further difficulties about comparing the happiness of different people. The weighing of consequences seems more often a matter of vague intuition than of scientific calculation.

Other objections are moral. The critics suggest that, even if utilitarianism is roughly workable, it gives the wrong answers.

Some object to the reduction of all value to happiness. Bentham said that happiness is pleasure and the absence of pain. But is cheerful hedonism really the only way of life that is valuable in itself? Others object that the largest total of happiness might be compatible with unjust inequalities in its distribution, or with policies that trample on people's rights. And utilitarianism has problems over life and death. Can it avoid saying that persistently unhappy people (or just people persistently below average happiness) should be killed if they cannot be cheered up? Would a utilitarian have a duty to have children if they were likely to be happy? Other objections have been to the way utilitarians seem to accept that "the end justifies the means." It is a form of consequentialism: the view that acts are never right or wrong in themselves, but only because of their consequences. But can it be right that whether or not to torture a child should be decided by cool calculation of consequences? What sort of people would we become if we adopted this attitude?

The moral objections, together with utilitarian attempts to meet them, are the topic of this book. No attractive morality could easily accept some of the apparent consequences of utilitarianism. And yet no attractive morality could avoid giving happiness and misery a central place. One strong stimulus to progress in ethics is the love-hate relationship with utilitarianism that this tension can generate.

PART ONE
UTILITARIANISM AND ITS FOUNDATIONS

PART OF THE attraction of utilitarianism is that it seems simpler and more coherent than the miscellaneous set of moral rules we may have been taught. The principle of utility seems to provide an answer to such questions as *"Why* is it wrong to lie or break promises?" But perhaps explaining how actions make for more or less happiness only defers the problem. *Why* is it right to increase happiness and wrong to diminish it?

One kind of answer appeals to what we are like. Bentham believed in a hedonist psychology: he thought of it as a scientific law that people always seek pleasure and avoid pain. He thought that morality is intelligible only as a means of realizing these unalterable goals. Many have thought this psychology excessively crude. Surely people often desire things other than their own pleasure? What about the desires for power, or fame, or virtue? Or altruistic desires? John Stuart Mill considered this objection when producing his own account of the basis of utilitarianism. He accepted that people want a great variety of things, but said that when people want to be, for instance, virtuous, this becomes part of their happiness. On this view, a less narrow psychology than Bentham's leaves the essential premise intact: the only thing people desire is their happiness.

Mill's "proof" of the principle of utility attempts to derive it from this hedonist psychology. The derivation has two stages. He first has to show that happiness is not only what people do want, but also something that they should want. And then he has to show that wanting one's own happiness justifies pursuit of the general happiness.

Both parts of the derivation seem likely to have problems. From the fact that someone wants something, it does not seem intuitively to follow that what they want is morally desirable. (There are people who, for reasons of sadism or revenge, want others to suffer.) And the second step may also be hard to make. Perhaps there is a conflict between my own happiness and that of people in general. (I inherit some money. Giving it to charity may do most for the general happiness, but spending it on a trip around the world may do most for my happiness.) Unless such conflicts can be explained away, the psychological derivation of the utilitarian morality seems to be in trouble. The morality tells me to do what the psychology says is impossible. The truth of the hedonist psychology may exclude rather than support utilitarianism. Mill believes that these difficulties can be overcome, and his "proof" is a classic attempt to do this. G.E. Moore's discussion of the attempt is a classic statement of the criticisms of it.

An alternative defense of utilitarianism starts not with what we desire, but with our intuitive beliefs about right and wrong: our "moral intuitions," as philosophers sometimes call them. Henry Sidgwick's claim is that "the Morality of Common Sense may be truly represented as unconsciously Utilitarian." The suggestion is not that every rule of commonsense morality is precisely fitted to increase happiness. It is rather that the rules have a tendency to do so and that the utilitarian principle is the most plausible way of explaining them in terms of a systematic basis. Sidgwick thinks that utilitarians can succeed in showing their principle to be "the scientifically complete and systematically reflective form of that regulation of conduct, which through the whole course of human history has always tended substantially in the same direction."

One problem for this view concerns the moral consensus that the principle of utility is supposed to fit. In many societies there are deep moral divisions, so that it may be hard to see what counts as the Morality of Common Sense. And the differences of outlook between different societies may raise doubts about generalizations as to the direction in which morality has tended "through the whole course of human history." Perhaps many of the differences can be explained away. After all, utilitarians consciously aiming at maximizing happiness may differ about the best way of doing so. But one danger is that the hypothesis loses tautness, with believers showing a relaxed willingness to see any rule as being in some way utilitarian. It is worth bearing in mind alternative accounts, such as sociobiological explanations of moral rules in terms of gene survival, or Marxist explanations of moral codes in terms of the interests of a dominant class, or feminist explanations in terms of male dominance. These different accounts can all be made to fit quite a lot of the facts about morality, but the question is whether the evidence supports the hypothesis of "unconscious utilitarianism" (or whichever other is the preferred theory) so much better than the others as to establish its truth. (There is also a pluralistic view, that the morality of any given society may have arisen from a multitude of sources, being shaped by religious beliefs, by conflicts or compromises between different groups, by genetic factors, and so on.)

Utilitarianism's evolution from Bentham through Mill to Sidgwick was one of growing intellectual sophistication. Bentham wrote primarily as a propagandist of political and social reform, with a robustness and vigor that perhaps made up for the simplicity of his philosophical and psychological views, his obsessive impulse to classify, and even for his cranky and fussy stipulations about such details as the bedding to be used in workhouses. Mill had far more awareness of psychological complexity and of the strength of outlooks other than the utilitarian one. And Sidgwick's *Methods of Ethics*, although one of the most boring books in moral philosophy, is also, through its thoroughness and awareness of intellectual complexity, one of the greatest. But there is another contrast that is at least as marked: between the utilitarian radicalism of Bentham and Mill and the utilitarian conservatism of Sidgwick. Bentham saw commonsense morality as something needing surgery on utilitarian lines: "Hence we see the emptiness of all those rhapsodies of common-place morality, which consist in the taking of such names as lust, cruelty, and avarice, and branding them with marks of reprobation: applied to the *thing*, they are false; applied to the *name*, they are true indeed, but nugatory. Would you do a real service to mankind, show then the cases in which sexual desire *merits* the name of lust; displeasure, that of cruelty; and pecuniary interest, that of avarice." Sidgwick, on the other hand, can seem very comfortable with the English code of morals as it was in 1874: "It is only on Utilitarian principles that we can account for anomalous difference which the morality of Common Sense has always made between the two sexes as regards the simple offence of unchastity . . . [This] can only be justified by taking into account the greater interest that society has in maintaining a high standard of female chastity. For the degradation of this standard must strike at the root of family life, by impairing men's security in the exercise of their parental affections: but there is no corresponding consequence of male unchastity, which may therefore prevail to a considerable extent without imperilling the very existence of the family, though it impairs its wellbeing."

This raises another problem for Sidgwick's defense of utilitarianism. Suppose the moral sense *is* unconsciously utilitarian. How impressive we find this will depend on how impressed we are with conventional morality. How far would the truth of Sidgwick's hypothesis give someone a reason for being a utilitarian? (Suppose it could be shown that commonsense morality had been shaped by unconscious racism or, as Sidgwick's remarks may suggest, by unconscious sexism?)

Some ways of arguing for utilitarianism are based neither on psychology nor on appeals to moral intuitions. R.M. Hare's derivation is a case in point. He believes that purely logical investigation of the properties of moral judgments shows that they are universalizable: that they entail identical judgments about the rightness or wrongness of all relevantly similar cases. So, if I say that I ought to behave in a certain way toward others, it follows that, if the situation were exactly reversed, they ought to behave in the same way toward me. On this basis, he argues that making moral judgments constrains us within the perspective of utilitarian impartiality, where desires count equally, no matter whose they are.

Both the premise about moral judgments and the derivation from it of utilitarianism are controversial. But, independent of those issues, Hare's claim is a striking articulation of one side of a central debate in ethics. Should we see our moral intuitions as an unreliable product of social conditioning, and look for some independent guide to right and wrong? Or is ethics, because a matter of working out *our* values, unavoidably rooted in moral intuitions?

JEREMY BENTHAM*

Of the Principle of Utility

I. NATURE HAS PLACED mankind under the governance of two sovereign masters, *pain* and *pleasure*. It is for them alone to point out what we ought to do, as well as to determine what we shall do. On the one hand the standard of right and wrong, on the other the chain of causes and effects, are fastened to their throne. They govern us in all we do, in all we say, in all we think: every effort we can make to throw off our subjection, will serve but to demonstrate and confirm it. In words a man may pretend to abjure their empire: but in reality he will remain subject to it all the while. The *principle of utility*[1] recognises this subjection, and assumes it for the foundation of that system, the object of which is to rear the fabric of felicity by the hands of reason and of

---

*From *An Introduction to the Principles of Morals and Legislation*, Chapter 1.
[1]Note by the author, July 1822.
To this denomination has of late been added, or substituted, the *greatest happiness* or *greatest felicity principle*: this for shortness, instead of saying at length *that principle* which states the greatest happiness of all those whose interest is in question, as being the right and proper, and only right and proper and universally desirable, end of human action: of human action in every situation, and in particular in that of a functionary or set of functionaries exercising the powers of Government. The word *utility* does not so clearly point to the ideas of *pleasure* and *pain* as the words *happiness* and *felicity* do: nor does it lead us to the consideration of the *number*, of the interests affected; to the *number*, as being the circumstance, which contributes, in the largest proportion, to the formation of the standard here in question, the *standard of right and wrong*, by which alone the propriety of human conduct, in every situation, can with propriety be tried. This want of a sufficiently manifest connexion between the ideas of *happiness* and *pleasure* on the one hand, and the idea of *utility* on the other, I have every now and then found operating, and with but too much efficiency, as a bar to the acceptance, that might otherwise have been given, to this principle.

law. Systems which attempt to question it, deal in sounds instead of senses, in caprice instead of reason, in darkness instead of light.

But enough of metaphor and declamation: it is not by such means that moral science is to be improved.

2. The principle of utility is the foundation of the present work: it will be proper therefore at the outset to give an explicit and determinate account of what is meant by it. By the principle[2] of utility is meant that principle which approves or disapproves of every action whatsoever, according to the tendency which it appears to have to augment or diminish the happiness of the party whose interest is in question: or, what is the same thing in other words, to promote or to oppose that happiness. I say of every action whatsoever; and therefore not only of every action of a private individual, but of every measure of government.

3. By utility is meant that property in any object, whereby it tends to produce benefit, advantage, pleasure, good, or happiness, (all this in the present case comes to the same thing) or (what comes again to the same thing) to prevent the happening of mischief, pain, evil, or unhappiness to the party whose interest is considered: if that party be the community in general, then the happiness of the community: if a particular individual, then the happiness of that individual.

4. The interest of the community is one of the most general expressions that can occur in the phraseology of morals: no wonder that the meaning of it is often lost. When it has a meaning, it is this. The community is a fictitious *body*, composed of the individual persons who are considered as constituting as it were its *members*. The interest of the community then is, what? — the sum of the interests of the several members who compose it.

5. It is in vain to talk of the interest of the community, without understanding what is the interest of the individual.[3] A thing is said to promote the interest, or to be *for* the interest, of an individual, when it tends to add to the sum total of his pleasures: or, what comes to the same thing, to diminish the sum total of his pains.

6. An action then may be said to be conformable to the principle of

---

[2] The word principle is derived from the Latin *principium*: which seems to be compounded of the two words *primus*, first, or chief, and *cipium*, a termination which seems to be derived from *capio*, to take, as in *mancipium, municipium*; to which are analogous, *auceps, forceps*, and others. It is a term of very vague and very extensive signification: it is applied to any thing which is conceived to serve as a foundation or beginning to any series of operations: in some cases, of physical operations; but of mental operations in the present case.

The principle here in question may be taken for an act of the mind; a sentiment; a sentiment of approbation; a sentiment which, when applied to an action, approves of its utility, as that quality of it by which the measure of approbation or disapprobation bestowed upon it ought to be governed.

[3] Interest is one of those words, which not having any superior *genus*, cannot in the ordinary way be defined.

utility, or, for shortness' sake, to utility, (meaning with respect to the community at large) when the tendency it has to augment the happiness of the community is greater than any it has to diminish it.

7. A measure of government (which is but a particular kind of action, performed by a particular person or persons) may be said to be conformable to or dictated by the principle of utility, when in like manner the tendency which it has to augment the happiness of the community is greater than any which it has to diminish it.

8. When an action, or in particular a measure of government, is supposed by a man to be conformable to the principle of utility, it may be convenient, for the purposes of discourse, to imagine a kind of law or dictate, called a law or dictate of utility; and to speak of the action in question, as being conformable to such law or dictate.

9. A man may be said to be a partisan of the principle of utility, when the approbation or disapprobation he annexes to any action, or to any measure, is determined by and proportioned to the tendency which he conceives it to have to augment or to diminish the happiness of the community: or in other words, to its conformity or uncomformity to the laws or dictates of utility.

10. Of an action that is conformable to the principle of utility one may always say either that it is one that ought to be done, or at least that it is not one that ought not to be done. One may say also, that it is right it should be done; at least that it is not wrong it should be done: that it is a right action; at least that it is not a wrong action. When thus interpreted, the words *ought*, and *right* and *wrong*, and others of that stamp, have a meaning: when otherwise, they have none.

11. Has the rectitude of this principle been ever formally contested? It should seem that it had, by those who have not known what they have been meaning. Is it susceptible of any direct proof? it should seem not: for that which is used to prove every thing else, cannot itself be proved: a chain of proofs must have their commencement somewhere. To give such proof is as impossible as it is needless.

12. Not that there is or ever has been that human creature breathing, however stupid or perverse, who has not on many, perhaps on most occasions of his life, deferred to it. By the natural constitution of the human frame, on most occasions of their lives men in general embrace this principle, without thinking of it: if not for the ordering of their own actions, yet for the trying of their own actions, as well as of those of other men. There have been, at the same time, not many, perhaps, even of the most intelligent, who have been disposed to embrace it purely and without reserve. There are even few who have not taken some occasion or other to quarrel with it, either on account of their not understanding always how to apply it, or on account of some prejudice or other which they were afraid to examine into, or could not bear to part with. For such is the stuff that man is made of: in principle and in

practice, in a right track and in a wrong one, the rarest of all human qualities is consistency.

13. When a man attempts to combat the principle of utility, it is with reasons drawn, without his being aware of it, from that very principle itself.[4] His arguments, if they prove any thing, prove not that the principle is *wrong*, but that, according to the applications he supposes to be made of it, it is *misapplied.* Is it possible for a man to move the earth? Yes; but he must first find out another earth to stand upon.

14. To disprove the propriety of it by arguments is impossible; but, from the causes that have been mentioned, or from some confused or partial view of it, a man may happen to be disposed not to relish it. Where this is the case, if he thinks the settling of his opinions on such a subject worth the trouble, let him take the following steps and at length, perhaps, he may come to reconcile himself to it.

1. Let him settle with himself, whether he would wish to discard this

---

[4]"The principle of utility (I have heard it said) is a dangerous principle: it is dangerous on certain occasions to consult it.' This is as much as to say, what? that it is not consonant to utility, to consult utility: in short, that it is *not* consulting it, to consult it.

Addition by the Author, July 1822.

Not long after the publication of the Fragment on Government, anno 1776, in which, in the character of an all-comprehensive and all-commanding principle, the principle of *utility* was brought to view, one person by whom observation to the above effect was made was *Alexander Wedderburn*, at that time Attorney or Solicitor General, afterwards successively Chief Justice of the Common Pleas, and Chancellor of England, under the successive titles of Lord Loughborough and Earl of Rosslyn. It was made — not indeed in my hearing, but in the hearing of a person by whom it was almost immediately communicated to me. So far from being self-contradictory, it was a shrewd and perfectly true one. By that distinguished functionary, the state of the Government was thoroughly understood: by the obscure individual, at that time not so much as supposed to be so: his disquisitions had not been as yet applied, with any thing like a comprehensive view, to the field of Constitutional Law, nor therefore to those features of the English Government, by which the greatest happiness of the ruling *one* with or without that of a favoured few, are now so plainly seen to be the only ends to which the course of it has at any time been directed. The *principle of utility* was an appellative, at that time employed — employed by me, as it had been by others, to designate that which in a more perspicuous and instructive manner, may, as above, be designated by the name of the *greatest happiness principle.* 'This principle (said Wedderburn) is a dangerous one.' Saying so, he said that which, to a certain extent, is strictly true: a principle, which lays down, as the only *right* and justifiable end of Government, the greatest happiness of the greatest number — how can it be denied to be a dangerous one? dangerous it unquestionably is, to every government which has for its *actual* end or object, the greatest happiness of a certain *one*, with or without the addition of some comparatively small number of others, whom it is a matter of pleasure or accommodation to him to admit, each of them, to a share in the concern, on the footing of so many junior partners. *Dangerous* it therefore really was, to the interest — the sinister interest — of all those functionaries, himself included, whose interest it was, to maximise delay, vexation, and expense, in judicial and other modes of procedure, for the sake of the profit, extractible out of the expense. In a Government which had for its end in view the greatest happiness of the greatest number, Alexander Wedderburn might have been Attorney General and then Chancellor: but he would not have been Attorney General with £15,000 a year, nor Chancellor, with a peerage with a veto upon all justice, with £25,000 a year, and with 500 sinecures at his disposal, under the name of Ecclesiastical Benefices, besides *et caeteras.*

principle altogether; if so, let him consider what it is that all his reasonings (in matters of politics especially) can amount to?

2. If he would, let him settle with himself, whether he would judge and act without any principle, or whether there is any other he would judge and act by?

3. If there be, let him examine and satisfy himself whether the principle he thinks he has found is really any separate intelligible principle; or whether it be not a mere principle in words, a kind of phrase, which at bottom expresses neither more nor less than the mere averment of his own unfounded sentiments; that is, what in another person he might be apt to call caprice?

4. If he is inclined to think that his own approbation or disapprobation, annexed to the idea of an act, without any regard to its consequences, is a sufficient foundation for him to judge and act upon, let him ask himself whether his sentiment is to be a standard of right and wrong, with respect to every other man, or whether every man's sentiment has the same privilege of being a standard to itself?

5. In the first case, let him ask himself whether his principle is not despotical, and hostile to all the rest of human race?

6. In the second case, whether it is not anarchical, and whether at this rate there are not as many different standards of right and wrong as there are men? and whether even to the sane man, the same thing, which is right to-day, may not (without the least change in its nature) be wrong to-morrow? and whether the same thing is not right and wrong in the same place at the same time? and in either case, whether all argument is not at an end? and whether, when two men have said, "I like this," and "I don't like it," they can (upon such a principle) have any thing more to say?

7. If he should have said to himself, No: for that the sentiment which he proposes as a standard must be grounded on reflection, let him say on what particulars the reflection is to turn? if on particulars having relation to the utility of the act, then let him say whether this is not deserting his own principle, and borrowing assistance from that very one in opposition to which he sets it up: or if not on those particulars, on what other particulars?

8. If he should be for compounding the matter, and adopting his own principle in part, and the principle of utility in part, let him say how far he will adopt it?

9. When he has settled with himself where he will stop, then let him ask himself how he justifies to himself the adopting it so far? and why he will not adopt it any farther?

10. Admitting any other principle than the principle of utility to be a right principle, a principle that it is right for a man to pursue; admitting (what is not true) that the word *right* can have a meaning without reference to utility, let him say whether there is any such thing as a

motive that a man can have to pursue the dictates of it: if there is, let him say what that motive is, and how it is to be distinguished from those which enforce the dictates of utility: if not, then lastly let him say what it is this other principle can be good for?

JOHN STUART MILL*

Of What Sort of Proof the Principle of Utility is Susceptible

IT HAS ALREADY been remarked, that questions of ultimate ends do not admit of proof, in the ordinary acceptation of the term. To be incapable of proof by reasoning is common to all first principles; to the first premises of our knowledge, as well as to those of our conduct. But the former, being matters of fact, may be the subject of a direct appeal to the faculties which judge of fact — namely, our senses, and our internal consciousness. Can an appeal be made to the same faculties on questions of practical ends? Or by what other faculty is cognisance taken of them?

Questions about ends are, in other words, questions what things are desirable. The utilitarian doctrine is, that happiness is desirable, and the only thing desirable, as an end; all other things being only desirable as means to that end. What ought to be required of this doctrine — what conditions is it requisite that the doctrine should fulfil — to make good its claim to be believed?

The only proof capable of being given that an object is visible, is that people actually see it. The only proof that a sound is audible, is that people hear it: and so of the other sources of our experience. In like manner, I apprehend, the sole evidence it is possible to produce that anything is desirable, is that people do actually desire it. If the end which the utilitarian doctrine proposes to itself were not, in theory and in practice, acknowledged to be an end, nothing could ever convince any person that it was so. No reason can be given why the general

*From John Stuart Mill: *Utilitarianism*, Chapter 4.

happiness is desirable, except that each person, so far as he believes it to be attainable, desires his own happiness. This, however, being a fact, we have not only all the proof which the case admits of, but all which it is possible to require, that happiness is a good: that each person's happiness is a good to that person, and the general happiness, therefore, a good to the aggregate of all persons. Happiness has made out its title as *one* of the ends of conduct, and consequently one of the criteria of morality.

But it has not, by this alone, proved itself to be the sole criterion. To do that, it would seem, by the same rule, necessary to show, not only that people desire happiness, but that they never desire anything else. Now it is palpable that they do desire things which, in common language, are decidedly distinguished from happiness. They desire, for example, virtue, and the absence of vice, no less really than pleasure and the absence of pain. The desire of virtue is not as universal, but it is as authentic a fact, as the desire of happiness. And hence the opponents of the utilitarian standard deem that they have a right to infer that there are other ends of human action besides happiness, and that happiness is not the standard of approbation and disapprobation.

But does the utilitarian doctrine deny that people desire virtue, or maintain that virtue is not a thing to be desired? The very reverse. It maintains not only that virtue is to be desired, but that it is to be desired disinterestedly, for itself. Whatever may be the opinion of utilitarian moralists as to the original conditions by which virtue is made virtue; however they may believe (as they do) that actions and dispositions are only virtuous because they promote another end than virtue; yet this being granted, and it having been decided, from considerations of this description, what *is* virtuous, they not only place virtue at the very head of the things which are good as means to the ultimate end, but they also recognise as a psychological fact the possibility of its being, to the individual, a good in itself, without looking to any end beyond it; and hold, that the mind is not in a right state, not in a state conformable to Utility, not in the state most conducive to the general happiness, unless it does love virtue in this manner — as a thing desirable in itself, even although, in the individual instance, it should not produce those other desirable consequences which it tends to produce, and on account of which it is held to be virtue. This opinion is not, in the smallest degree, a departure from the Happiness principle. The ingredients of happiness are very various, and each of them is desirable in itself, and not merely when considered as swelling an aggregate. The principle of utility does not mean that any given pleasure, as music, for instance, or any given exemption from pain, as for example health, is to be looked upon as means to a collective something termed happiness, and to be desired on that account. They are desired and desirable in and for themselves; besides being means, they are a part of the end. Virtue, according to the utilitarian doctrine, is not naturally and originally part of the end, but it is capable of becoming so; and in those who love it disinterestedly it has become so, and is desired and cherished, not as a means to happiness, but as a part of their happiness.

To illustrate this farther, we may remember that virtue is not the only thing, originally a means, and which if it were not a means to anything else, would be and remain indifferent, but which by association with what it is a means to, comes to be desired for itself, and that too with the utmost intensity. What, for example, shall we say of the love of money? There is nothing originally more desirable about money than about any heap of glittering pebbles. Its worth is solely that of the things which it will buy; the desires for other things than itself, which it is a means of gratifying. Yet the love of money is not only one of the strongest moving forces of human life, but money is, in many cases, desired in and for itself; the desire to possess it is often stronger than the desire to use it, and goes on increasing when all the desires which point to ends beyond it, to be compassed by it, are falling off. It may, then, be said truly, that money is desired not for the sake of an end, but as part of the end. From being a means to happiness, it has come to be itself a principal ingredient of the individual's conception of happiness. The same may be said of the majority of the great objects of human life — power, for example, or fame; except that to each of these there is a certain amount of immediate pleasure annexed, which has at least the semblance of being naturally inherent of fame, is the immense aid they give to the attainment of in them; a thing which cannot be said of money. Still, however, the strongest natural attraction, both of power and our other wishes; and it is the strong association thus generated between them and all our objects of desire, which gives to the direct desire of them the intensity it often assumes, so as in some characters to surpass in strength all other desires. In these cases the means have become a part of the end, and a more important part of it than any of the things which they are means to. What was once desired as an instrument for the attainment of happiness, has come to be desired for its own sake. In being desired for its own sake it is, however, desired as *part* of happiness. The person is made, or thinks he would be made, happy by its mere possession; and is made unhappy by failure to obtain it. The desire of it is not a different thing from the desire of happiness, any more than the love of music, or the desire of health. They are included in happiness. They are some of the elements of which the desire of happiness is made up. Happiness is not an abstract idea, but a concrete whole; and these are some of its parts. And the utilitarian standard sanctions and approves their being so. Life would be a poor thing, very ill provided with sources of happiness, if there were not this provision of nature, by which things originally indifferent, but conducive to, or otherwise associated with, the satisfaction of our primitive desires, become in themselves sources of pleasure more valuable than the primitive pleasures, both in permanency, in the space of human existence that they are capable of covering, and even in intensity.

Virtue, according to the utilitarian conception, is a good of this description. There was no original desire of it, or motive to it, save its conduciveness to pleasure, and especially to protection from pain. But through the association thus formed, it may be felt a good in itself, and desired as such with as great intensity as any other good; and with this difference between it and the love of money, of power, or of fame, that all of these may, and often do, render the individual noxious to the other members of the society to which he belongs, whereas there is nothing which makes him so much a blessing to them as the cultivation of the disinterested love of virtue. And consequently, the utilitarian standard, while it tolerates and approves those other acquired desires, up to the point beyond which they would be more injurious to the general happiness than promotive of it, enjoins and requires the cultivation of the love of virtue up to the greatest strength possible, as being above all things important to the general happiness.

It results from the preceding considerations, that there is in reality nothing desired except happiness. Whatever is desired otherwise than as a means to some end beyond itself, and ultimately to happiness, is desired as itself a part of happiness, and is not desired for itself until it has become so. Those who desire virtue for its own sake, desire it either because the consciousness of it is a pleasure, or because the consciousness of being without it is a pain, or for both reasons united; as in truth the pleasure and pain seldom exist separately, but almost always together, the same person feeling pleasure in the degree of virtue attained, and pain in not having attained more. If one of these gave him no pleasure, and the other no pain, he would not love or desire virtue, or would desire it only for the other benefits which it might produce to himself or to persons whom he cared for.

We have now, then, an answer to the question, of what sort of proof the principle of utility is susceptible. If the opinion which I have now stated is psychologically true — if human nature is so constituted as to desire nothing which is not either a part of happiness or a means of happiness, we can have no other proof, and we require no other, that these are the only things desirable. If so, happiness is the sole end of human action, and the promotion of it the test by which to judge of all human conduct; from whence it necessarily follows that it must be the criterion of morality, since a part is included in the whole.

And now to decide whether this is really so; whether mankind does desire nothing for itself but that which is a pleasure to them, or of which the absence is a pain; we have evidently arrived at a question of fact and experience, dependent, like all similar questions, upon evidence. It can only be determined by practised self-consciousness and self-observation, assisted by observation of others. I believe that these sources of evidence, impartially consulted, will declare that desiring a thing and finding it pleasant, aversion to it and thinking of it as painful, are phenomena entirely inseparable, or rather two parts of the same phenomenon; in strictness of language, two different modes of naming the same psychological fact: that to think of an object as desirable (unless for the sake of its consequences), and to think of it as pleasant, are one and the same thing; and that to desire anything, except in proportion as the idea of it is pleasant, is a physical and metaphysical impossibility.

So obvious does this appear to me, that I expect it will hardly be disputed: and the objection made will be, not that desire can possibly be directed to anything ultimately except pleasure and exemption from pain, but that the will is a different thing from desire; that a person of confirmed virtue, or any other person whose purposes are fixed, carries out his purposes without any thought of the pleasure he has in contemplating them, or expects to derive from their fulfilment; and persists in acting on them, even though these pleasures are much diminished, by changes in his character or decay of his passive sensibilities, or are out-weighed by the pains which the pursuit of the purposes may bring upon him. All this I fully admit, and have stated it elsewhere, as positively and emphatically as any one. Will, the active phenomenon, is a different thing from desire, the state of passive sensibility, and though originally an offshoot from it, may in time take root and detach itself from the parent stock; so much so, that in the case of an habitual purpose, instead of willing the thing because we desire it, we often desire it only because we will it. This, however, is but an instance of that familiar fact, the power of habit, and is nowise confined to the case of virtuous actions. Many indifferent things, which men originally did from a motive of some sort, they continue to do from habit. Sometimes this is done unconsciously, the consciousness coming only after the action: at other times with conscious volition, but volition which has become habitual, and is put in operation by the force of habit, in opposition perhaps to the deliberate preference, as often happens with those who have contracted habits of vicious or hurtful indulgence. Third and last comes the case in which the habitual act of will in the individual instance is not in contradiction to the general intention prevailing at other times, but in fulfilment of it; as in the case of the person of confirmed virtue, and of all who pursue deliberately and consistently any determinate end. The distinction between will and desire thus understood is an authentic and highly important psychological fact; but the fact consists solely in this—that will, like all other parts of our constitution, is amenable to habit, and that we may will from habit what we no longer desire for itself, or desire only because we will it. It is not the less true that will, in the beginning, is entirely produced by desire; including in that term the repelling influence of pain as well as the attractive one of pleasure. Let us take into consideration, no longer the person who has a confirmed will to do right, but him in whom that virtuous will is still feeble, conquerable by temptation, and not to be fully relied on; by what means can it be strengthened? How can the will to be virtuous, where it does not exist in sufficient force, be implanted or awakened? Only by making the person *desire* virtue — by making him think of it in a pleasurable light, or of its absence in a painful one. It is by associating the doing right with pleasure, or the doing wrong with pain, or by eliciting and impressing and bringing home to the person's experience the pleasure naturally involved in the one or the pain in the other, that it is possible to call forth that will to be virtuous, which, when confirmed, acts without any thought of either pleasure or pain. Will is the child of desire, and passes out of the dominion of its parent only to come under that of habit. That which is the result of habit affords no presumption of being intrinsically good; and there would be no reason for wishing that the purpose of virtue should become independent of pleasure and pain, were it not that the influence of the pleasurable and painful associations which prompt to virtue is not sufficiently to be depended on for unerring constancy of action until it has acquired the support of habit. Both in feeling and in conduct, habit is the only thing which imparts certainty; and it is because of the importance to others of being able to rely absolutely on one's feelings and conduct, and to oneself of being able to rely on one's own, that the will to do right ought to be cultivated into this habitual independence. In other words, this state of the will is a means to good, not intrinsically a good; and does not contradict the doctrine that nothing is a good to human beings but in so far as it is either itself pleasurable, or a means of attaining pleasure or averting pain.

But if this doctrine be true, the principle of utility is proved. Whether it is or not must now be left to the consideration of the thoughtful reader.

G.E. MOORE*

⁂

Criticism of Mill's "Proof"

⁂

MILL HAS MADE as naïve and artless a use of the naturalistic fallacy as anybody could desire. "Good," he tells us, means "desirable," and you can only find out what is desirable by seeking to find out what is actually desired. This is, of course, only one step towards the proof of Hedonism; for it may be, as Mill goes on to say, that other things beside pleasure are desired. Whether or not pleasure is the only thing desired is, as Mill himself admits, (p. 58), a psychological question, to which we shall presently proceed. The important step for Ethics is this one just taken, the step which pretends to prove that "good" means "desired."

Well, the fallacy in this step is so obvious, that it is quite wonderful how Mill failed to see it. The fact is that "desirable" does not mean "able to be desired" as "visible" means "able to be seen." The desirable means simply what *ought* to be desired or *deserves* to be desired; just as the detestable means not what can be but what ought to be detested and the damnable what deserves to be damned. Mill has, then, smuggled in, under cover of the word "desirable," the very notion about which he ought to be quite clear. 'Desirable' does indeed mean "what it is good to desire"; but when this is understood, it is no longer plausible to say that our only test of *that*, is what is actually desired. Is it merely a tautology when the Prayer Book talks of *good* desires? Are not *bad* desires also possible? Nay, we find Mill himself talking of a "better and nobler object of desire" (p. 10), as if, after all, what is desired were not *ipso facto* good, and good in proportion to the amount it is desired.

*From *Principia Ethica*, Chapter 3.

Moreover, if the desired is *ipso facto* the good; then the good is *ipso facto* the motive of our actions, and there can be no question of finding motives for doing it, as Mill is at such pains to do. If Mill's explanation of "desirable" be *true*, then his statement (p. 26) that the rule of action may be *confounded* with the motive of it is untrue: for the motive of action will then be according to him *ipso facto* its rule; there can be no distinction between the two, and therefore no confusion, and thus he has contradicted himself flatly. These are specimens of the contradictions, which, as I have tried to shew, must always follow from the use of the naturalistic fallacy; and I hope I need now say no more about the matter.

Well, then, the first step by which Mill has attempted to establish his Hedonism is simply fallacious. He has attempted to establish the identity of the good with the desired, by confusing the proper sense of "desirable," in which it denotes that which it is good to desire, with the sense which it would bear if it were analogous to such words as "visible." If "desirable" is to be identical with "good," then it must bear one sense; and if it is to be identical with 'desired,' then it must bear quite another sense. And yet to Mill's contention that the desired is necessarily good, it is quite essential that these two senses of "desirable" should be the same. If he holds they are the same, then he has contradicted himself elsewhere; if he holds they are not the same, then the first step in his proof of Hedonism is absolutely worthless. . . .

Mill admits, as I have said, that pleasure is not the only thing we actually desire. "The desire of virtue," he says, "is not as universal, but it is as authentic a fact, as the desire of happiness." [1] And again, "Money is, in many cases, desired in and for itself." [2] These admissions are, of course, in naked and glaring contradiction with his argument that pleasure is the only thing desirable, because it is the only thing desired. How then does Mill even attempt to avoid this contradiction? His chief argument seems to be that "virtue," "money" and other such objects, when they are thus desired in and for themselves, are desired only as "a part of happiness." [3] Now what does this mean? Happiness, as we saw, has been defined by Mill, as "pleasure and the absence of pain." Does Mill mean to say that "money," these actual coins, which he admits to be desired in and for themselves, are a part either of pleasure or of the absence of pain? Will he maintain that those coins themselves are in my mind, and actually a part of my pleasant feelings? If this is to be said, all words are useless: nothing can possibly be distinguished from anything else; if these two things are not distinct, what on earth is? We shall hear next that this table is really and truly

[1] p. 53.
[2] p. 55.
[3] pp. 56–57.

the same thing as this room; that a cab-horse is in fact indistinguishable from St Paul's Cathedral; that this book of Mill's which I hold in my hand, because it was his pleasure to produce it, is now and at this moment a part of the happiness which he felt many years ago and which has so long ceased to be. Pray consider a moment what this contemptible nonsense really means. "Money," says Mill, "is only desirable as a means to happiness." Perhaps so; but what then? "Why," says Mill, "money is undoubtedly desired for its own sake." "Yes, go on," say we. "Well," says Mill, 'if money is desired for its own sake, it must be desirable as an end-in-itself: I have said so myself." "Oh," say we, "but you also said just now that it was only desirable as a means." "I own I did," says Mill, "but I will try to patch up matters, by saying that what is only a means to an end, is the same thing as a part of that end." I daresay the public won't notice." And the public haven't noticed. Yet this is certainly what Mill has done. He has broken down the distinction between means and ends, upon the precise observance of which his Hedonism rests. And he has been compelled to do this, because he has failed to distinguish "end" in the sense of what is desirable, from "end" in the sense of what is desired: a distinction which, nevertheless, both the present argument and his whole book presupposes. . .

Mill, for instance, as we saw, declares: "Each person, so far as he believes it to be attainable, desires his own happiness" (p. 53). And he offers this as a reason why the general happiness is desirable. We have seen that to regard it as such, involves, in the first place, the naturalistic fallacy. But moreover, even if that fallacy were not a fallacy, it could only be a reason for Egoism and not for Utilitarianism. Mill's argument is as follows: A man desires his own happiness; therefore his own happiness is desirable. Further: A man desires nothing but his own happiness; therefore his own happiness is alone desirable. We have next to remember, that everybody, according to Mill, so desires his own happiness: and then it will follow that everybody's happiness is alone desirable. And this is simply a contradiction in terms.

HENRY SIDGWICK*

Utilitarianism and Commonsense Morality

CAN WE THEN, between this Scylla and Charybdis of ethical inquiry, avoiding on the one hand doctrines that merely bring us back to common opinion with all its imperfections, and on the other hand doctrines that lead us round in a circle, find any way of obtaining self-evident moral principles of real significance? It would be disheartening to have to regard as altogether illusory the strong instinct of Common Sense that points to the existence of such principles, and the deliberate convictions of the long line of moralists who have enunciated them. At the same time, the more we extend our knowledge of man and his environment, the more we realise the vast variety of human natures and circumstances that have existed in different ages and countries, the less disposed we are to believe that there is any definite code of absolute rules, applicable to all human beings without exception. And we shall find, I think, that the truth lies between these two conclusions. There are certain absolute practical principles, the truth of which, when they are explicitly stated, is manifest; but they are of too abstract a nature, and too universal in their scope, to enable us to ascertain by immediate application of them what we ought to do in any particular case; particular duties have still to be determined by some other method.

One such principle was given in . . . this Book; where I pointed out that whatever action any of us judges to be right for himself, he implicitly judges to be right for all similar persons in similar circumstances. Or, as we may otherwise put it, "if a kind of conduct that is right (or

*From *The Methods of Ethics*, Book 3, Chapter 13, and Book 4, Chapters 2 and 3.

wrong) for me is not right (or wrong) for some one else, it must be on the ground of some difference between the two cases, other than the fact that I and he are different persons." A corresponding proposition may be stated with equal truth in respect of what ought to be done to—not by—different individuals. These principles have been most widely recognised, not in their most abstract and universal form, but in their special application to the situation of two (or more) individuals similarly related to each other: as so applied, they appear in what is popularly known as the Golden Rule, "Do to others as you would have them do to you." This formula is obviously unprecise in statement; for one might wish for another's co-operation in sin, and be willing to reciprocate it. Nor is it even true to say that we ought to do to others only what we think it right for them to do to us; for no one will deny that there may be differences in the circumstances—and even in the natures—of two individuals, A and B, which would make it wrong for A to treat B in the way in which it is right for B to treat A. In short the self-evident principle strictly stated must take some such negative form as this; 'it cannot be right for A to treat B in a manner in which it would be wrong for B to treat A, merely on the ground that they are two different individuals, and without there being any difference between the natures or circumstances of the two which can be stated as a reasonable ground for difference of treatment.' Such a principle manifestly does not give complete guidance—indeed its effect, strictly speaking, is merely to throw a definite *onus probandi* on the man who applies to another a treatment of which he would complain if applied to himself; but Common Sense has amply recognised the practical importance of the maxim: and its truth, so far as it goes, appears to me self-evident.

A somewhat different application of the same fundamental principle that individuals in similar conditions should be treated similarly finds its sphere in the ordinary administration of Law, or (as we say) of "Justice." Accordingly in § 1 of chap. v. of this Book I drew attention to 'impartiality in the application of general rules,' as an important element in the common notion of Justice; indeed, there ultimately appeared to be no other element which could be intuitively known with perfect clearness and certainty. Here again it must be plain that this precept of impartiality is insufficient for the complete determination of just conduct, as it does not help us to decide what kind of rules should be thus impartially applied; though all admit the importance of excluding from government, and human conduct generally, all conscious partiality and "respect of persons."

The principle just discussed, which seems to be more or less clearly implied in the common notion of "fairness" or "equity," is obtained by considering the similarity of the individuals that make up a Logical Whole or Genus. There are others, no less important, which emerge in the consideration of the similar parts of a Mathematical or Quantitative Whole. Such a Whole is presented in the common notion of the Good —or, as is sometimes said, "good on the whole"—of any individual human being. The proposition "that one ought to aim at one's own good" is sometimes given as the maxim of Rational Self-love or Prudence: but as so stated it does not clearly avoid tautology; since we may define 'good' as 'what one ought to aim at." If, however, we say "one's good on the whole," the addition suggests a principle which, when explicitly stated, is, at any rate, not tautological. I have already referred to this principle as that "of impartial concern for all parts of our conscious life":—we might express it concisely by saying "that Hereafter *as such* is to be regarded neither less nor more than Now." It is not, of course, meant that the good of the present may not reasonably be preferred to that of the future on account of its greater certainty: or again, that a week ten years hence may not be more important to us than a week now, through an increase in our means or capacities of happiness. All that the principle affirms is that the mere difference of priority and posteriority in time is not a reasonable ground for having more regard to the consciousness of one moment than to that of another. The form in which it practically presents itself to most men is "that a smaller present good is not to be preferred to a greater future good" (allowing for difference of certainty): since Prudence is generally exercised in restraining a present desire (the object or satisfaction of which we commonly regard as *pro tanto* 'a good'), on account of the remoter consequences of gratifying it. The commonest view of the principle would no doubt be that the present *pleasure* or *happiness* is reasonably to be foregone with the view of obtaining greater pleasure or happiness hereafter: but the principle need not be restricted to a hedonistic application; it is equally applicable to any other interpretation of "one's own good," in which good is conceived as a mathematical whole, of which the integrant parts are realised in different parts or moments of a lifetime. And therefore it is perhaps better to distinguish it here from the principle "that Pleasure is the sole Ultimate Good," which does not seem to have any logical connexion with it.

So far we have only been considering the "Good on the Whole" of a single individual: but just as this notion is constructed by comparison and integration of the different "goods" that succeed one another in the series of our conscious states, so we have formed the notion of Universal Good by comparison and integration of the goods of all individual human—or sentient—existences. And here again, just as in the former case, by considering the relation of the integrant parts to the whole and to each other, I obtain the self-evident principle that the good of any one individual is of no more importance, from the point of view (if I may say so) of the Universe, than the good of any other; unless, that is, there are special grounds for believing that more good is likely to be realised in the one case than in the other. And it is evident to me that as a rational being I am bound to aim at good generally, — so far as it is attainable by my efforts, — not merely at a particular part of it.

From these two rational intuitions we may deduce, as a necessary inference, the maxim of Benevolence in an abstract form: viz. that each one is morally bound to regard the good of any other individual as much as his own, except in so far as he judges it to be less, when impartially viewed, or less certainly knowable or attainable by him.

Chapter II
The Proof of Utilitarianism

The principle of aiming at universal happiness is more generally felt to require some proof, or at least (as Mill puts it) some "considerations determining the mind to accept it," than the principle of aiming at one's own happiness. From the point of view, indeed, of abstract philosophy, I do not see why the Egoistic principle should pass unchallenged any more than the Universalistic. I do not see why the axiom of Prudence should not be questioned, when it conflicts with present inclination, on a ground similar to that on which Egoists refuse to admit the axiom of Rational Benevolence. If the Utilitarian has to answer the question, "Why should I sacrifice my own happiness for the greater happiness of another?" it must surely be admissible to ask the Egoist, "Why should I sacrifice a present pleasure for a greater one in the future? Why should I concern myself about my own future feelings any more than about the feelings of other persons?" It undoubtedly seems to Common Sense paradoxical to ask for a reason why one should seek one's own happiness on the whole; but I do not see how the demand can be repudiated as absurd by those who adopt the views of the extreme empirical school of psychologists, although those views are commonly supposed to have a close affinity with Egoistic Hedonism. Grant that the Ego is merely a system of coherent phenomena, that the permanent identical "I" is not a fact but a fiction, as Hume and his followers maintain; why, then, should one part of the series of feelings into which the Ego is resolved be concerned with another part of the same series, any more than with any other series?

However, I will not press this question now; since I admit that Common Sense does not think it worth while to supply the individual with reasons for seeking his own interest.[1] Reasons for doing his duty —according to the commonly accepted standard of duty — are not held

---

[1] The relation of Egoistic to Universalistic Hedonism is further examined in the concluding chapter [not reprinted here].

to be equally superfluous: indeed we find that utilitarian reasons are continually given for one or other of the commonly received rules of morality. Still the fact that certain rules are commonly received as binding, though it does not establish their self-evidence, renders it generally unnecessary to prove their authority to the Common Sense that receives them: while for the same reason a Utilitarian who claims to supersede them by a higher principle is naturally challenged, by Intuitionists no less than by Egoists, to demonstrate the legitimacy of his claim. To this challenge some Utilitarians would reply by saying that it is impossible to "prove" a first principle; and this is of course true, if by proof we mean a process which exhibits the principle in question as an inference from premises upon which it remains dependent for its certainty; for these premises, and not the inference drawn from them, would then be the real first principles. Nay, if Utilitarianism is to be *proved* to a man who already holds some other moral principles, — whether he be an Intuitional moralist, who regards as final the principles of Truth, Justice, Obedience to authority, Purity, etc., or an Egoist who regards his own interest as the ultimately reasonable end of his conduct, — it would seem that the process must be one which establishes a conclusion actually *superior* in validity to the premises from which it starts. For the Utilitarian prescriptions of duty are *prima facie* in conflict, at certain points and under certain circumstances, both with rules which the Intuitionist regards as self-evident, and with the dictates of Rational Egoism; so that Utilitarianism, if accepted at all, must be accepted as overruling Intuitionism and Egoism. At the same time, if the other principles are not throughout taken as valid, the so-called proof does not seem to be addressed to the Intuitionist or Egoist at all. How shall we deal with this dilemma? How is such a process — clearly different from ordinary proof — possible or conceivable? Yet there certainly seems to be a general demand for it. Perhaps we may say that what is needed is a line of argument which on the one hand allows the validity, to a certain extent, of the maxims already accepted, and on the other hand shows them to be not absolutely valid, but needing to be controlled and completed by some more comprehensive principle.

Such a line of argument, addressed to Egoism, was given in chap. xiii. of the foregoing book. It should be observed that the applicability of this argument depends on the manner in which the Egoistic first principle is formulated. If the Egoist strictly confines himself to stating his conviction that he ought to take his own happiness or pleasure as his ultimate end, there seems no opening for any line of reasoning to lead him to Universalistic Hedonism as a first principle;[2] it cannot be proved that the difference between his own happiness and another's happiness

---

[2] It is to be observed that he may be led to it in other ways than that of argument: *i.e.* by appeals to his sympathies, or to his moral or quasi-moral sentiments.

is not *for him* all-important. In this case all that the Utilitarian can do is to effect as far as possible a reconciliation between the two principles, by expounding to the Egoist the *sanctions* of rules deduced from the Universalistic principle, — *i.e.* by pointing out the pleasures and pains that may be expected to accrue to the Egoist himself from the observation and violation respectively of such rules. It is obvious that such an exposition has no tendency to make him accept the greatest happiness of the greatest number as his ultimate end; but only as a means to the end of his own happiness. It is therefore totally different from a *proof* (as above explained) of Universalistic Hedonism. When, however, the Egoist puts forward, implicitly or explicitly, the proposition that his happiness or pleasure is Good, not only *for him* but from the point of view of the Universe, — as (*e.g.*) by saying that "nature designed him to seek his own happiness," — it then becomes relevant to point out to him that *his* happiness cannot be a more important part of Good, taken universally, than the equal happiness of any other person. And thus, starting with his own principle, he may be brought to accept Universal happiness or pleasure as that which is absolutely and without qualification Good or Desirable: as an end, therefore, to which the action of a reasonable agent as such ought to be directed.

This, it will be remembered, is the reasoning[3] that I used in chap. xiii. of the preceding book in exhibiting the principle of Rational Benevolence as one of the few Intuitions which stand the test of rigorous criticism. It should be observed, however, that as addressed to the Intuitionist, this reasoning only shows the Utilitarian first principle to be *one* moral axiom: it does not prove that it is *sole* or *supreme*. The premises with which the Intuitionist starts commonly include other formulae held as independent and self-evident. Utilitarianism has therefore to exhibit itself in the twofold relation above described, at once negative and positive, to these formulae. The Utilitarian must, in the first place, endeavour to show to the Intuitionist that the principles of Truth, Justice,[4] etc. have only a dependent and subordinate validity: arguing either that the principle is really only affirmed by Common Sense as a general rule admitting of exceptions and qualifications, as in the case of Truth, and that we require some further principle for systematising these exceptions and qualifications; or that the fundamental notion is vague and needs further determination, as in the case of Justice;[4] and further, that the different rules are liable to conflict with each other, and that we require some higher principle to decide

---

[3] I ought to remind the reader that the argument in chap. xiii. only leads to the first principle of Utilitarianism, if it be admitted that Happiness is the only thing ultimately and intrinsically Good or Desirable. I afterwards in chap. xiv. endeavoured to bring Common Sense to this admission.

[4] That is, so far as we mean by Justice anything more than the simple negation of arbitrary inequality.

the issue thus raised; and again, that the rules are differently formulated by different persons, and that these differences admit of no Intuitional solution, while they show the vagueness and ambiguity of the common moral notions to which the Intuitionist appeals.

This part of the argument I have perhaps sufficiently developed in the preceding book. It remains to supplement this line of reasoning by developing the positive relation that exists between Utilitarianism and the Morality of Common Sense: by showing how Utilitarianism sustains the general validity of the current moral judgments, and thus supplements the defects which reflection finds in the intuitive recognition of their stringency; and at the same time affords a principle of synthesis, and a method for binding the unconnected and occasionally conflicting principles of common moral reasoning into a complete and harmonious system. If systematic reflection upon the morality of Common Sense thus exhibits the Utilitarian principle as that to which Common Sense naturally appeals for that further development of its system which this same reflection shows to be necessary, the proof of Utilitarianism seems as complete as it can be made. And since, further — apart from the question of proof — it is important in considering the method of Utilitarianism to determine exactly its relation to the commonly received rules of morality, it will be proper to examine this relation at some length in the following chapter.

Chapter III
Relation of Utilitarianism to The Morality of Common Sense

It has been before observed (Book i. chap. vi.) that the two sides of the double relation in which Utilitarianism stands to the Morality of Common Sense have been respectively prominent at two different periods in the history of English ethical thought. Since Bentham we have been chiefly familiar with the negative or aggressive aspect of the Utilitarian doctrine. But when Cumberland, replying to Hobbes, put forward the general tendency of the received moral rules to promote the "common good[5] of all Rationals" his aim was simply Conservative: it never occurs to him to consider whether these rules as commonly formulated are in any way imperfect, and whether there are any discrepancies between such common moral opinions and the conclusions of Rational Benevolence. So in Shaftesbury's system the "Moral" or

---

[5] It ought to be observed that Cumberland does not adopt a hedonistic interpretation of Good. Still, I have followed Hallam in regarding him as the founder of English Utilitarianism: since it seems to have been by a gradual and half-unconscious process that "Good" came to have the definitely hedonistic meaning which it has implicitly in Shaftesbury's system, and explicitly in that of Hume.

"Reflex Sense" is supposed to be always pleased with that "balance" of the affections which tends to the good or happiness of the whole, and displeased with the opposite. In Hume's treatise this coincidence is drawn out more in detail, and with a more definite assertion that the perception of utility[6] (or the reverse) is in each case the source of the moral likings (or aversions) which are excited in us by different qualities of human character and conduct. And we may observe that the most penetrating among Hume's contemporary critics, Adam Smith, admits unreservedly the objective coincidence of Rightness or Approvedness and Utility: though he maintains, in opposition to Hume, that "it is not the view of this utility or hurtfulness, which is either the first or the principal source of our approbation or disapprobation." After stating Hume's theory that "no qualities of the mind are approved of as virtuous, but such as are useful or agreeable either to the person himself or to others, and no qualities are disapproved of as vicious but such as have a contrary tendency"; he remarks that "Nature seems indeed to have so happily adjusted our sentiments of approbation and disapprobation to the conveniency both of the individual and of the society, that after the strictest examination it will be found, I believe, that this is universally the case."

And no one can read Hume's *Inquiry into the First Principles of Morals* without being convinced of this at least, that if a list were drawn up of the qualities of character and conduct that are directly or indirectly productive of pleasure to ourselves or to others, it would include all that are commonly known as virtues. Whatever be the origin of our notion of moral goodness or excellence, there is no doubt that "Utility" is a general characteristic of the dispositions to which we apply it: and that, so far, the Morality of Common Sense may be truly represented as at least unconsciously Utilitarian. But it may still be objected, that this coincidence is merely general and qualitative, and that it breaks down when we attempt to draw it out in detail, with the quantitative precision which Bentham introduced into the discussion. And no doubt there is a great difference between the assertion that virtue is always productive of happiness, and the assertion that the right action is under all circumstances that which will produce the greatest possible happiness on the whole. But it must be borne in mind that Utilitarianism is not concerned to prove the absolute coincidence in results of the

---

[6] I should point out that Hume uses "utility" in a narrower sense than that which Bentham gave it, and one more in accordance with the usage of ordinary language. He distinguishes the "useful" from the "immediately agreeable": so that while recognising "utility" as the main ground of our moral approbation of the more important virtues, he holds that there are other elements of personal merit which we approve because they are "immediately agreeable," either to the person possessed of them or to others. It appears, however, more convenient to use the word in the wider sense in which it has been current since Bentham.

Intuitional and Utilitarian methods. Indeed, if it could succeed in proving as much as this, its success would be almost fatal to its practical claims; as the adoption of the Utilitarian principle would then become a matter of complete indifference. Utilitarians are rather called upon to show a natural transition from the Morality of Common Sense to Utilitarianism, somewhat like the transition in special branches of practice from trained instinct and empirical rules to the technical method that embodies and applies the conclusions of science: so that Utilitarianism may be presented as the scientifically complete and systematically reflective form of that regulation of conduct, which through the whole course of human history has always tended substantially in the same direction. For this purpose it is not necessary to prove that existing moral rules are *more* conducive to the general happiness than any others: but only to point out in each case some manifest felicific tendency which they possess.

Hume's dissertation, however, incidentally exhibits much more than a simple and general harmony between the moral sentiments with which we commonly regard actions and their foreseen pleasurable and painful consequences. And, in fact, the Utilitarian argument cannot be fairly judged unless we take fully into account the cumulative force which it derives from the complex character of the coincidence between Utilitarianism and Common Sense.

It may be shown, I think, that the Utilitarian estimate of consequences not only supports broadly the current moral rules, but also sustains their generally received limitations and qualifications: that, again, it explains anomalies in the Morality of Common Sense, which from any other point of view must seem unsatisfactory to the reflective intellect; and moreover, where the current formula is not sufficiently precise for the guidance of conduct, while at the same time difficulties and perplexities arise in the attempt to give it additional precision, the Utilitarian method solves these difficulties and perplexities in general accordance with the vague instincts of Common Sense, and is naturally appealed to for such solution in ordinary moral discussions. It may be shown further, that it not only supports the generally received view of the relative importance of different duties, but is also naturally called in as arbiter, where rules commonly regarded as co-ordinate come into conflict: that, again, when the same rule is interpreted somewhat differently by different persons, each naturally supports his view by urging its Utility, however strongly he may maintain the rule to be self-evident and known *a priori:* that where we meet with marked diversity of moral opinion on any point, in the same age and country, we commonly find manifest and impressive utilitarian reasons on both sides: and that finally the remarkable discrepancies found in comparing the moral codes of different ages and countries are for the most part strikingly correlated to differences in the effects of actions on happiness, or in men's foresight of, or concern for, such effects.

R. M. HARE*

Universalizability and Utilitarianism

MORAL JUDGEMENTS are, I claim, universalizable in only one sense, namely that they entail identical judgements about all cases identical in their universal properties.

It follows from universalizability that if I now say that I ought to do a certain thing to a certain person, I am committed to the view that the very same thing ought to be done to me, were I in exactly his situation, including having the same personal characteristics and in particular the same motivational states. But the motivational states he actually now has may run quite counter to my own present ones. For example, he may very much want not to have done to him what I am saying I ought to do to him (which involves prescribing that I do it). But we have seen that if I fully represent to myself his situation, including his motivations, I shall myself acquire a corresponding motivation, which would be expressed in the prescription that the same thing *not be* done to me, were I to be forthwith in just that situation. But this prescription is inconsistent with my original "ought"-statement, if that was, as we have been assuming, prescriptive. For, as we have just seen, the statement that I ought to do it to him commits me to the view that it ought to be done to me, were I in his situation. And this, since "ought" is prescriptive, entails the prescription that the same *be* done to me in that situation. So, if I have this full knowledge of his situation, I am left with two inconsistent prescriptions. I can avoid this "contradiction in the will" (cf. Kant, 1785:58) only by abandoning my original "ought"-statement, given my present knowledge of my proposed victim's situation.

A problem arises here, however, about this conflict between my own and my victim's preferences. There is first of all the difficulty, which

*From *Moral Thinking, Its Levels, Method and Point,* Chapter 6.

we shall be dealing with in the next chapter, of comparing his preferences with mine in respect of intensity. How am I to say which is the greater, and by how much? But even if we assume that this difficulty can be overcome, the problem remains of why my preferences, even if they are less intense, should be subordinated to his. And if mine are more intense than his, ought they to be subordinated at all? Suppose, for example, that all I think I ought to do to him is move his bicycle so that I can park my car, and he has a mild aversion to my doing this (not because he dislikes someone else interfering with his property, but simply because he wants it to stay where it is). This problem seems even more pressing in multilateral cases in which the preferences of many people are affected; but it will do no harm to deal with it in this simple bilateral case first.

I can see no reason for not adopting the same solution here as we do in cases where our own preferences conflict with one another. For example, let us change the case and suppose that it is my own bicycle, and that it is moderately inconvenient to move it, but highly inconvenient not to be able to park my car; I shall then naturally move the bicycle, thinking that that is what, prudentially speaking, I ought to do, or what I most want, all in all, to do. Reverting now to the bilateral case: we have established that, if I have full knowledge of the other person's preferences, I shall myself have acquired preferences equal to his regarding what should be done to me were I in his situation; and these are the preferences which are now conflicting with my original prescription. So we have in effect not an interpersonal conflict of preferences or prescriptions, but an intrapersonal one; both the conflicting preferences are mine. I shall therefore deal with the conflict in exactly the same way as with that between two original preferences of my own.

Multilateral cases now present less difficulty than at first appeared. For in them too the interpersonal conflicts, however complex and however many persons are involved, will reduce themselves, given full knowledge of the preferences of others, to intrapersonal ones. And since we are able, in our everyday life, to deal with quite complex intrapersonal conflicts of preferences, I can see no reason why we should not in the same way deal with conflicts of this special sort, which have arisen through our awareness of the preferences of others combined with the requirement that we universalize our moral prescriptions.

Let us apply this to our simple bilateral car-bicycle case. The other party wants me not to move his bicycle, but I want more to move it in order to park my car. I am fully aware of the strength of his desire, and therefore have a desire of equal strength that, were I in his situation, the bicycle should stay where it is. But I also have my original desire to move it in order to park my car. This latter desire wins by superior strength. On the other hand, if the positions were reversed (the bicycle mine, the car his), and I could somehow prevent the bicycle being moved, the case would be from my individual point of view different (though not different in its universal properties). Suppose that, in this different case, my desire not to have the bicycle moved is far weaker than the other party's desire to park his car; and suppose that I am fully aware of the strength of his desire and therefore have an equal desire that, were I in his position, I should be able to park my car. I shall then, in this different situation, have again two desires: the original desire to leave my bicycle where it is, and my acquired desire that were I the other party I should be able to park my car; and the latter will be the stronger. So in this different situation I shall think that the bicycle ought to be moved.

Note that, although the situations are different, they differ only in what *individuals* occupy the two roles; their *universal* properties are all the same. That is why (and this is interesting and significant) in both cases the conclusion is that the bicycle ought to be moved; this is because in each case its owner's desire to leave it where it is is less than the car-owner's desire to park his car. We see here in miniature how the requirement to universalize our prescriptions generates utilitarianism. And we see also how in principle unanimity can be reached by our method of reasoning, once each fully represents to himself the situation of the other. And there is in principle no difficulty in extending the method to multilateral cases; the difficulties are all practical ones of acquiring the necessary knowledge and correctly performing some very complex thought-processes. In difficult cases it would take an archangel to do it.

The thesis of universalizability itself was established by arguments of a philosophical-logical sort.* The most important of these consists in showing that a person who makes different moral judgements about cases which he admits to be identical in their non-moral universal properties encounters the same kind of incomprehension as is encountered by a logical inconsistency (for example a self-contradiction). If any dispute arises about precisely what properties are to count as universal for the purposes of the thesis, the same test can be applied again. For example, it is usually held that spatial and temporal properties do not count (because they cannot be defined without reference to an individual point of origin of the coordinate system); and they can be shown not to count by pointing out that the sort of logical incomprehension just described would arise if somebody treated the date (irrespective of what sorts of things happened on that or on related dates) as morally relevant; and similarly for the grid map reference (irrespective of what was at that or at related locations).

---

*FR and LM refers to Hare's previous books: *Freedom and Reason* (Oxford U. Press, 1963) and *The Language of Morals.* (Oxford U. Press, 1952).

The same move can be made in the present case. If somebody says "I ought to do it to him, but nobody ought to do it to me if I were in precisely his position with his preferences," and gives as his reason, not that he is he, nor that today is today, but that this is the actual case and that merely hypothetical, then, I claim, the same logical incomprehension would arise as if he had said either of those two other things. I am here appealing to our *linguistic* intuitions, being confident of my own, and confident that they are linguistic not moral (because they must be shared by anybody who understands the use of "ought," whatever his moral opinions).

PART TWO
HAPPINESS

UTILITARIANS AIM TO maximize happiness. But what is happiness? Very different answers have been given to this question, and from those answers very different ways of life follow.

Bentham was characteristically untroubled: happiness was a mental state. Someone is happy when in a state of pleasure and no pain. But many utilitarians have been troubled about this. A.J. Ayer, in his discussion of Bentham, proposes a revision: happiness should be thought of, not as a mental state, but as having what one wants. Mental state versions and desire versions both have their supporters and critics.

Mental State Versions

One problem is: what are the distinguishing features of the mental state of happiness? Sexual happiness, the happiness of helpless laughter, the happiness of discovering the structure of DNA, a week of happiness cycling in France, being happily married for years. It is hard to believe that what these have in common is a detectable inner sensation. But if the "sensation" view of happiness is naive, what *do* all these states have in common?

Another problem is that blissful mental states of any kind may not add up to a life we would choose. Robert Nozick's "experience machine" makes the point. You could be plugged into a machine that would feed signals into your brain so that you had wonderful experiences, though you would not any longer experience the real world. If offered the chance of being plugged in for life, would you take it? Many people would refuse, however much the experiences were tailored to their requirements. This suggests that many people value things other than such experiences. Happiness, interpreted as a mental state, may be too thin an account of what is valuable in itself.

Desire Versions

The experience machine may not provide the kind of life we want. But this is not fatal to versions of utilitarianism where happiness is interpreted as getting what you want. On those versions, if people want other things more than blissful experiences, those other things are of greater utility. And problems about what different happy mental states have in common are also sidestepped.

Desire versions have their problems, too. Start with the simplest version, according to which the utilitarian should aim to satisfy as many desires as possible (weighted for strength, so that intense desires count for more). As R.B. Brandt points out, it is not clear how we are to compare the alternatives between which we are choosing, as desires change. What about desires I once had about my future, which have now faded? If when I was ten I very much wanted to be a policeman, does that past desire carry any weight now? Or should past desires be excluded? What about the desires of dead people? On one view, the desires of the dead should be excluded, because they will not know whether their desires have been satisfied. But what about spreading slanders about people, so subtly that they never know about it? Can the desire not to be slandered be ignored because the person will not know whether it has been satisfied?

Mill, in a state of depression when he was twenty, asked himself whether achieving all his current goals would make him happy, and realized that it would not. (His description of how he overcame this gives a picture — rare in utilitarian writings — of belief being shaped by personal experience and emotion.) This case suggests that the relationship between happiness and desires can be complicated: even the satisfaction of desires that have not faded may not give happiness. And, conversely, things that were not desired may bring happiness with them.

Not all of people's desires are satisfied. Perhaps what matters is the proportion that are. A person with a severe mental handicap may have only a very limited range of simple and rather weak desires. Perhaps nearly all of them are satisfied. Yet it seems hard to believe that such a life comes closer to the ideal than that of someone with a much wider range of desires including a larger proportion of unsatisfied ones. Perhaps a more adequate idea of the good life gives weight to having a wide range of desires, and perhaps also to having strong desires, as well as to having a reasonable proportion of them satisfied.

But even this will not do. Suppose you are offered a place on a life-enhancing course, which guarantees to develop in you a wide range of new and intense desires, all of which will be satisfied. You enroll, and when you turn up you are taken by a robot to a private room. The robot takes hold of you and starts to bang your head against the wall. You have a very strong desire for this to stop, which the robot soon satisfies. It then holds your head under water, arousing a very strong desire to surface before you drown, which it again satisfies. It then starts attaching electrodes to your body . . . if you would prefer not to have your life enhanced in this way, perhaps this more global preference needs to be included in some way before the desire version of utilitarianism is adequate.

Utility and Pluralism

Much work has been done to produce both mental state and desire versions of utilitarianism that are sufficiently sophisticated to cope with the criticisms of the simpler accounts. James Griffin's account of "well-being" is a sophisticated development of a desire version. The desires that count are informed ones and are subject to restrictions as to the kind of role they play in a person's life. Griffin then turns to the objection made by pluralist critics: that utilitarianism assumes only one thing is of value, when in fact we value many irreducibly different kinds of thing. He argues that the informed desire account is compatible with accepting pluralism about values. The problem that remains (and which Griffin discusses) is whether this leaves utilitarianism with any distinct content. Where happiness is interpreted as pleasurable mental states, there is a clear disagreement between utilitarianism and other views where value is placed on honesty, dignity, knowledge, liberty, etc., independent of their contribution to pleasure. But the sophisticated desire utilitarian seems to say, "If those are things people care about, they are part of happiness." We may lose grip on what the point of disagreement is between utilitarians and others.

Some versions of utilitarianism are too crude to be plausible. Others are sophisticated enough to be very attractive. Some non-utilitarian moralities are unattractive through having rules that do not seem rooted in the contribution they make to people's lives. Others do make people and their experiences and desires central. If the most attractive view about what is intrinsically valuable is somewhere in the intersection between this second kind of pluralism and the more sophisticated versions of utilitarianism, perhaps it does not matter much whether it is called utilitarian or not.

JEREMY BENTHAM*

⤴

Happiness as Pleasure and No Pain

⤴

Of the Four Sanctions or Sources of Pain and Pleasure

1. It has been shown that the happiness of the individuals, of whom a community is composed, that is their pleasures and their security, is the end and the sole end which the legislator ought to have in view: the sole standard, in conformity to which each individual ought, as far as depends upon the legislator, to be *made* to fashion his behaviour. But whether it be this or any thing else that is to be *done*, there is nothing by which a man can ultimately be *made* to do it, but either pain or pleasure. Having taken a general view of these two grand objects (*viz.,* pleasure, and what comes to the same thing, immunity from pain) in the character of *final* causes; it will be necessary to take a view of pleasure and pain itself, in the character of *efficient* causes or means.

  2. There are four distinguishable sources from which pleasure and pain are in use to flow: considered separately, they may be termed the *physical,* the *political,* the *moral,* and the *religious:* and inasmuch as the pleasures and pains belonging to each of them are capable of giving a binding force to any law or rule of conduct, they may all of them be termed *sanctions.*[1]

---

*From Jeremy Bentham: *An Introduction to the Principles of Morals and Legislation,* Chapters 3 and 4.

[1]Sanctio, in Latin, was used to signify the *act of binding,* and, by a common grammatical transition, *any thing which serves to bind a man:* to wit, to the observance of such or such a mode of conduct. According to a Latin grammarian,[a] the import of the word is derived

[a]Servius. See Ainsworth's Dict. ad verbum *Sanctio.*

41

3. If it be in the present life, and from the ordinary course of nature, not purposely modified by the interposition of the will of any human being, nor by any extraordinary interposition of any superior invisible being, that the pleasure or the pain takes place or is expected, it may be said to issue from or to belong to the *physical sanction*.

4. If at the hands of a *particular* person or set of persons in the community, who under names correspondent to that of *judge*, are chosen for the particular purpose of dispensing it, according to the will of the sovereign or supreme ruling power in the state, it may be said to issue from the *political sanction*.

5. If at the hands of such *chance* persons in the community, as the party in question may happen in the course of his life to have concerns with, according to each man's spontaneous disposition, and not according to any settled or concerted rule, it may be said to issue from the *moral* or *popular sanction*.[2]

6. If from the immediate hand of a superior invisible being, either in the present life, or in a future, it may be said to issue from the *religious sanction*.

7. Pleasures or pains which may be expected to issue from the *physical, political,* or *moral* sanctions, must all of them be expected to be experienced, if ever, in the *present* life: those which may be expected to issue from the *religious* sanction, may be expected to be experienced either in the *present* life or in a *future*.

8. Those which can be experienced in the present life, can of course be no others than such as human nature in the course of the present life is susceptible of: and from each of these sources may flow all the pleasures or pains of which, in the course of the present life, human nature is susceptible. With regard to these then (with which alone we have in this place any concern) those of them which belong to any one of those sanctions, differ not ultimately in kind from those which be-

---

by rather a far-fetched process (such as those commonly are, and in a great measure indeed must be, by which intellectual ideas are derived from sensible ones) from the word *sanguis*, blood: because, among the Romans, with a view to inculcate into the people a persuasion that such or such a mode of conduct would be rendered obligatory upon a man by the force of which I call the religious sanction (that is, that he would be made to suffer by the extraordinary interposition of some superior being, if he failed to observe the mode of conduct in question) certain ceremonies were contrived by the priests: in the course of which ceremonies the blood of victims was made use of.

A Sanction then is a source of obligatory powers or *motives*: that is, of *pains* and *pleasures*; which, according as they are connected with such or such modes of conduct, operate, and are indeed the only things which can operate, as *motives*.

[2]Better termed *popular*, as more directly indicative of its constituent cause; as likewise of its relation to the more common phrase *public opinion*, in French *opinion publique*, the name there given to that tutelary power, of which of late so much is said, and by which so much is done. The latter appellation is however unhappy and inexpressive; since if *opinion* is material, it is only in virtue of the influence it exercises over action, through the medium of the affections and the will.

long to any one of the other three: the only difference there is among them lies in the circumstances that accompany their production. A suffering which befalls a man in the natural and spontaneous course of things, shall be styled, for instance, a *calamity*; in which case, if it be supposed to befall him through any imprudence of his, it may be styled a punishment issuing from the physical sanction. Now this same suffering, if inflicted by the law, will be what is commonly called a *punishment*; if incurred for want of any friendly assistance, which the misconduct, or supposed misconduct, of the sufferer has occasioned to be withholden, a punishment issuing from the *moral* sanction; if through the immediate interposition of a particular providence, a punishment issuing from the religious sanction.

9. A man's goods, or his person, are consumed by fire. If this happened to him by what is called an accident, it was a calamity: if by reason of his own imprudence (for instance, from his neglecting to put his candle out) it may be styled a punishment of the physical sanction: if it happened to him by the sentence of the political magistrate, a punishment belonging to the political sanction; that is, what is commonly called a punishment: if for want of any assistance which his *neighbour* withheld from him out of some dislike to his *moral* character, a punishment of the *moral* sanction: if by an immediate act of *God's* displeasure, manifested on account of some *sin* committed by him, or through any distraction of mind, occasioned by the dread of such displeasure, a punishment of the *religious* sanction.[3]

10. As to such of the pleasures and pains belonging to the religious sanction, as regard a future life, of what kind these may be we cannot know. These lie not open to our observation. During the present life they are matter only of expectation: and, whether that expectation be derived from natural or revealed religion, the particular kind of pleasure or pain, if it be different from all those which lie open to our observation, is what we can have no idea of. The best ideas we can obtain of such pains and pleasures are altogether unliquidated in point of quality. In what other respects our ideas of them *may* be liquidated will be considered in another place.

11. Of these four sanctions the physical is altogether, we may observe, the ground-work of the political and the moral: so is it also of the religious, in as far as the latter bears relation to the present life. It is included in each of those other three. This may operate in any case, (that is, any of the pains or pleasures belonging to it may operate) independently of *them*: none of *them* can operate but by means of this. In a word, the powers of nature may operate of themselves; but neither

[3]A suffering conceived to befall a man by the immediate act of God, as above, is often, for shortness' sake, called a *judgment*: instead of saying, a suffering inflicted on him in consequence of a special judgment formed, and resolution thereupon taken, by the Deity.

the magistrate, nor men at large, *can* operate, nor is God in the case in question *supposed* to operate, but through the powers of nature.

12. For these four objects, which in their nature have so much in common, it seemed of use to find a common name. It seemed of use, in the first place, for the convenience of giving a name to certain pleasures and pains, for which a name equally characteristic could hardly otherwise have been found: in the second place, for the sake of holding up the efficacy of certain moral forces, the influence of which is apt not to be sufficiently attended to. Does the political sanction exert an influence over the conduct of mankind? The moral, the religious sanctions do so too. In every inch of his career are the operations of the political magistrate liable to be aided or impeded by these two foreign powers: who, one or other of them, or both, are sure to be either his rivals or his allies. Does it happen to him to leave them out of his calculations? he will be sure almost to find himself mistaken in the result. Of all this we shall find abundant proofs in the sequel of this work. It behoves him, therefore, to have them continually before his eyes; and that under such a name as exhibits the relation they bear to his own purposes and designs.

Value of a Lot of Pleasure or Pain, How to be Measured

1. Pleasures then, and the avoidance of pains, are the *ends* which the legislator has in view: it behoves him therefore to understand their *value*. Pleasures and pains are the *instruments* he has to work with: it behoves him therefore to understand their force, which is again, in other words, their value.

2. To a person considered *by himself*, the value of a pleasure or pain considered *by itself*, will be greater or less, according to the four following circumstances[1]:

1. Its *intensity.*

2. Its *duration.*

3. Its *certainty* or *uncertainty.*

4. Its *propinquity* or *remoteness.*

---

[1]These circumstances have since been denominated *elements* or *dimensions* of *value* in a pleasure or a pain.

Not long after the publication of the first edition, the following memoriter verses were framed, in the view of lodging more effectually, in the memory, these points, on which the whole fabric of morals and legislation may be seen to rest.

> *Intense, long, certain, speedy, fruitful, pure* —
> Such marks in *pleasures* and in *pains* endure.
> Such pleasures seek if *private* be thy end:
> If it be *public*, wide let them *extend.*
> Such *pains* avoid, whichever be thy view:
> If pains *must* come, let them *extend* to few.

3. These are the circumstances which are to be considered in estimating a pleasure or a pain considered each of them by itself. But when the value of any pleasure or pain is considered for the purpose of estimating the tendency of any *act* by which it is produced, there are two other circumstances to be taken into account; these are,

5. Its *fecundity*, or the chance it has of being followed by sensations of the *same* kind; that is, pleasures, if it be a pleasure: pains, if it be a pain.

6. Its *purity*, or the chance it has of *not* being followed by sensations of the *opposite* kind: that is, pains, if it be a pleasure: pleasures, if it be a pain.

   These two last, however, are in strictness scarcely to be deemed properties of the pleasure or the pain itself; they are not, therefore, in strictness to be taken into the account of the value of that pleasure or that pain. They are in strictness to be deemed properties only of the act, or other event, by which such pleasure or pain has been produced; and accordingly are only to be taken into the account of the tendency of such act or such event.

4. To a *number* of persons, with reference to each of whom the value of a pleasure or a pain is considered, it will be greater or less, according to seven circumstances: to wit, the six preceding ones; *viz.*

1. Its *intensity*.

2. Its *duration*.

3. Its *certainty* or *uncertainty*.

4. Its *propinquity* or *remoteness*.

5. Its *fecundity*.

6. Its *purity*.

And one other; to wit:

7. Its *extent*; that is, the number of persons to whom it *extends*; or (in other words) who are affected by it.

5. To take an exact account then of the general tendency of any act, by which the interests of a community are affected, proceed as follows. Begin with any one person of those whose interests seem most immediately to be affected by it: and take an account,

1. Of the value of each distinguishable *pleasure* which appears to be produced by it in the *first* instance.

2. Of the value of each *pain* which appears to be produced by it in the *first* instance.

3. Of the value of each pleasure which appears to be produced by it *after* the first. This constitutes the *fecundity* of the first *pleasure* and the *impurity* of the first *pain*.

4. Of the value of each *pain* which appears to be produced by it after the first. This constitutes the *fecundity* of the first *pain*, and the *impurity* of the first pleasure.

5. Sum up all the values of all the *pleasures* on the one side, and those of all the pains on the other. The balance, if it be on the side of pleasure, will give the *good* tendency of the act upon the whole, with respect to the interests of that *individual* person; if on the side of pain, the *bad* tendency of it upon the whole.

6. Take an account of the *number* of persons whose interests appear to be concerned; and repeat the above process with respect to each. *Sum up* the numbers expressive of the degrees of *good* tendency, which the act has, with respect to each individual, in regard to whom the tendency of it is *good* upon the whole: do this again with respect to each individual, in regard to whom the tendency of it is *bad* upon the whole. Take the *balance*; which, if on the side of *pleasure*, will give the general *good tendency* of the act, with respect to the total number or community of individuals concerned; if on the side of pain, the general *evil tendency*, with respect to the same community.

6. It is not to be expected that this process should be strictly pursued previously to every moral judgment, or to every legislative or judicial operation. It may, however, be always kept in view: and as near as the process actually pursued on these occasions approaches to it, so near will such process approach to the character of an exact one.

7. The same process is alike applicable to pleasure and pain, in whatever shape they appear: and by whatever denomination they are distinguished: to pleasure, whether it be called *good* (which is properly the cause or instrument of pleasure) or *profit* (which is distant pleasure, or the cause or instrument of distant pleasure,) or *convenience*, or *advantage, benefit, emolument, happiness*, and so forth: to pain, whether it be called *evil*, (which corresponds to *good*) or *mischief*, or *inconvenience*, or *disadvantage*, or *loss*, or *unhappiness*, and so forth.

8. Nor is this a novel and unwarranted, any more than it is a useless theory. In all this there is nothing but what the practice of mankind, wheresoever they have a clear view of their own interest, is perfectly conformable to. An article of property, an estate in land, for instance, is valuable, on what account? On account of the pleasures of all kinds which it enables a man to produce, and what comes to the same thing

the pains of all kinds which it enables him to avert. But the value of such an article of property is universally understood to rise or fall according to the length or shortness of the time which a man has in it: the certainty or uncertainty of its coming into possession: and the nearness or remoteness of the time at which, if at all, it is to come into possession. As to the *intensity* of the pleasures which a man may derive from it, this is never thought of, because it depends upon the use which each particular person may come to make of it; which cannot be estimated till the particular pleasures he may come to derive from it, or the particular pains he may come to exclude by means of it, are brought to view. For the same reason, neither does he think of the *fecundity* or *purity* of those pleasures.

Thus much for pleasure and pain, happiness and unhappiness, in *general*. We come now to consider the several particular kinds of pain and pleasure.

A. J. AYER*

Happiness as Satisfaction of Desires

THE STOCK OBJECTION to Bentham's system is that it is based upon a false psychology.[1] Not all human action is purposive; and of those actions which are purposive it is not true that they are always such as the agent thinks will bring him the most happiness. For the most part people aim at particular objects; they set out to accomplish certain tasks, to indulge their emotions, to satisfy their physical needs, to fulfil their obligations, to outwit their neighbours, to gratify their friends. These, and many others, are their ends, and while they are engaged in pursuing them they do not look beyond them. It may be that the achievement of these ends will actually give them pleasure, but this does not imply that they have had this pleasure in view all along. It is, indeed, possible to pursue an object, say, that of gratifying a friend, not even immediately for its own sake, but solely for the sake of the pleasure that one expects oneself to derive from its attainment; but this is a sophisticated attitude, which even in the case of purely selfish action furnishes the exception rather than the rule. Nevertheless, it may be objected, whatever ends a person may in fact pursue, it is surely the case that he would not pursue them unless he liked doing so. And to say that he does what he likes is to say that he acts with a view to his own happiness, whether he be conscious of doing so or not. But now the question is, By what criterion are we to establish that a person is "doing what he likes"? If our

*From A. J. Ayer: "The Principle of Utility," in A. J. Ayer: *Philosophical Essays*.
[1] For elaborations of this criticism *vide* G. E. Moore, *Principia Ethica*, chap. 3, and F. H. Bradley, *Ethical Studies*, chap. 3.

measure of what a person likes is simply what he does, then to say, in this sense, that every man acts with a view to his own happiness is just to assert a tautology. It is to say no more than that every man does what he does. But if, on the other hand, our criterion of a person's liking one thing better than another is his saying to himself that he will derive more pleasure from it, then the proposition that every man, who acts purposively, does what he likes best is psychologically false; and so, consequently, is the proposition that every man seeks his own greatest happiness.

I think that this objection is certainly valid against Bentham, but I do not think that it is so fatal an objection as some of his critics have supposed. For one thing, it is still possible to hold that pleasure is the only thing which is good in itself, even if one gives up the contention that it is the only thing which is ever actually desired. One can still encourage people to pursue pleasure, and nothing but pleasure, as an end, even while admitting that there are other ends which they can pursue. But I do not think that many people would be inclined to take this view, unless they also held the psychological doctrine that there could be no other end but pleasure. Once this psychological doctrine was shown to them to be false, I think that they would mostly not take pleasure as their only value. They would say that pleasure was sometimes to be aimed at, but sometimes not; and that some types of pleasure were more worth having than others. There is, however, a more subtle way of preserving the essential part of Bentham's system, and that is to maintain his proposition that every one seeks happiness, not in the way that he maintained it, as a psychological generalization, but as a tautology. Thus, we may agree to understand the word "happiness" as referring, in this context, not to some particular object of desire, but to any object of desire whatsoever. That is to say, we can identify the "happiness" of a person with the class of ends that he in fact pursues, whatever these may happen to be. No doubt this is not quite what is ordinarily meant by happiness, but that does not matter for our purpose. Then Bentham's principle of utility becomes the principle that we are always to act in such a way as to give as many people as possible as much as possible of whatever it is that they want. I think that this interpretation preserves the essence of Bentham's doctrine, and it has the advantage of making it independent of any special psychological theory.

A much more serious objection than the one that we have just now tried to meet is that Bentham's criterion is not practically workable. For, in the first place, it is impossible for any one to estimate *all* the consequences of any given action; they may extend over centuries. If Bentham had not written as he did, I should not now be writing this. I do not know in what way my writing will affect the ratio of pleasure to pain that Bentham's actions have so far produced; but presumably it will alter it in some way, if only for its effect upon myself; yet this is not a circumstance that Bentham could conceivably have taken into account. Besides, we are required to consider not merely the actual consequences of our actions but also what would have been the consequences of the actions that we might have done in their place. Ought Brutus to have murdered Caesar? Would someone else have murdered Caesar if Brutus had not? Suppose that but for Brutus Caesar would not have been murdered, what difference would this have made to the history of the Roman Empire? And what further difference would that have made to the history of Europe? Would Shakespeare still have existed? If he had still existed, he presumably would not have written the play of *Julius Caesar* in the form in which he did. And how much difference would that have made to the general happiness? Plainly the whole question succumbs into absurdity.

It is clear then that if we are to make any sense at all of Bentham's principle we must confine its application to a limited number of the consequences of our actions, namely to those consequences that the agent can reasonably be expected to foresee. And, in fact, if Bentham's principle is to be regarded, as I think that he himself wished it to be regarded, not as a rule for passing moral judgements after the event, but as a practical guide to action, we are bound to interpret it in this restricted way. For to a man who is considering how he ought to act the only consequences that can be relevant are those that he foresees. Even so, when it comes to the assessment of these consequences, the problem is by no means so straightforward as Bentham seems to have assumed. Suppose that I am hesitating between two courses of action, both of which, so far as I can see, will affect only five people. And suppose that I have reason to believe that if I do action A three of these people will obtain some satisfaction from it, whereas only two of them will be satisfied if I do action B. But suppose also that the amount of dissatisfaction that I shall cause to the remainder is likely to be somewhat greater in each instance if I do action A than if I do action B. How, even in such a simplified example, can I possibly work out the sum? In virtue of what standard of measurement can I set about adding the satisfaction of one person to that of another and subtracting the resultant quantity from the dissatisfaction of someone else? Clearly there is no such standard, and Bentham's process of "sober calculation" turns out to be a myth.

Here again the answer is that to do justice to Bentham's principle we must consider it as applying not to individuals but to a society. The amount of happiness that is likely to follow from any particular action cannot be calculated with any nicety, though even so it will often be reasonably safe to judge that one course of action will produce more happiness than another; and in these cases there will be no difficulty in making Bentham's principle apply. But what can be judged with very much greater certainty is that the general observance of a certain set of rules throughout a given society will contribute more to the happiness of the members of that society than will the general neglect of those rules, or the observance of some other set of rules which might be adopted in their place. Our proposition is, in short, that the members of a given community will be more likely to obtain what they want on the whole, if they habitually behave towards one another in certain ways rather than in certain other ways, if they are, for example, habitually kind rather than cruel. And it seems to me that this is a type of proposition that can be practically verified. It is not indeed a question that can be settled by mathematical calculation. Our estimates of what it is that people "really" want and how far they are satisfied are bound to be somewhat rough and ready. Nevertheless I think that by observing people's behaviour one can become reasonably sure that their general adherence to certain rules of conduct would on the whole promote the satisfaction of their wants. And it is just the discovery and application of such rules that Bentham's principle of utility recommends.

My conclusion is then that, while he did not succeed in setting either morals or politics "upon the sure path of a science," Bentham did produce a guide for action which it is possible to follow, though not perhaps exactly in the form in which he stated it. Whether one follows it or not is then a matter for a moral decision. If any one chooses to adopt what Bentham called the principle of asceticism and set about making himself and everyone around him as miserable as possible he can be remonstrated with but, strictly speaking, not refuted. It is, however, unlikely that he would now get very many people to agree with him. Again, it might be urged against Bentham that the question which we have to consider is not what people actually want but what they ought to want, or what they must be made to want; and no doubt there is something to be said for this point of view. But Bentham's attitude is simpler and it is at least arguable that from the practical standpoint it should be preferred.

R. B. BRANDT*

Objections to Desire-Satisfaction Views of Happiness

A DECISION IS called for: whether fully rational persons will support a moral system which promises to *maximize happiness* in a society, or to provide the collection of events which sentient creatures in some sense *most want*. I shall contrast these as the "happiness theory" and the "desire theory."

These two theories are not the only possible ones. Various philosophers have thought that some things, different from happiness and possibly not desired by anyone or everyone, are worthwhile in themselves and worthy of being produced for no further reason, for instance: knowledge and virtue. This view, however, seems to be obsolescent, and I propose to ignore it.

For our purposes a decision between the happiness theory and the desire theory must be made, since otherwise an intelligent discussion of measurement of welfare and interpersonal comparisons would be precluded. For practical purposes, however, it might seem to make little difference which is chosen, at least after some necessary qualifications and restrictions are imposed on the desire theory, in view of the normally close relation between what a person wants and what will make him happy.

At the present time the desire theory enjoys widespread support among both philosophers and economists, in one or other of its possible forms; but I am going to opt for the unpopular happiness theory, on the

*From R. B. Brandt: *A Theory of the Right and the Good*, Chapter 13.

ground that the other proposal is not a plausible, or even an intelligible one, when we work it out in detail.

1. The Objection to Desire Theories

Let us initially and roughly define the "desire theory" as the theory which identifies welfare with desire-satisfaction and holds that ideally benevolent people would seek to maximize the desire-satisfaction of everyone. Some philosophers have held this theory in an unqualified form, but it is more usual for some distinctions to be made, for instance to identify welfare with the satisfaction of only some desires: ones that persist in the face of full information, or that occur in a normal (not angry) frame of mind, or, to use a conception discussed in an earlier chapter, ones that survive cognitive psychotherapy. But probably most philosophers would want a further restriction made. They would want to exclude altruistic or, more generally, non-self-interested desires . . . and as a result would want to define 'welfare' in terms of desire-satisfactions that would come about only while the person is still alive, or perhaps only in terms of those about which the person would know when they occurred. There are other possible restrictions.

It may seem inconsistent for desire theories to be rejected here. For the proposal I made about what is the best thing to do, from a person's own point of view, puts his desires squarely in the centre of the account. And I came very close to saying that if something is rationally desired for itself by a person, that thing is intrinsically good for him. Nevertheless, we shall see that the desire theory of welfare becomes elusive when we raise the question which programme of action would maximize the desire-satisfactions of an individual (or collection of individuals) over a lifetime. That question is one we do have to raise when we ask which moral system would produce most welfare for the individuals in a society over their whole lifetime. Whether an individual who visualized this difficulty clearly would experience some change in his own desires, in the direction of aiming at happiness only, is a question I leave to the reader for reflection.

In order to get the difficulty clear, let me first sketch the essence of the happiness theory, for which the problem does not arise. And, in order to simplify the problem to the bare essentials, let us consider just the case of one person X who can do either A or B, and wishes to do what will maximize the welfare of another person, Y, over his lifetime. Let us also ignore the fact that we can know only with probability what will happen, and let us suppose we can talk freely just of what will happen to Y if A is done, as compared with if B is done. We suppose, then, that for every future moment of time we can know what difference it will make to Y's life whether A or B is done, and hence can decide how much happier Y is at that moment given one act occurred than he would have been had the other occurred. Let us represent these results by a curve, plotting the points at which he is happier if A is done above the X axis, the distance above the axis fixed by how much happier he is than he would have been had B been done; and similarly plotting points below the X axis representing how much happier he is if B is done than he would have been had A been done. This operation will give us curve-segments both above and below the line. Let us then compute the area under these curves. When we know whether the area above the curve is larger or smaller than that under the curve, we know which act will contribute more to Y's happiness over his lifetime. Whatever the practical difficulties in measurement, this conception is at least clear.

Two points in support of the happiness theory of welfare were mentioned in Chapter 7. First, that what we seem to care about securing for other persons (e.g. our own children) is their happiness; and we seem to care about getting them what they want (or would want if they knew more, etc.) only to the extent we think that so doing will bring them happiness or avoid distress and depression. Second, the psychological theory of benevolence leads to the conclusion that what we are sympathetically motivated to secure for others is happiness and freedom from distress (although we may want desire-satisfaction because we believe it a means to these).

These two points suggest that a benevolent person will tend to support a moral code which he thinks will maximize expectable welfare in the sense of expectable happiness.

Let us now turn to the central awkwardness of the desire theory. We must first remind ourselves what it is to satisfy someone's desire. Suppose Mr. X at a time t wants an occurrence O at some time t', or at any one of many moments t_1 to t_n. Then, if O actually occurs at some one of these times, X's desire has been satisfied. And a greater satisfaction of desire has occurred, if the occurrent O was desired more intensely.

It is clear that the desire theory can take any one of several forms. In its simple unqualified form it affirms that a person's welfare has been increased if an O occurs which was or is or will be desired by him in fact. In a qualified form it affirms that a person's welfare has been increased if an O occurs which was or is or will be desired by him, if he is fully informed, and calm, and if the desire is not altruistic. We need not worry about the various possible forms of qualification. I shall consider the theory only in the simplest form, since the problem I wish to point out arises there (as well as in the other forms).

The desire theory holds, then, that greater welfare corresponds to greater satisfaction of desire, and that a benevolent person, in deciding what to do, does or at least ought to perform that act among the options open to him which will maximize desire-satisfaction. The idea seems to be that we consider all the desires a person has (and everyone has many occurrent desires at every moment), at some time or other, or many times, over a lifetime, and what that person—more particularly, for our problem, a moral code—should aim at is to maximize the satisfaction of these desires. This conception is unintelligible.

That there is a problem begins to appear when we reflect that we think some desires need not count. Suppose my six-year-old son has decided he would like to celebrate his fiftieth birthday by taking a roller-coaster ride. This desire now is hardly one we think we need attend to in planning to maximize his lifetime well-being. Notice that we pay no attention to our own past desires. Are we then to take into account only the desires we think my son will have at the time his desire would be 'satisfied', here at the age of fifty? If we take this line, we come close to the happiness theory—of providing that for each future moment he enjoys himself maximally at that moment.

The problem for the desire-satisfaction theory arises from two facts: first, that occurrent desires at a time t are for something to occur (to have occurred) at some other time; and second, that desires change over time.

The second fact merits dilation. Notice that one acquires some desires and loses others as one matures: loses one's desire to be an airline pilot, perhaps, and acquires one to provide for one's family. There are temporary fancies: a person suddenly wants to learn French, works at it, and then loses interest before achieving mastery. Most notably, some desires are cyclical, in the sense that after satisfaction there is a period of no desire for a whole family of events, followed by a recovery of interest. Some desires, as in morphine addiction, are the result of an earlier sequence of activities. As a person approaches the end of his life, he may lose his hedonic interests and want to make some contribution to the world, and wish perhaps to have done things differently in the past.

In view of these facts, what is a would-be maximizer of satisfaction of desires to do? If the other person's desires were fixed, you could identify his fixed long-term preference ordering of biographies for himself or the world, and then move him up to the highest indifference curve your resources permit. Since the desires are not fixed, you cannot pursue this programme.

Does the length of time a person entertains a desire make a difference, so that a sadistic wish for an angry hour counts less than a wish entertained for a whole month (say, only 1/720 as much)? You might say that such comparisons are irrelevant; it is desires at the time of satisfaction that count. But consider an objection to this[1]: a convinced sceptic who has rebelled against a religious background wants, most of his life, no priest to be called when he is about to die. But he weakens on his deathbed, and asks for a priest. Do we maximize his welfare by

---

[1]For the example, I am indebted to Derek Parfit and James Griffin.

summoning a priest? Some would say not, in view of his past desires. The programme also ignores future regrets.

What, then, is the programme of desire-satisfaction maximization to be, if different from happiness-maximization? As far as I know, no proposal has been put forward by advocates of the desire theory which tells us in principle, and generally, how to decide which of two possible courses of action would produce more desire-satisfaction, even if we can predict the impact of the events on the individual, and how long and how intensely each of the several outcomes has been or will be desired.[2] I have the temerity to suggest that the whole concept is unintelligible.

I make this suggestion with hesitation, since someone may produce an intelligible and attractive programme which I have overlooked. And there are intelligible programmes; the only question is, how convincing are they? Let me suggest one. Suppose we give up the idea of an overall general programme which I might adopt now for maximizing the desire-satisfaction of my young son, given information about his future desires. Let us suppose rather that I adopt a flexible plan, and whenever the time comes to make a choice, say, between actions A and B which expectably affect his welfare, I adopt his set of priorities at that time (or, perhaps, his system of ideal priorities). The procedure then, for any choice, is to go along with the other person's vote, or his rational vote, at the time. Thus the procedure is flexible over time: if and when my son's desires shift in intensity, my programme of assistance will shift accordingly. A result of this programme will be that, if and to the extent that he ignores his past desires, I am to ignore them. I also ignore his future desires to the extent that he does (or would, if he were rational). Another implication is that if he is dead on a certain date and has no desires, the programme calls for no satisfaction of earlier desires. In the case of the dying sceptic, the programme calls for a priest to be summoned, since that is what he now wants.

This programme seems arbitrary and unsatisfactory compared with the original tidy goal of satisfying a person's desires, past and future, maximally, based on a picture of all desires he will have at every moment of his life. Nor can it be recommended on the ground that it is the most efficient way to maximize lifetime desire-satisfaction when all desires are taken into account, because we have no general conception of such a programme.

There is another problem about implementing the foregoing desire theory, for the theory must find a plan for aggregating the desire-satisfactions of everybody whose welfare is concerned. How will this be done? Suppose a choice has to be made between plan A and plan B. A

---

[2]Thomas Nagel, 1970, is possibly an exception; R. B. Perry had a solution for certain obvious cases.

prospective beneficiary, Mr. X, votes for A, whereas the other prospective beneficiary, Mr. Y, votes for B. How will a decision be made? Evidently the above plan will need extension. Suppose we are able to compare the intensity of X's preference for A over B, and equally that of Y for B over A. Is the programme to call for acting in line with the stronger preference? This might be unconvincing, say, if Mr. X happens to want a great many things more than Mr. Y, and perhaps more intensely. That would seem strange—although it does not seem strange to adopt a programme which produces the most happiness, however divided between the two. One different programme that might be adopted is simply to allocate to each individual an equal share of the resources of the community over a lifetime. But this is not attractive either, in view of the special claims of the ill or handicapped. I must leave open the question what a desire-satisfaction theorist would say rational benevolent persons would prefer to do.

The above problems with the desire-satisfaction theory may lead us to opt for the happiness theory, for reasons suggested by Sidgwick in a slightly different context. He wrote: "If we are not to systematise human activities by taking Universal Happiness as their common end, on what other principles are we to systematise them? I have failed to find—and am unable to construct—any systematic answer to this question that appears to me deserving of serious consideration." (1922, p. 406.)

The alternative theory is that fully rational and benevolent persons want a moral code to maximize the happiness, or net enjoyment, of sentient creatures. None of the foregoing problems arises for the happiness theory.

A happiness conception of utility or welfare is not popular in some quarters at present. Economists may reject it because it is no longer used in price theory; they can construct the indifference curves needed for prediction with choices or preferences alone. Another thought more widely persuasive is that the happiness theory suggests dictation to others about what they should do—not giving them what they want, but rather what is thought best for their happiness. This thought is seriously mistaken; for, as Mill made clear, it is important for happiness in the long-run that people should be secured in the direction of their own lives, both because this freedom is significant for growth in personal decision-making, and because people like to feel they can make their own decisions.[3]

---

[3]Some philosophers are moved by some differences between the desire theory and the happiness theory (which desire theory I leave to them). Suppose a man wants his wife to be faithful to him. She commits adultery but sees to it that he never knows about her unfaithfulness. Has his welfare been diminished? The desire theory would say that it has, because something has occurred which he wants not to occur. The happiness theory would say not, by this event in itself, although the question whether the long-range happiness of both has not been subtly damaged is another matter.

ROBERT NOZICK*

The Experience Machine

THERE ARE ALSO substantial puzzles when we ask what matters other than how *people's* experiences feel "from the inside." Suppose there were an experience machine that would give you any experience you desired. Superduper neuropsychologists could stimulate your brain so that you would think and feel you were writing a great novel, or making a friend, or reading an interesting book. All the time you would be floating in a tank, with electrodes attached to your brain. Should you plug into this machine for life, preprogramming your life's experiences? If you are worried about missing out on desirable experiences, we can suppose that business enterprises have researched thoroughly the lives of many others. You can pick and choose from their large library or smorgasbord of such experiences, selecting your life's experiences for, say, the next two years. After two years have passed, you will have ten minutes or ten hours out of the tank, to select the experiences of your *next* two years. Of course, while in the tank you won't know that you're there; you'll think it's all actually happening. Others can also plug in to have the experiences they want, so there's no need to stay unplugged to serve them. (Ignore problems such as who will service the machines if everyone plugs in.) Would you plug in? *What else can matter to us, other than how our lives feel from the inside?* Nor should you refrain because of the few moments of distress between the moment you've decided and the moment you're plugged. What's a

*From Robert Nozick: *Anarchy, State and Utopia*, Chapter 3.

few moments of distress compared to a lifetime of bliss (if that's what you choose), and why feel any distress at all if your decision *is* the best one?

What does matter to us in addition to our experiences? First, we want to *do* certain things, and not just have the experience of doing them. In the case of certain experiences, it is only because first we want to do the actions that we want the experiences of doing them or thinking we've done them. (But *why* do we want to do the activities rather than merely to experience them?) A second reason for not plugging in is that we want to *be* a certain way, to be a certain sort of person. Someone floating in a tank is an indeterminate blob. There is no answer to the question of what a person is like who has long been in the tank. Is he courageous, kind, intelligent, witty, loving? It's not merely that it's difficult to tell; there's no way he is. Plugging into the machine is a kind of suicide. It will seem to some, trapped by a picture, that nothing about what we are like can matter except as it gets reflected in our experiences. But should it be surprising that what *we are* is important to us? Why should we be concerned only with how our time is filled, but not with what we are?

Thirdly, plugging into an experience machine limits us to a manmade reality, to a world no deeper or more important than that which people can construct. There is no *actual* contact with any deeper reality, though the experience of it can be simulated. Many persons desire to leave themselves open to such contact and to a plumbing of deeper significance.[1] This clarifies the intensity of the conflict over psychoactive drugs, which some view as mere local experience machines, and others view as avenues to a deeper reality; what some view as equivalent to surrender to the experience machine, others view as following one of the reasons *not* to surrender!

We learn that something matters to us in addition to experience by imagining an experience machine and then realizing that we would not use it. We can continue to imagine a sequence of machines each designed to fill lacks suggested for the earlier machines. For example, since the experience machine doesn't meet our desire to *be* a certain way, imagine a transformation machine which transforms us into whatever sort of person we'd like to be (compatible with our staying us). Surely one would not use the transformation machine to become as one

---

[1]Traditional religious views differ on the *point* of contact with a transcendent reality. Some say that contact yields eternal bliss or Nirvana, but they have not distinguished this sufficiently from merely a *very* long run on the experience machine. Others think it is intrinsically desirable to do the will of a higher being which created us all, though presumably no one would think this if we discovered we had been created as an object of amusement by some superpowerful child from another galaxy or dimension. Still others imagine an eventual merging with a higher reality, leaving unclear its desirability, or where that merging leaves *us*.

would wish, and thereupon plug into the experience machine![2] So something matters in addition to one's experiences *and* what one is like. Nor is the reason merely that one's experiences are unconnected with what one is like. For the experience machine might be limited to provide only experiences possible to the sort of person plugged in. Is it that we want to make a difference in the world? Consider then the result machine, which produces in the world any result you would produce and injects your vector input into any joint activity. We shall not pursue here the fascinating details of these or other machines. What is most disturbing about them is their living of our lives for us. Is it misguided to search for *particular* additional functions beyond the competence of machines to do for us? Perhaps what we desire is to live (an active verb) ourselves, in contact with reality. (And this, machines cannot do *for* us.) Without elaborating on the implications of this, which I believe connect surprisingly with issues about free will and causal accounts of knowledge, we need merely note the intricacy of the question of what matters *for people* other then their experiences. Until one finds a satisfactory answer, and determines that this answer does not *also* apply to animals, one cannot reasonably claim that only the felt experiences of animals limit what we may do to them.

---

[2]Some wouldn't use the transformation machine at all; it seems like *cheating.* But the one-time use of the transformation machine would not remove all challenges; there would still be obstacles for the new us to overcome, a new plateau from which to strive even higher. And is this plateau any the less earned or deserved than that provided by genetic endowment and early childhood environment? But if the transformation machine could be used indefinitely often, so that we could accomplish anything by pushing a button to transform ourselves into someone who could do it easily, there would remain no limits we *need* to strain against or try to transcend. Would there be anything left *to do*? Do some theological views place God outside of time because an omniscient omnipotent being couldn't fill up his days?

JOHN STUART MILL*

Higher and Lower Pleasures

THE CREED WHICH accepts as the foundation of morals, Utility, or the Greatest Happiness Principle, holds that actions are right in proportion as they tend to promote happiness, wrong as they tend to produce the reverse of happiness. By happiness is intended pleasure, and the absence of pain; by unhappiness, pain, and the privation of pleasure. To give a clear view of the moral standard set up by the theory, much more requires to be said; in particular, what things it includes in the ideas of pain and pleasure; and to what extent this is left an open question. But these supplementary explanations do not affect the theory of life on which this theory of morality is grounded—namely, that pleasure, and freedom from pain, are the only things desirable as ends; and that all desirable things (which are as numerous in the utilitarian as in any other scheme) are desirable either for the pleasure inherent in themselves, or as means to the promotion of pleasure and the prevention of pain.

Now, such a theory of life excites in many minds, and among them in some of the most estimable in feeling and purpose, inveterate dislike. To suppose that life has (as they express it) no higher end than pleasure—no better and nobler object of desire and pursuit—they designate as utterly mean and grovelling; as a doctrine worthy only of swine, to whom the followers of Epicurus were, at a very early period, contemptuously likened; and modern holders of the doctrine are occasionally made the subject of equally polite comparisons by its German, French, and English assailants.

*From John Stuart Mill: *Utilitarianism*, Chapter 2.

When thus attacked, the Epicureans have always answered, that it is not they, but their accusers, who represent human nature in a degrading light; since the accusation supposes human beings to be capable of no pleasures except those of which swine are capable. If this supposition were true, the charge could not be gainsaid, but would then be no longer an imputation; for if the sources of pleasure were precisely the same to human beings and to swine, the rule of life which is good enough for the one would be good enough for the other. The comparison of the Epicurean life to that of beasts is felt as degrading, precisely because a beast's pleasures do not satisfy a human being's conception of happiness. Human beings have faculties more elevated than the animal appetites, and when once made conscious of them, do not regard anything as happiness, which does not include their gratification. I do not, indeed, consider the Epicureans to have been by any means faultless in drawing out their scheme of consequences from the utilitarian principle. To do this in any sufficient manner, many Stoic, as well as Christian elements require to be included. But there is no known Epicurean theory of life which does not assign to the pleasures of the intellect, of the feelings and imagination, and of the moral sentiments, a much higher value as pleasures than to those of mere sensation. It must be admitted, however, that utilitarian writers in general have placed the superiority of mental over bodily pleasures chiefly in the greater permanency, safety, uncostliness, etc., of the former — that is, in their circumstantial advantages rather than in their intrinsic nature. And on all these points utilitarians have fully proved their case; but they might have taken the other, and, as it may be called, higher ground, with entire consistency. It is quite compatible with the principle of utility to recognise the fact, that some *kinds* of pleasure are more desirable and more valuable than others. It would be absurd that while, in estimating all other things, quality is considered as well as quantity, the estimation of pleasures should be supposed to depend on quantity alone.

If I am asked, what I mean by difference of quality in pleasures, or what makes one pleasure more valuable than another, merely as a pleasure, except its being greater in amount, there is but one possible answer. Of two pleasures, if there be one to which all or almost all who have experience of both give a decided preference, irrespective of any feeling of moral obligation to prefer it, that is the more desirable pleasure. If one of the two is, by those who are competently acquainted with both, placed so far above the other that they prefer it, even though knowing it to be attended with a greater amount of discontent, and would not resign it for any quantity of the other pleasure which their nature is capable of, we are justified in ascribing to the preferred enjoyment a superiority in quality, so far out-weighing quantity as to render it, in comparison, of small account.

Now it is an unquestionable fact that those who are equally acquainted with, and equally capable of appreciating and enjoying, both, do give a most marked preference to the manner of existence which employs their higher faculties. Few human creatures would consent to be changed into any of the lower animals, for a promise of the fullest allowance of a beast's pleasures; no intelligent human being would consent to be a fool, no instructed person would be an ignoramus, no person of feeling and conscience would be selfish and base, even though they should be persuaded that the fool, the dunce, or the rascal is better satisfied with his lot than they are with theirs. They would not resign what they possess more than he for the most complete satisfaction of all the desires which they have in common with him. If they ever fancy they would, it is only in cases of unhappiness so extreme, that to escape from it they would exchange their lot for almost any other, however undesirable in their own eyes. A being of higher faculties requires more to make him happy, is capable probably of more acute suffering, and certainly accessible to it at more points, than one of an inferior type; but in spite of these liabilities, he can never really wish to sink into what he feels to be a lower grade of existence. We may give what explanation we please of this unwillingness; we may attribute it to pride, a name which is given indiscriminately to some of the most and to some of the least estimable feelings of which mankind are capable: we may refer it to the love of liberty and personal independence, an appeal to which was with the Stoics one of the most effective means for the inculcation of it; to the love of power, or to the love of excitement, both of which do really enter into and contribute to it: but its most appropriate appellation is a sense of dignity, which all human beings possess in one form or another, and in some, though by no means in exact, proportion to their higher faculties, and which is so essential a part of the happiness of those in whom it is strong, that nothing which conflicts with it could be, otherwise than momentarily, an object of desire to them. Whoever supposes that this preference takes place at a sacrifice of happiness — that the superior being, in anything like equal circumstances, is not happier than the inferior — confounds the two very different ideas, of happiness, and content. It is indisputable that the being whose capacities of enjoyment are low, has the greatest chance of having them fully satisfied; and a highly endowed being will always feel that any happiness which he can look for, as the world is constituted, is imperfect. But he can learn to bear its imperfections, if they are at all bearable; and they will not make him envy the being who is indeed unconscious of the imperfections, but only because he feels not at all the good which those imperfections qualify. It is better to be a human being dissatisfied than a pig satisfied; better to be Socrates dissatisfied than a fool satisfied. And if the fool, or the pig, are of a different opinion, it is because they only know their own side of the question. The other party to the comparison knows both sides.

It may be objected, that many who are capable of the higher pleasures, occasionally, under the influence of temptation, postpone them to the lower. But this is quite compatible with a full appreciation of the intrinsic superiority of the higher. Men often, from infirmity of character, make their election for the nearer good, though they know it to be the less valuable; and this no less when the choice is between two bodily pleasures, than when it is between bodily and mental. They pursue sensual indulgences to the injury of health, though perfectly aware that health is the greater good. It may be further objected, that many who begin with youthful enthusiasm for everything noble, as they advance in years sink into indolence and selfishness. But I do not believe that those who undergo this very common change, voluntarily choose the lower description of pleasures in preference to the higher. I believe that before they devote themselves exclusively to the one, they have already become incapable of the other. Capacity for the nobler feelings is in most natures a very tender plant, easily killed, not only by hostile influences, but by mere want of sustenance; and in the majority of young persons it speedily dies away if the occupations to which their position in life has devoted them, and the society into which it has thrown them, are not favourable to keeping that higher capacity in exercise. Men lose their high aspirations as they lose their intellectual tastes, because they have not time or opportunity for indulging them; and they addict themselves to inferior pleasures, not because they deliberately prefer them, but because they are either the only ones to which they have access, or the only ones which they are any longer capable of enjoying. It may be questioned whether any one who has remained equally susceptible to both classes of pleasures, ever knowingly and calmly preferred the lower; though many, in all ages, have broken down in an ineffectual attempt to combine both.

From this verdict of the only competent judges, I apprehend there can be no appeal. On a question which is the best worth having of two pleasures, or which of two modes of existence is the most grateful to the feelings, apart from its moral attributes and from its consequences, the judgment of those who are qualified by knowledge of both, or, if they differ, that of the majority among them, must be admitted as final. And there needs be the less hesitation to accept this judgment respecting the quality of pleasures, since there is no other tribunal to be referred to even on the question of quantity. What means are there of determining which is the acutest of two pains, or the intensest of two pleasurable sensations, except the general suffrage of those who are familiar with both? Neither pains nor pleasures are homogeneous, and pain is always heterogeneous with pleasure. What is there to decide whether a particular pleasure is worth purchasing at the cost of a particular pain, except the feelings and judgment of the experienced? When, therefore, those feelings and judgment declare the pleasures derived from the higher faculties to be preferable *in kind*, apart from the question of intensity, to those of which the animal nature, disjoined from the higher faculties, is susceptible, they are entitled on this subject to the same regard.

I have dwelt on this point, as being a necessary part of a perfectly just conception of Utility or Happiness, considered as the directive rule of human conduct. But it is by no means an indispensable condition to the acceptance of the utilitarian standard; for that standard is not the agent's own greatest happiness, but the greatest amount of happiness altogether; and if it may possibly be doubted whether a noble character is always the happier for its nobleness, there can be no doubt that it makes other people happier, and that the world in general is immensely a gainer by it. Utilitarianism, therefore, could only attain its end by the general cultivation of nobleness of character, even if each individual were only benefited by the nobleness of others, and his own, so far as happiness is concerned, were a sheer deduction from the benefit. But the bare enunciation of such an absurdity as this last, renders refutation superfluous.

JOHN STUART MILL*

A Crisis in My Mental History

FROM THE WINTER of 1821, when I first read Bentham, and especially from the commencement of the *Westminster Review,* I had what might truly be called an object in life; to be a reformer of the world. My conception of my own happiness was entirely identified with this object. The personal sympathies I wished for were those of fellow labourers in this enterprise. I endeavoured to pick up as many flowers as I could by the way; but as a serious and permanent personal satisfaction to rest upon, my whole reliance was placed on this; and I was accustomed to felicitate myself on the certainty of a happy life which I enjoyed, through placing my happiness in something durable and distant, in which some progress might be always making, while it could never be exhausted by complete attainment. This did very well for several years, during which the general improvement going on in the world and the idea of myself as engaged with others in struggling to promote it, seemed enough to fill up an interesting and animated existence. But the time came when I awakened from this as from a dream. It was in the autumn of 1826. I was in a dull state of nerves, such as everybody is occasionally liable to; unsusceptible to enjoyment or pleasurable excitement; one of those moods when what is pleasure at other times becomes insipid or indifferent; the state, I should think, in which converts to Methodism usually are, when smitten by their first "conviction of sin." In this frame of mind it occurred to me to put the question directly to myself: "Suppose that all your objects in life were

*From John Stuart Mill: *Autobiography,* Chapter 5.

66

realized; that all the changes in institutions and opinions which you are looking forward to, could be completely effected at this very instant: would this be a great joy and happiness to you?" And an irrepressible self-consciousness distinctly answered, "No!" At this my heart sank within me: the whole foundation on which my life was constructed fell down. All my happiness was to have been found in the continual pursuit of this end. The end had ceased to charm, and how could there ever again be any interest in the means? I seemed to have nothing left to live for.

At first I hoped that the cloud would pass away of itself; but it did not. A night's sleep, the sovereign remedy for the smaller vexations of life, had no effect on it. I awoke to a renewed consciousness of the woeful fact. I carried it with me into all companies, into all occupations. Hardly anything had power to cause me even a few minutes' oblivion of it. For some months the cloud seemed to grow thicker and thicker. The lines in Coleridge's "Dejection"—I was not then acquainted with them—exactly describe my case:

> A grief without a pang, void, dark and drear,
> A drowsy, stifled, unimpassioned grief,
> Which finds no natural outlet or relief
> In word, or sigh, or tear.

In vain I sought relief from my favourite books; those memorials of past nobleness and greatness from which I had always hitherto drawn strength and animation. I read them now without feeling, or with the accustomed feeling *minus* all its charm; and I became persuaded that my love of mankind, and of excellence for its own sake, had worn itself out. I sought no comfort by speaking to others of what I felt. If I had loved any one sufficiently to make confiding my griefs a necessity, I should not have been in the condition I was. I felt, too, that mine was not an interesting, or in any way respectable distress. There was nothing in it to attract sympathy. Advice, if I had known where to seek it, would have been most precious. The words of Macbeth to the physician often occurred to my thoughts. But there was no one on whom I could build the faintest hope of such assistance. My father, to whom it would have been natural to me to have recourse in any practical difficulties, was the last person to whom, in such a case as this, I looked for help. Everything convinced me that he had no knowledge of any such mental state as I was suffering from, and that even if he could be made to understand it, he was not the physician who could heal it. My education, which was wholly his work, had been conducted without any regard to the possibility of its ending in this result; and I saw no use in giving him the pain of thinking that his plans had failed, when the failure was probably irremediable, and, at all events, beyond the power of *his* remedies. Of other friends I had at that time none to whom I had any hope of making my condition intelligible. It was however abundantly intelligible to myself; and the more I dwelt upon it, the more hopeless it appeared.

My course of study had led me to believe that all mental and moral feelings and qualities, whether of a good or of a bad kind, were the results of association; that we love one thing, and hate another, take pleasure in one sort of action or contemplation, and pain in another sort, through the clinging of pleasurable or painful ideas to those things, from the effect of education or of experience. As a corollary from this, I had always heard it maintained by my father, and was myself convinced, that the object of education should be to form the strongest possible associations of the salutary class; associations of pleasure with all things beneficial to the great whole, and of pain with all things hurtful to it. This doctrine appeared inexpugnable; but it now seemed to me, on retrospect, that my teachers had occupied themselves but superficially with the means of forming and keeping up these salutary associations. They seemed to have trusted altogether to the old familiar instruments, praise and blame, reward and punishment. Now, I did not doubt that by these means, begun early, and applied unremittingly, intense associations of pain and pleasure, especially of pain, might be created, and might produce desires and aversions capable of lasting undiminished to the end of life. But there must always be something artificial and casual in associations thus produced. The pains and pleasures thus forcibly associated with things are not connected with them by any natural tie; and it is therefore, I thought, essential to the durability of these associations, that they should have become so intense and inveterate as to be practically indissoluble before the habitual exercise of the power of analysis had commenced. For I now saw, or thought I saw, what I had always before received with incredulity — that the habit of analysis has a tendency to wear away the feelings; as indeed it has, when no other mental habit is cultivated, and the analysing spirit remains without its natural complements and correctives. The very excellence of analysis (I argued) is that it tends to weaken and undermine whatever is the result of prejudice; that it enables us mentally to separate ideas which have only casually clung together; and no associations whatever could ultimately resist this dissolving force, were it not that we owe to analysis our clearest knowledge of the permanent sequences in nature; the real connexions between things, not dependent on our will and feelings; natural laws, by virtue of which, in many cases, one thing is inseparable from another in fact; which laws, in proportion as they are clearly perceived and imaginatively realized, cause our ideas of things which are always joined together in Nature to cohere more and more closely in our thoughts. Analytic habits may thus even strengthen the associations between causes and effects, means and ends, but tend altogether to weaken those which are, to speak familiarly, a *mere* matter of feeling. They are therefore (I thought) favourable to prudence and clear-sightedness, but a perpetual worm at the root both of the passions and of the virtues; and, above all, fearfully undermine all desires, and all pleasures, which are the effects of association, that is, according to the theory I held, all except the purely physical and organic; of the entire insufficiency of which to make life desirable no one had a stronger conviction than I had. These were the laws of human nature, by which, as it seemed to me, I had been brought to my present state. All those to whom I looked up were of opinion that the pleasure of sympathy with human beings, and the feelings which made the good of others, and especially of mankind on a large scale, the object of existence, were the greatest and surest sources of happiness. Of the truth of this I was convinced, but to know that a feeling would make me happy if I had it, did not give me the feeling. My education, I thought, had failed to create these feelings in sufficient strength to resist the dissolving influences of analysis, while the whole course of my intellectual cultivation had made precocious and premature analysis the inveterate habit of my mind. I was thus, as I said to myself, left stranded at the commencement of my voyage, with a well-equipped ship and a rudder, but no sail; without any real desire for the ends which I had been so carefully fitted out to work for: no delight in virtue, or the general good, but also just as little in anything else. The fountains of vanity and ambition seemed to have dried up within me, as completely as those of benevolence. I had had (as I reflected) some gratification of vanity at too early an age: I had obtained some distinction, and felt myself of some importance, before the desire of distinction and of importance had grown into a passion; and little as it was which I had attained, yet having been attained too early, like all pleasures enjoyed too soon, it had made me blasé and indifferent to the pursuit. Thus neither selfish nor unselfish pleasures were pleasures to me. And there seemed no power in nature sufficient to begin the formation of my character anew, and create, in a mind now irretrievably analytic, fresh associations of pleasure with any of the objects of human desire.

These were the thoughts which mingled with the dry heavy dejection of the melancholy winter of 1826–1827. During this time I was not incapable of my usual occupations. I went on with them mechanically, by the mere force of habit. I had been so drilled in a certain sort of mental exercise that I could still carry it on when all the spirit had gone out of it. I even composed and spoke several speeches at the debating society, how, or with what degree of success, I know not. Of four years continual speaking at that society, this is the only year of which I remember next to nothing. Two lines of Coleridge, in whom alone of all writers I have found a true description of what I felt, were often in my thoughts, not at this time (for I had never read them), but in a later period of the same mental malady:

> Work without hope draws nectar in a sieve,
> And hope without an object cannot live.

In all probability my case was by no means so peculiar as I fancied it, and I doubt not that many others have passed through a similar state; but the idiosyncrasies of my education had given to the general phenomenon a special character, which made it seem the natural effect of causes that it was hardly possible for time to remove. I frequently asked myself, if I could, or if I was bound to go on living, when life must be passed in this manner. I generally answered to myself that I did not think I could possibly bear it beyond a year. When, however, not more than half that duration of time had elapsed, a small ray of light broke in upon my gloom. I was reading, accidentally, Marmontel's *Memoires*, and came to the passage which relates his father's death, the distressed position of the family, and the sudden inspiration by which he, then a mere boy, felt and made them feel that he would be everything to them — would supply the place of all that they had lost. A vivid conception of the scene and its feelings came over me, and I was moved to tears. From this moment my burden grew lighter. The oppression of the thought that all feeling was dead within me was gone. I was no longer hopeless: I was not a stock or a stone. I had still, it seemed, some of the material out of which all worth of character, and all capacity for happiness, are made. Relieved from my ever-present sense of irremediable wretchedness, I gradually found that the ordinary incidents of life could again give me some pleasure; that I could again find enjoyment, not intense, but sufficient for cheerfulness, in sunshine and sky, in books, in conversation, in public affairs; and that there was, once more, excitement, though of a moderate kind, in exerting myself for my opinions, and for the public good. Thus the cloud gradually drew off, and I again enjoyed life; and though I had several relapses, some of which lasted many months, I never again was as miserable as I had been.

The experiences of this period had two very marked effects on my opinions and character. In the first place, they led me to adopt a theory of life, very unlike that on which I had before acted, and having much in common with what at that time I certainly had never heard of, the anti-self-consciousness theory of Carlyle. I never, indeed, wavered in the conviction that happiness is the test of all rules of conduct, and the end of life. But I now thought that this end was only to be attained by not making it the direct end. Those only are happy (I thought) who have their minds fixed on some object other than their own happiness; on the happiness of others, on the improvement of mankind, even on some art or pursuit, followed not as a means, but as itself an ideal end. Aiming thus at something else, they find happiness by the way. The enjoyments of life (such was now my theory) are sufficient to make it a pleasant thing, when they are taken *en passant*, without being made a principal object. Once make them so, and they are immediately felt to be insufficient. They will not bear a scrutinizing examination. Ask yourself whether you are happy, and you cease to be so. The only chance is to treat, not happiness, but some end external to it, as the purpose of life. Let your self-consciousness, your scrutiny, your self-interrogation, exhaust themselves on that; and if otherwise fortunately circumstanced, you will inhale happiness with the air you breathe, without dwelling on it or thinking about it, without either forestalling it in imagination, or putting it to flight by fatal questioning. This theory now became the basis of my philosophy of life. And I still hold to it as the best theory for all those who have but a moderate degree of sensibility and of capacity for enjoyment, that is, for the great majority of mankind.

The other important change which my opinions at this time underwent was that I, for the first time, gave its proper place, among the prime necessities of human well-being, to the internal culture of the individual. I ceased to attach almost exclusive importance to the ordering of outward circumstances, and the training of the human being for speculation and for action.

JAMES GRIFFIN*

A Sophisticated Version of the Desire Account

THERE ARE STRONG objections to such an account. Is it even intelligible? If our desires never changed with time, then each of us would have a single preference order, by reference to which what most fulfilled his desires over the course of his life could be calculated. However, life is not so simple; preferences change, and not always in a way that allows us totally to discount earlier ones. Suppose that for much of his life a person wanted his friends to keep him from vegetating when he retired but, now that he is retired, wants to be left to vegetate. Is there any intelligible programme for weighing desires that change with time and hence for maximizing fulfilment?

The breadth of the account, which is its attraction, is also its great flaw. The account drops the Experience Requirement [as we called it]. It allows my utility to be determined not only by things that I am not aware of (that seems right: if you cheat me out of an inheritance that I never expected, I might not know but still be worse off for it), but also by things that do not affect my life in any way at all. The trouble is that one's desires spread themselves so widely over the world that their objects extend far outside the bound of what, with any plausibility, one could take as touching one's own well-being. The restriction to *informed* desire is no help here. I might meet a stranger on a train and, listening to his ambitions, form a strong, informed desire that he succeed, but never hear of him again. And any moderately decent person

*From James Griffin: *Well-Being, Its Meaning, Measurement and Moral Importance*, Chapters 1 and 2.

wants people living in the twenty-second century to be happy and prosperous. And we know that Leonardo had an informed desire that humans fly, which the Wright brothers fulfilled centuries later. Indeed, without the Experience Requirement, why would utility not include the desires of the dead? And would that not mean the account had gone badly awry? And if we exclude these desires that extend beyond the bounds of what affects well-being, would we not, in order to avoid arbitrariness, have to reintroduce the Experience Requirement, thereby losing the breadth that makes the informed-desire account attractive? The difficulty goes deep in the theory. In fact, it goes deep, one way or other, in any account of well-being.

How May We Restrict the Desire Account?

The informed-desire account will have to be abandoned unless we can find a way to restrict the desires that count. But we cannot do it with the Experience Requirement.

The notion we are after is not the notion of value in general, but the narrower notion of a life's being valuable solely to the person who lives it. And this must itself impose restrictions on which desires count. As these examples show, the desires that count have to enter our lives in a way beyond just being our desires. So what we need to do is to make clear the sense in which only certain informed desires enter our lives in this further way. Think of the difference between my desire that the stranger succeed and my desire that my children prosper. I want both, but they enter my life in different ways. The first desire does not become one of my aims. The second desire, on the other hand, is one of my central ends, on the achievement of which the success of my life will turn. It is not that, deep down, what I really want is my own achievement, and that I want my children's prosperity only as a means to it. What I want is *their* prosperity, and it distorts the value I attach to it to make it only a means to such a purely personal end as my own achievement. It is just that their prosperity also becomes part of my life's being successful in a way that the prosperity of the stranger on the train does not.

But that can be only part of the story. It is not that informed desires count only if they become the sort of aims or goals or aspirations on which the success of a life turns. Good things can just happen; manna from heaven counts too. So we should try saying, to introduce more breadth, that what count are what we aim at and what we would not avoid or be indifferent to getting. What counts for me, therefore, is what enters my life with no doing from me, what I bring into my life, and what I do with my life. The range of that list is not so great as to include things that I cannot (e.g. the prosperity of our twenty-second-century successors) or do not (e.g. the sympathetic stranger's success) take into my life as an aim or goal. And Leonardo's wanting humans to fly would not count either; to the extent it became an aim of his life it was unsuccessful, and to the extent it was merely a wish it does not count.

In a way the account is now circular. I appeal to our rough notion of well-being in deciding which informed desires to exclude from this account of well-being. But that, I think, does not matter. If what we were doing were taking a totally empty term, "well-being," and stipulating a sense for it, then we could not, in the middle of the job, appeal to "well-being." But our job is not that. The notion of 'well-being' we want to account for is not empty to start with; utilitarians use our everyday notion, and our job is to make it clearer. So we are free to move back and forth between our judgments about which cases fall inside the boundary and our descriptions of the boundary. Every account of this type will do the same. There is the same sort of undamaging circularity in mental state and enjoyment accounts, because they need to get beyond the ordinary senses of "pleasure" and "enjoyment," and they would have to go about fixing a new boundary in just the same way.

This narrowing of the desire account still does not get rid of the great embarrassment of the desires of the dead. Of course, a lot of the desires of the dead do count morally, but that is because they affect the living. There is a good case for honouring wishes expressed in wills. Inheritance satisfies the desires of the living to provide for their offspring and encourages saving that benefits society generally. There is a good case, too, for granting rights to the dead — say, to determine whether their bodies are used for medical purposes. But that, again, does not require appeal beyond the well-being of the living. And, anyway, that a desire of a dead person counts *morally* does not show that it counts towards his well-being.

The real trouble is our counting the fulfilment of aims even if (as it seems we must) we do not require that the fulfilment enter experience. Some of our aims are not fulfilled until we are dead; some, indeed, being desires for then, could not be. But is this so embarrassing, after all? You might have a desire — it could be an informed one, I think — to have your achievements recognized and acknowledged. An enemy of yours might go around slandering you behind your back, successfully persuading everyone that you stole all your ideas, and they, to avoid unpleasantness, pretend in your presence to believe you. If that could make your life less good, then why could it not be made less good by his slandering you with the extra distance behind your back that death brings? You might well be willing to exert yourself, at risk of your life, to prevent these slanders being disseminated after your death. You might, with eyes full open, prefer that course to longer life with a ruined reputation after it. There seems nothing irrational in attaching this value to posthumous reputation. And the value being attached to it does not seem to be moral or aesthetic or any kind other than the value to be attached to the life as a life to be lived. Here is another example. It would not have been at all absurd for Bertrand Russell to have thought that if his work for nuclear disarmament had, after his death, actually reduced the risk of nuclear war, his last years would have been more worthwhile, and his life altogether more valuable, than if it all proved futile. True, if Russell had indeed succeeded, his life clearly would have been more valuable to others. But Russell could also have considered it more valuable from the point of view of his own self-interest. For instance, it would not have been absurd for Russell to think the same about devoting his last years to some purely intellectual project without effects on others' well-being, such as patching up the holes in the Theory of Descriptions. A lot of desires of the dead would be ruled out on the grounds we have already mentioned, but it seems right for some still to count.

A Formal Account

An old and potent objection to the utilitarian way of thinking is that it assumes that we value only one kind of thing, whereas we value many irreducibly different kinds of things. It seems to me undeniable that we do value irreducibly different kinds of things. But that point counts against certain mental state accounts, not against the informed-desire account. On the desire account one can allow that when I fully understand what is involved, I may end up valuing many things and valuing them for themselves. The desire account is compatible with a strong form of pluralism about values.

However, the desire account may purchase its pluralism at the price of emptiness. If I advise you to maximize the fulfilment of your desires, I have not helped you much. I have not supplied you with the dominant end of human action by appeal to which you can resolve conflict between your subordinate ends. Nor have I given you a principle of choice of ends. It is no use to you to be told that you should decide what to go for by seeing what gives you most of what you decide to go for. Maximizing the fulfilment of one's desires does not yield, but presupposes, a hierarchy of goals. In contrast to this, the old notion of utility as a pleasurable mental state was both of these things — a dominant end and a principle of choice. And this contrast can easily give the impression that the desire account makes 'utility' almost empty.

But the charge that the new notion of "utility" is empty is, I think, partly the charge that it does not do what the old notion would do, and that is certainly correct. "Utility," on the old monistic interpretation, was the super, over-arching, substantive value. But now, "utility," on the desire account, is not to be seen as the single over-arching value, in fact not as a substantive value at all, but instead as a formal analysis of what it is for something to be prudentially valuable to some person. Therefore, utility will be related to substantive values such as pleasure or accomplishment or autonomy, not by being the dominant value that subsumes them, but by providing a way of understanding the notion "(prudentially) valuable" and hence the notions "more valuable" and "less valuable."

So when, for whatever purposes, we shift from everyday talk of pursuing various different ends to theoretical talk of maximizing a single quantity, "utility," this quantity should not be understood as an end of the same kind, only grander. There is simply no case for reducing these various ends to a single end in this sense. The most that can be said is that a person's ends are unified only in being his *ends,* things he *values.* When our various values conflict, we may attempt to resolve the conflict by trying to realize as much "value" as possible, but the only substantive values present remain the various values that originally appear in our system of ends. We are still able to go for the most "value," to step far enough back from all of our various particular ends and sacrifice the lesser for the greater, even in the absence of a single substantive end as mediator. We mediate, but without such a mediating value.

Is this then a "neutral" account of utility, in the sense in which accounts in recent economics and decision theory are? Yes and no. Yes, because this account, unlike hedonism or ideal utilitarianism, mentions no substantive values. But no, if the account is taken more widely to include the arguments for it, because then substantive values have to appear.

Is this account "objective" or "subjective"? By "subjective," I mean an account that makes well-being depend upon an individual's own desires, and by "objective" one that makes well-being independent of desires. It may look as if an informed-desire account could not be anything but subjective, since it makes "desire" part of the explanation of prudential value. But that entirely depends upon how we take the phrase "an *individual's own* desires." Values do not rest upon *one* person's desire. Values cannot be entirely personal, the result simply of someone's wanting the thing. That would not even be intelligible; persons generally have to be able to see a prudential value as something to go for if it is to be a prudential value at all. But the informed-desire account does make well-being depend upon variant, individual desires in this sense; it gives a place to both actual and ideal desires. *Lafite* may be worth much more than *Coke,* and might be to anyone at all if he appreciated all the flavours they contain, but is worth less to me with my untrained palate. And the account is certainly incompatible with some versions of an objective-list approach to well-being. An objective-list approach says that a person's well-being can be affected by the presence of certain values (which it lists) even if they are not what he wants. The informed-desire account can allow that the values on the list (enjoyment, accomplishment, autonomy, etc.) are values for everyone, but it also allows that there may be very special persons for whom any value on the list (say, accomplishment), though valuable for them as for everybody, conflicts enough with another value (say, freedom from anxiety) for it not, all things considered, to be valuable for them to have. If a certain objective-list approach denies this, then it is different from the informed-desire approach. If it does not deny it, and even plausibly includes enjoyment on its list, and furthermore accepts the complex view about the relation of value and desire that I set out in the last section, then it gets very hard to distinguish from the informed-desire approach. Some philosophers treat the distinction between objective and subjective as if it marked a crucial distinction between accounts of well-being. They do, because they attach great importance to whether or not well-being is made to depend upon an individual's desires, tastes, feelings, or attitudes. But, as we just saw in the last section, the dependence of prudential value on desire is much less simple, less a matter of all or nothing, than they assume. The best account of "utility" makes it depend on some desires and not on others. So the distinction between objective and subjective, defined in the common way that I have defined it, does not mark an especially crucial distinction. It would be better if these terms (at least in this sense) were put into retirement. But if they are not, if the question "Subjective or objective?" is pressed, then the answer has to be "Both."

That answer shows how far what seems to me the best account of "utility" has to move away from its classical beginnings. It has to move from mental state accounts to a desire account; it has to move from an actual-desire to an informed-desire account; and it has to set the standards for a desire's being "informed" in a place not too distant from an objective-list account. This is a stiffer standard for "informed" or "rational" desire than other writers have wished to adopt, so much so that it might seem that I should use a different label. But this label, it seems to me, has merits. It records the fact that this account is a development of one utilitarian tradition, that there is no plausible stopping point for the notion of "utility" short of it, but that this point is still short of objective-list accounts.

AMARTYA SEN*

Plural Utility

1. *The Vector View.* In this paper I am concerned with the advantages of viewing utility primarily as a vector (with several distinct components), and only secondarily as some homogeneous magnitude, possibly a numerical index.

There is nothing controversial in asserting that utility can be viewed as a vector since any real number can be trivially split into components. Furthermore, few would in fact deny that it is possible to distinguish between utilities of different types, or arising from different activities. What is less straightforward is the assertion that there are substantial advantages in choosing the vector view. It is argued that this is indeed the case.

While a significantly richer descriptive account of a person's well-being is a possible advantage (and one that is given some attention here), perhaps the most useful part of the contrast lies in the possible use of the vector view in getting a wider class of interesting moralities than utilitarianism and—more generally—welfarism permit.[1] The class of "utility-supported moralities" permits evaluation of states of affairs distinguishing between different *components* of each person's utility, and possibly weighting them differently. After investigation of various features of the vector approach to utility (sections 2–7), the

*From Amartya Sen: *Plural Utility, Proceedings of the Aristotelian Society*, 1980–1981.
[1]Welfarism defines a restricted class of moralities which make the goodness of any state an increasing function of the aggregate individual utilities in that state. See my "Utilitarianism and Welfarism", *Journal of Philosophy*, 76 (1979).

scope and adequacy of utility-supported moralities is examined in the last section of this paper. Non-utilitarian outcome moralities can be partitioned into utility-supported moralities and others, and the distinction is of some considerable interest.

A vector view of utility should not be confused with the fact that utility has many *alternative interpretations*. There is the contrast between utility as pleasure and utility as desire fulfilment.[2] There are other interpretations, based on such notions as liking, enjoying, the sense of well-being, etc. and while they have various things in common, they are not the same, at least not under some plausible set of interpretations. The vector view of utility is not concerned with the existence of *alternative interpretations* as such, but with the existence of many *coexisting aspects* of utility. It is, of course, possible to get a vector view of utility from a set of alternative interpretations by insisting on the relevance of each of the different interpretations in catching a particular aspect of utility. But the vector view can be adopted even *within* any one interpretation of utility, e.g., pleasure or desire. Desires, for example, can be distinguished between types, or discriminated in some other way, giving us a vector view of utility within the *one* interpretation of utility as desire fulfilment.

4. Desire Fulfilment. There is a basic asymmetry between the pleasure-based view of utility and the desire-based view. Pleasures are reasonably seen as being utilities themselves; desires are not. It is the *fulfilment* of desires that can be reasonably seen as being utility. The primary view of utility as desires can, thus, be seen as being conditional on their fulfilment. This duality of (i) desiring, and (ii) having that desire fulfilled, immediately raises some problems which do not arise with the pleasure-based view.

First, there is the issue of the fulfilment of so-called "irrational" desires. This is a complex notion, and here I will concentrate only on the simple case of factual errors. You desire fame because you think you would adore it, but suppose it is the case that if you were in fact to get there, you would not really be able to work up much adoration. The mistakes can, of course, be more complicated and more interesting. Proposals for "rational assessment" of desires have been suggested, and the case for concentrating on "rational desires" or "rational preference" has been argued.

Second, there is also the question of the timing of the desire vis-a-vis the timing of the fulfilment. It is generally thought to be an advantage of the desire account over the pleasure account that the desires of the dead can be given a status in the former approach. On the other hand, this opens up a new and important problem. If you desire in time 1 that

[2]See the helpful analysis of this contrast in J. C. B. Gosling, *Pleasure and Desire* (Oxford: Clarendon Press, 1969).

you should have x_2 rather than y_2 in period 2, while when period 2 comes you desire that you should have y_2 *rather than* x_2, does the former desire have any status at all? It is tempting to think that it should not have any status since the old preference no longer obtains, but examples can be constructed (e.g., of a firm non-believer all one's life asking for religious performance on his death bed), in which this appears to be too crude a solution. These conflicts are serious enough to lead Richard Brandt to the view that the whole concept of "desire-satisfaction maximization" is "unintelligible".

Third, there is the issue of "awareness" of desire fulfilment and violation. Jonathan Glover illustrates the problem with the case in which a woman says: "My husband wants me to be faithful to him while he is in prison, but he will never know about this."Can a state or an action of which you are unaware be taken to change your utility level? Insofar as your desire is for the occurrence of a state or an action, not for your belief in it, awareness cannot be crucial. But insofar as your own utility cannot be easily taken to have changed without your *perceiving* any change at all, awareness will seem to be relevant.

I have listed a few of the open problems with the desire view of utility. How do we resolve them? What I would like to argue here is that it could be a mistake to seek a resolution in the form of choosing one alternative or the other in each case. With a vector view utility, the claim of one alternative can be accepted without denying the claim of the other.

Consider the question of awareness first. Glover tells you the story of the prisoner and his unfaithful wife. You presume that the prisoner never knew, but you still feel *sorry* for him. "Did he ever know?" you ask Glover. "Yes," says Glover, "it got to him eventually". You feel *sorrier* for the prisoner. Is your sympathy a good indicator of the prisoner's utility? I don't see why not. The *fact* of the desire fulfilment and the awareness of it can be *both* relevant, and the relevance of one does not rule out the relevance of the other. The requirement of "exclusiveness" seems quite arbitrary and uncalled for.

A similar remark applies to the case of mistakes. Take A, B and C, three aspiring authors. A would love success, knows it, and desires success strongly. B would not, in fact, like success if he got there, but does not know this, and so desires success as strongly as A. C would not like success either, but unlike B he knows this, and is too wise to seek success. None of them succeed. It is, of course, quite straightforward to claim that in terms of desire fulfilment regarding literary success, A has failed in a manner that C has not. But what about B? There is some "error" in his seeking literary success, and in terms of "rational desire" his position may be similar to that of C. But is his position really the same as C's? After all he did desire success strongly, and the fact that this desire itself was not rational, could scarcely wipe out his loss. If the three cases are treated in three different ways, then it is reasonable to conclude that *both* the fulfilment of actual desire as well as the fulfilment of rational desire are relevant.

The case of change of desire over time can possibly also make more than one set of desires relevant. Galileo did not, it appears, lose his desire to stand up for the truth when he was forced to recant. But suppose he had. Would that make his recantation no tragedy at all in terms of his own desire fulfilment? Past desires need not lose their relevance altogether *just because* they happened to have been supplanted by later desires, and the question of what importance, *if any*, to attach to past desires must be faced as an issue requiring more of an analysis than just noting the existence of a later contrary desire.

This does not answer the question: "Which *one* alternative?" It disputes the cogency of the question. It could, of course, be the case that a past desire is rightly taken to be of no value (i.e., the frustration of someone's childhood ambition of being a locomotive driver need not get any value in judging the desire fulfilment of an otherwise successful person who later chose a different walk of life). Or it may get a great deal of value (e.g., in the case of the broken and intimidated Galileo). In deciding on what weights to put, there will be, of course, need for theories taking us well beyond the current discourse. What is being asserted here is the elementary claim that the weighting issue is an open one and cannot be arbitrarily closed by taking past desires to be valueless simply because of the existence of contrary desires later. The vector view permits this variability.

But what about Richard Brandt's view that the existence of different —and contrary — views of desires makes the whole concept of "desire-satisfaction maximisation," in fact, "unintelligible?" Obviously, many goals make optimization more difficult than one goal. But an optimization exercise involving many goals need not be unintelligible. Different goals can be ranked in terms of priorities, or weighted vis-a-vis each other or otherwise combined into a consistent "objective function". The co-existence of several relevant indicators of desire-fulfilment only entails that all of them count, not that each is an irresistible force. Indeed, even if weights are unspecified, some intelligible rankings can be immediately asserted, viz., those given by the partial ordering of the *intersection* of the different desire-fulfilment orderings. How much further we can go depends on how precisely the weights can be specified.

5. *Partial Orderings of Aggregate Utility.* With the primary (vector) view of utility — interpreted in terms of desires, or pleasures, or some other elements, or some mixture of these — there is a minimal partial ranking of secondary utility given by the intersection of the rankings reflecting the different elements. If x ranks higher than y according to each element, then x must yield higher total utility than y.

If the weights to be put on the different components of the vector of utility are fully specified, then the secondary view of utility will be a complete ordering based on the weighted sum of the different components. While these two cases reflect the minimum (the intersection partial ordering) and the maximum (a complete ordering), there are many intermediate possibilities. The weights may be partially specified as lying within some *ranges*, in which case the partial ordering of secondary utility will lie somewhere in between the intersection partial order and a complete order. The narrower the ranges, the more extensive the partial ordering of secondary utility.

The weights will, of course, depend on the nature of the exercise in which a secondary view of utility is to be used. The exercise can be, as discussed earlier, a moral one (e.g., using utilitarian morality based on, say, pleasures), a predictive one (e.g., anticipating particular actions), or descriptive in some other way (e.g., describing a person's misery or happiness). The possibility of incompleteness is present in each case. Indeed the vector view of utility suggests that there is nothing "unnatural" about personal utility being a partial ordering. The complete ordering is often just a special case.

For the sake of simplicity, the following discussion takes one particular interpretation of utility, viz., desire fulfilment. In this case, a utility-supported morality may be called—without (I hope) causing confusion—a desire-supported morality. A desire-supported morality can discriminate between different types of desires (e.g., between desires for different kinds of activity, or between desires related to different types of family and social relations, or between desires at various points of time). Desire-based utilitarianism is a special case of desire-based welfarism, which reflects a subclass of desire-supported moralities.

By admitting a good deal of pluralism *within* the framework of utility itself, the class of desire-supported moralities permits a wide variety of moral approaches, but it retains the requirement that for something to be morally valuable, it must be a part of a person's desire. It should be noted that the class is broad enough to admit moralities that contradict the Pareto principle. For example, the desire for one's own lifestyle may be *part* of each person's desires but overwhelmed by each person's "nosey" desires in the individual utility-*totals*; and still the first set of self-regarding desires can be made to win in a desire-supported morality. Given support from any part of a person's desires, an objective can be made much more important through appropriate weighting than would be the case with intensity-aggregation.

While the class of desire-supported moralities is very broad, it must be clarified that some types of moral considerations will find no room in it. First of all, a desire-supported morality is one type of "outcome morality," judging states of affairs only, and the issues connected with consequentialism, deontological considerations, etc., are left unattended. While this leaves some questions open, the class of desire-supported moralities also involves far-reaching constraints. I shall note three types of moral considerations that are positively excluded from finding any room in desire-supported moralities except through some indirect channel.

First, any objective notion of a person's well-being or interest which is independent of his desires has no status.

Second, it may be noticed that a basic capability index not only shifts attention from utility to some human functions (e.g., to move freely, not to be hungry), it also shifts attention from actual performance to *capabilities* (what a person *can* do rather than what he *does* do). The entire perspective of *opportunities* as opposed to chosen positions will be missed by any desire-supported morality. Once again, it may well be the case that everyone will desire, *inter alia,* to have a wider set of opportunities and a wider choice. But if the opportunities available (and the alternatives to choose from) *shrink* (i) without affecting the actually chosen positions and desires for them, and (ii) with such a change of desire strengths for opportunities that the reduced opportunity sets involve the *same* extent of desire fulfilment, then any desire-supported morality will ignore the reduction of opportunities and of choice. Opportunities have no value in a desire-supported system, only *desires* for opportunities have, and objective contraction of opportunities can be washed out by subjective change of desires.

Third, moral theories that treat exploitation as a disvalue, or sexual or racial discrimination as morally wrong, and do this independently of the *strength* of the individual desires for the elimination of these vices, cannot be accommodated within the desire-supported class. The reasoning is similar to that in the previous two cases.

The vector view of utility substantially extends the scope of using utility in moral arguments. Even though the welfarist—and (consequently) the utilitarian—necessity to relate moral goodness ultimately to *aggregate* utilities of individuals is dropped, the necessity of linking with some *component* of utility is retained. Utility-supported moralities (e.g., desire-supported systems) form a very much wider class than welfarism (e.g., desire-based welfarism). Nevertheless, the need to justify all moral values with reference to some aspect of utility (e.g., the fulfilment of some desires) continues to act as a binding and powerful constraint.

The class of utility-supported moralities imposes a different boundary than does welfarism, covering a good deal more. But despite pushing utility-justified arguments as far as they would go, what it leaves out is still quite vast. Critical assessment of the more relaxed restriction of being utility-supported (as opposed to the stricter requirement of being welfarist) is an interesting question in ethics. I have tried to argue that it is also an important question.

PART THREE
PERSONS, JUSTICE, AND RIGHTS

MANY CRITICS HAVE thought the utilitarian goal of the highest total happiness disturbingly impersonal. On the utilitarian view, it may be relatively unimportant if some particular people do badly, so long as the benefits to others outweigh these losses. And freedom to run your own life may also sometimes be removed: if you are going to do things that will bring you less happiness than you could have, there is a utilitarian case for someone else acting paternalistically: intervening to save you from your own mistakes. These criticisms of utilitarianism may be based on a commitment to equality, or to individual rights, or to liberty. What they have in common is well summed up by John Rawls: "Utilitarianism does not take seriously the distinction between persons."

Is it right that some people in a society are very rich and others very poor? Many who think this unjust or immoral are critical of utilitarianism on the grounds that it could justify such inequalities.

As Bentham's comments on Alexander Wedderburn suggest, there is an egalitarian side to utilitarianism. In the utilitarian calculation, everyone is to count for one and no one for more than one. And, in the distribution of wealth, a bias in favor of equality comes from the diminishing marginal utility of money: $100 means more to someone poor than to someone rich.

But it is also possible for utilitarianism to justify inequality. Some economists and others think that, since inequalities include rewards earned by harder work or by innovation and enterprise, they encourage economic growth, with the result that the unequal societies are likely to be richer. In considering the total happiness, the results of growth could outweigh the effects of the diminishing marginal utility of money. Sometimes the "incentives" policy is defended on the grounds that, in the long run, everyone will benefit from the greater wealth, which, it is held, will "trickle down" from rich to poor. But the benefits do not always trickle down to everybody. And the cases where they do not are those most offensive to egalitarians. Yet in such cases total happiness could be maximized, despite very uneven distribution. The criticism is that utilitarians are not concerned with equality or unequality as such: they are only interested in distribution to the extent that it affects the total sum of happiness. Huge inequalities with a slightly greater total would be preferred to equal distribution of a marginally smaller total. Critics see utilitarians as blind to a major dimension of moral assessment. For a single person, it may be worth putting up with unhappiness now, if this leads to greater happiness later. Perhaps happiness across a lifetime is what matters. One charge is that utilitarians' indifference to equality comes about because they assume that one person's gain can compensate for another's loss in the way later gains can compensate for present losses. Underrating the separateness of persons leads to casualness about justice.

Parfit's partial defense against this charge depends on questioning a common view of personal identity. We normally assume that, although in thirty years time I will have changed in appearance and character, I will still be fully *me*. Parfit thinks that the persisting ego is an illusion: there is no further fact beyond a person's history of physical and psychological characteristics, which persist or fade to varying degrees. He believes that the person I am now may only partly survive into my old age. On this account, the differences between me now and me then may become closer than we normally suppose to the differences between you and me. The separateness of persons may not be so important as we suppose. The evaluation of Parfit's case depends on whether one accepts that there is no persisting ego. And if there is no ego, the case depends on the absence of other characteristics stable enough to give people the required unity.

Another egalitarian objection to utilitarianism also rests, in a different way, on the separateness of persons. Utilitarians, in aiming to satisfy people's preferences, may fail to distinguish between *personal* preferences (people's preferences for goods or opportunities for themselves) and *external* preferences (their preferences for goods or opportunities for other people). Ronald Dworkin believes that people have a right to be treated as equals and that this is incompatible with the utilitarian willingness to give weight to external preferences. When such preferences are included, the egalitarian character of a utilitarian argument "is corrupted, because the chance that anyone's preferences have to succeed will then depend, not only on the demands that the personal preferences of others make on scarce resources, but on the respect or affection they have for him or for his way of life." Dworkin believes this to be a form of double counting and that equality of treatment requires the recognition of rights that protect individuals against the result of the "corrupted" version of utilitarianism. These objections to the inclusion of external preferences are criticized by H. L. A. Hart, who denies that their inclusion is necessarily a form of double counting and who is dubious about Dworkin's account of the basis of rights.

One worry about utilitarianism is that it may justify trampling on particular individuals in pursuit of the general happiness. Some utilitarians have resisted this claim. Mill, for instance, argued that understanding the importance of self-expression provides a utilitarian case for liberty in which individuality can flourish. Similar arguments have been used in the case of other interests that have a special importance for us, such as not being killed or tortured. It has been held that people will feel secure only if these vital interests are protected. Many utilitarians have on these grounds been prepared to justify rules protecting them, even in circumstances where other interests appear at first sight to outweigh them.

A sophisticated utilitarian can accept that limitations on the scope of utilitarian calculation can themselves be justified on utilitarian grounds. Utilitarians do not believe in "natural rights" (described by Bentham as "nonsense on stilts"). But the utilitarian case for restricting the scope of utilitarian calculation produces a recognition of frontiers that often closely correspond to those of "natural rights."

The utilitarian argument for recognizing the frontiers is based on the beneficial consequences of doing so. Happiness is increased through there being more room for self-expression, or a greater sense of security. But there is always the possibility that, in a particular case, there may be even stronger utilitarian reasons for violating the "right." Take the case of medical experiments on patients. It is widely accepted that people have a right not to have experiments carried out on them without their free and informed consent. Utilitarians can give general support to this. The code of practice requiring informed consent avoids all kinds of horrors that might otherwise be inflicted on people. It also greatly increases our sense of security when going to the hospital.

But there could be a case where the utilitarian is pushed the other way. Perhaps an experiment involving extreme risk to those it is carried out on would save huge numbers of future lives. In such a case, to stick to the rule about informed consent would prevent the experiment, and so would have worse consequences in the long run. It seems that keeping to the rule would be to abandon utilitarianism. And making the utilitarian choice is to violate what others take to be a right. Those who believe in such rights may feel that utilitarianism does not provide a secure enough basis for them.

The most common alternative view of rights is that the case for respecting them does not depend on the good consequences of doing so. It is thought to be rooted in the separateness of persons. This is held to require that, in pursuing our goals, we respect, in an absolute way, certain limitations on what we can do to people. These "side constraints," as they are sometimes called, cannot be overridden by beneficial consequences. In an image drawn from card playing, Ronald Dworkin has suggested that rights are trumps. This brings out the way rights function as a powerful defense of the individual, but also brings out a certain rigidity in rights theory. Just as all cards are either trumps or not trumps, so it is suggested that any claim is either a right with trumping power or else a mere interest. The least right trumps any claim in the other category, no matter how substantial. There is perhaps something Procrustean about this. There are borderline cases where we may be unsure whether to count, say, a paid vacation from work every year, or an unpolluted place of work, as rights or merely as interests. Suppose we decide that people have a right to an unpolluted place of work, but that a paid vacation is not a right. Then freedom from pollution is in the same league as the right to life or the right to freedom of expression, whereas the annual paid vacation is down there competing with the desires of others for uninterrupted room service at a hotel. Perhaps things do not fall so neatly into these two categories.

In constraining what we can do to people in pursuit of the best consequences, rights theories risk boxing us in. We may be unable to avoid a disaster, because the only way of doing so would involve a minor rights violation. One way of escaping from this rigidity borrows both from utilitarianism and from rights theory. Amartya Sen's approach keeps the distinction between rights and mere interests, but uses it as part of a consequentialist theory: one in which the consequences of actions are what matter for its morality. But consequences are not to be assessed merely by adding up totals of happiness. They are to be judged by the rights that are respected or violated. On this approach, it becomes possible to justify an act that violates someone's right, if this is necessary to avert some greater violation of a right. This view is still left with what utilitarians will see as the rigidity to the two-tier separation of rights from other interests. (Though rights theorists would argue that this is inevitable in any morality giving adequate protection to the individual.) But it shows how the other rigidity (inability to violate minor rights in order to avoid catastrophes) can be avoided in a rights theory that borrows consequentialism from utilitarians.

Crude forms of utilitarianism and of rights theory are both open to powerful objections. Sophisticated forms of both theories tend to converge. The important question is what the best sophisticated theory will be like. It may be only of secondary importance whether it looks more like a modified rights theory or more like modified utilitarianism.

JOHN STUART MILL*

Liberty and Individuality

HE WHO LETS the world, or his own portion of it, choose his plan of life for him, has no need of any other faculty than the ape-like one of imitation. He who chooses his plan for himself, employs all his faculties. He must use observation to see, reasoning and judgment to foresee, activity to gather materials for decision, discrimination to decide, and when he has decided, firmness and self-control to hold to his deliberate decision. And these qualities he requires and exercises exactly in proportion as the part of his conduct which he determines according to his own judgment and feelings is a large one. It is possible that he might be guided in some good path, and kept out of harm's way, without any of these things. But what will be his comparative worth as a human being? It really is of importance, not only what men do, but also what manner of men they are that do it. Among the works of man, which human life is rightly employed in perfecting and beautifying, the first in importance surely is man himself. Supposing it were possible to get houses built, corn grown, battles fought, causes tried, and even churches erected and prayers said, by machinery — by automatons in human form — it would be a considerable loss to exchange for these automatons even the men and women who at present inhabit the more civilised parts of the world, and who assuredly are but starved specimens of what nature can and will produce. Human nature is not a machine to be built after a model, and set to do exactly the work prescribed for it, but a tree, which requires to grow and develop itself on all sides, according to the tendency of the inward forces which make it a living thing.

*From John Stuart Mill: *On Liberty*, Chapter 3.

It will probably be conceded that it is desirable people should exercise their understandings, and that an intelligent following of custom, or even occasionally an intelligent deviation from custom, is better than a blind and simply mechanical adhesion to it. To a certain extent it is admitted that our understanding should be our own: but there is not the same willingness to admit that our desires and impulses should be our own likewise; or that to possess impulses of our own, and of any strength, is anything but a peril and a snare. Yet desires and impulses are as much a part of a perfect human being as beliefs and restraints: and strong impulses are only perilous when not properly balanced; when one set of aims and inclinations is developed into strength, while others, which ought to co-exist with them, remain weak and inactive. It is not because men's desires are strong that they act ill; it is because their consciences are weak. There is no natural connection between strong impulses and a weak conscience. The natural connection is the other way. To say that one person's desires and feelings are stronger and more various than those of another, is merely to say that he has more of the raw material of human nature, and is therefore capable, perhaps of more evil, but certainly of more good. Strong impulses are but another name for energy. Energy may be turned to bad uses; but more good may always be made of an energetic nature, than of an indolent and impassive one. Those who have most natural feeling are always those whose cultivated feelings may be made the strongest. The same strong susceptibilities which make the personal impulses vivid and powerful, are also the source from whence are generated the most passionate love of virtue, and the sternest self-control. It is through the cultivation of these that society both does its duty and protects its interests: not by rejecting the stuff of which heroes are made, because it knows not how to make them. A person whose desires and impulses are his own — are the expression of his own nature, as it has been developed and modified by his own culture — is said to have a character. One whose desires and impulses are not his own, has no character, no more than a steam-engine has a character. If, in addition to being his own, his impulses are strong, and are under the government of a strong will, he has an energetic character. Whoever thinks that individuality of desires and impulses should not be encouraged to unfold itself, must maintain that society has no need of strong natures — is not the better for containing many persons who have much character — and that a high general average of energy is not desirable.

JOHN RAWLS*

The "Separateness of Persons" Objection

THE STRIKING FEATURE of the utilitarian view of justice is that it does not matter, except indirectly, how this sum of satisfactions is distributed among individuals any more than it matters, except indirectly, how one man distributes his satisfactions over time. The correct distribution in either case is that which yields the maximum fulfillment. Society must allocate its means of satisfaction whatever these are, rights and duties, opportunities and privileges, and various forms of wealth, so as to achieve this maximum if it can. But in itself no distribution of satisfaction is better than another except that the more equal distribution is to be preferred to break ties.[1] It is true that certain common sense precepts of justice, particularly those which concern the protection of liberties and rights, or which express the claims of desert, seem to contradict this contention. But from a utilitarian standpoint the explanation of these precepts and of their seemingly stringent character is that they are those precepts which experience shows should be strictly respected and departed from only under exceptional circumstances if the sum of advantages is to be maximized.[2] Yet, as with all other precepts, those of justice are derivative from the one end of attaining the greatest balance of satisfaction. Thus there is no reason in principle why the greater gains of some should not compensate for the lesser losses of others; or more importantly, why the violation of the liberty of

*From John Rawls: A Theory of Justice, section 5.
[1]On this point see Sidgwick, The Methods of Ethics, pp. 416f.
[2]See J. S. Mill, Utilitarianism, ch. IV, last two pars.

a few might not be made right by the greater good shared by many. It simply happens that under most conditions, at least in a reasonably advanced stage of civilization, the greatest sum of advantages is not attained in this way. No doubt the strictness of common sense precepts of justice has a certain usefulness in limiting men's propensities to injustice and to socially injurious actions, but the utilitarian believes that to affirm this strictness as a first principle of morals is a mistake. For just as it is rational for one man to maximize the fulfillment of his system of desires, it is right for a society to maximize the net balance of satisfaction taken over all of its members.

The most natural way, then, of arriving at utilitarianism (although not, of course, the only way of doing so) is to adopt for society as a whole the principle of rational choice for one man. Once this is recognized, the place of the impartial spectator and the emphasis on sympathy in the history of utilitarian thought is readily understood. For it is by the conception of the impartial spectator and the use of sympathetic identification in guiding our imagination that the principle for one man is applied to society. It is this spectator who is conceived as carrying out the required organization of the desires of all persons into one coherent system of desire; it is by this construction that many persons are fused into one. Endowed with ideal powers and sympathy and imagination, the impartial spectator is the perfectly rational individual who identifies with and experiences the desires of others as if these desires were his own. In this way he ascertains the intensity of these desires and assigns them their appropriate weight in the one system of desire the satisfaction of which the ideal legislator then tries to maximize by adjusting the rules of the social system. On this conception of society separate individuals are thought of as so many different lines along which rights and duties are to be assigned and scarce means of satisfaction allocated in accordance with rules so as to give the greatest fulfillment of wants. The nature of the decision made by the ideal legislator is not, therefore, materially different from that of an entrepreneur deciding how to maximize his profit by producing this or that commodity, or that of a consumer deciding how to maximize his satisfaction by the purchase of this or that collection of goods. In each case there is a single person whose system of desires determines the best allocation of limited means. The correct decision is essentially a question of efficient administration. This view of social cooperation is the consequence of extending to society the principle of choice for one man, and then, to make this extension work, conflating all persons into one through the imaginative acts of the impartial sympathetic spectator. Utilitarianism does not take seriously the distinction between persons.

DEREK PARFIT*

Personal Identity and the Separateness of Persons

UTILITARIANS REJECT DISTRIBUTIVE principles. They aim for the greatest net sum of benefits minus burdens, whatever its distribution. I shall say that they *maximize.*

When our acts can affect only one person, most of us accept maximization. We do not believe that we ought to give someone fewer happy days so as to be more fair in the way we spread them out over the parts of his life. There are, of course, arguments for spreading out enjoyments. We remain fresh, and have more to look forward to. But these arguments do not count against maximization; they remind us how to achieve it.

When our acts can affect several different people, Utilitarians make similar claims. They admit new arguments for spreading out enjoyments, such as that which appeals to the effects of relative deprivation, or to diminishing marginal utility. But Utilitarians treat equality as a mere means, not a separate aim.

Since their attitude to sets of lives is like ours to single lives, Utilitarians ignore the boundaries between lives. We may ask, 'Why?'

Here are three suggestions:

1. Their method of moral reasoning leads them to overlook these boundaries.

2. They believe that the boundaries are unimportant, because they think that sets of lives are like single lives.

*From Derek Parfit, *Reasons and Persons,* Chapter 15.

93

3. They accept the Reductionist View about personal identity.

Suggestion (1) has been made by Rawls. It can be summarized like this. Many Utilitarians answer moral questions with the method called that of an *Impartial Observer*. When such a Utilitarian asks himself, as an observer, what would be right, or what he would impartially prefer, he may *identify* with all of the affected people. He may imagine that he himself would be all of these different people. This will lead him to ignore the fact that *different* people are affected, and so to ignore the claims of just distribution as between these people.

Suggestion (2) has been made by Gauthier, and others. On this suggestion, Utilitarians mustmankind is a super-organism, or believe, like some Hindus, in a single *World Soul*. If suggestions (1) or (2) were true, they explain the Utilitarian View in ways that undermine this view. It is clearly a mistake to ignore the fact that we live different lives. And mankind is not a super-organism.

I suggest (3). On this suggestion, Utilitarians reject distributive principles because they believe in the Reductionist View. If the Reductionist View supports the rejection of these principles, this third explanation supports rather than undermines the Utilitarian View.

In the case of some Utilitarians, suggestion (1) may be correct. Many Utilitarians consider moral questions as if they were Impartial Observers. Some of these may be, as Rawls claims, *identifying* observers. But there can also be *detached* observers. While an identifying observer imagines himself as being *all* of the affected people, and a Rawlsian imagines himself as being *one* of the affected people, without knowing whom, a detached observer imagines himself as being *none* of the affected people.

Some Utilitarians have been detached Impartial Observers. These Utilitarians do not overlook the distinction between people. And, as Rawls remarks, there seems little reason why detached observers should be led to ignore the principles of distributive justice. If we approach morality in this detached way—if we do not think of ourselves as potentially involved—we may be somewhat more inclined to reject these principles. This is because we would not fear that we ourselves might become one of the people who are worst off. But this particular approach to moral questions does not sufficiently explain why these Utilitarians reject distributive principles.

Is suggestion (2) correct? As an *explanation* of the Utilitarian View, (2) is false. Some followers of Hegel believed that a nation was a Super-Organism. To quote one writer, a nation 'is a living being, like an individual'. But Utilitarians ignore national boundaries, and they do not believe that Mankind is such a single being.

Suggestion (2) is better taken, not as an explanation of the Utilitarian

View, but as an objection to this view. The suggestion may be that this view cannot be justified unless mankind is a super-organism. Since this is false, Utilitarians are wrong to reject distributive principles.

I suggest a different explanation. On suggestion (3), Utilitarians ignore distribution because they accept the Reductionist View. (3) is compatible with (1). Some Utilitarians may both be identifying observers, and accept the Reductionist View. But (3) conflicts with (2).

There may seem to be a puzzle here. On suggestion (2), a group of people must be assumed to be like a single person. This is the reverse of the Reductionist View, which compares a person's history to that of a nation, or a group of people. Since both these views compare nations to people, how can they be different views?

The answer is this. When we consider nations, most of us are Reductionists. We believe that the existence of a nation involves nothing more than the existence of its citizens, living together on its territory, and acting together in certain ways. In contrast, when considering persons, most of us believe the Non-Reductionist View. We believe that our identity must be determinate. This cannot be true unless a person is a separately existing entity, distinct from his brain and body, and his experiences. Most of us are thus Reductionists about nations but not about people. It is the difference between these common views which explains the two comparisons. The claim that X is like Y typically assumes the common view of Y. We shall therefore say, "People are like nations" if we are Reductionists about both. If we are Non-Reductionists about both, we shall instead say, "Nations are like people." The belief in super-organisms is the Non-Reductionist View about nations.

Changing a Principle's Scope

Since Utilitarians reject distributive principles, they believe that the boundaries of lives have no moral significance. On their view, the separateness of persons can be ignored. I have described three explanations for this view. I shall now argue that, despite some complications, mine is the best explanation.

> Consider *The Child's Burden*. We must decide whether to impose on some child some hardship. If we do, this will either
> (i) be for this child's own greater benefit in adult life, or
> (ii) be for the similar benefit of someone else — such as this child's younger brother.

Does it matter morally whether (i) or (ii) is true?

Most of us would answer: "Yes. If it is for the child's own later benefit, there can at least be no unfairness." We might add the general claim that imposing useful burdens is more likely to be justified if these burdens are for a person's own good.

Utilitarians would accept this claim, but explain it in a different way. Rather than claiming that such burdens cannot be unfair, they would claim that they are in general easier to bear.

To block this reply, we can suppose that our child is too young to be cheered up in this way. This simplifies the disagreement. Utilitarians would say: "Whether it is right to impose this burden on this child depends only on how great the later benefit will be. It does not depend upon who benefits. It would make no moral difference if the benefit comes, not to the child himself, but to someone else." Non-utilitarians would reply: "On the contrary, if it comes to the child himself, this helps to justify the burden. If it comes to someone else, that is unfair."

Do the two views about the nature of personal identity support different sides in this disagreement?

Part of the answer is clear. Non-utilitarians think it a morally important fact that it be the child himself who, as an adult, benefits. This fact is more important on the Non-Reductionist View, for it is on this view that the identity between the child and the adult is in its nature deeper. On the Reductionist View, what is involved in this identity is less deep, and it holds, over adolescence, to a reduced degree. If we are Reductionists, we may compare the absence of many connections between the child and his adult self to the absence of connections between different people. We shall give more weight to the fact that, in this example, this child does not care what will happen to his adult self. That it will be *he* who receives the benefit may thus seem to us less important. We might say, "It will not be *he* who benefits. It will only be his adult self."

The Non-Reductionist View supports the Non-utilitarian reply. Does it follow that the Reductionist View supports the Utilitarian claim? It does not. We might say, "Just as it would be unfair if it is someone else who benefits, so if it won't be the child, but only his adult self, this would also be unfair."

The point is a general one. If we are Reductionists, we regard the rough subdivisions within lives as, in certain ways, like the divisions between lives. We may therefore come to treat alike two kinds of distribution: within lives, and between lives. But there are two ways of treating these alike. We can apply distributive principles to both, or to neither.

Which of these might we do? I distinguished two ways in which our moral view may change. We may give to distributive principles a different scope, and a different weight. If we become Reductionists, we may be led to give these principles *greater* scope. Since we regard the subdivisions within lives as, in certain ways, like the divisions between lives, we may apply distributive principles even within lives, as in the claim just made about imposing burdens on a child. By widening the scope of distributive principles, we would be moving further away from the Utilitarian view. In this respect the Reductionist View counts against rather than in favour of the Utilitarian view.

Changing a Principle's Weight

Return next to the second explanation of the Utilitarian view. Gauthier suggests that to suppose that we should maximize for mankind "is to suppose that mankind is a super-person."

To understand this suggestion we should first ask why we can ignore distributive principles within a single life. Why is it morally permissible here simply to maximize? It might be thought that this is permissible because it is not a moral matter what we do with our own lives. Even if this was true, it cannot be the explanation. We believe that it can be right to maximise within the life of someone else. Medicine provides examples. We think it right for doctors to maximize on behalf of their unconscious patients. They would be right to choose some operation which would give their patients a smaller total sum of suffering, even though this suffering would all come within one period. We do not believe that this would be unfair to this person during this period.

Some claim: "We are free to maximize within one life only because it is *one* life." This claim supports Gauthier's charge against Utilitarians. It supports the claim that we could be free to maximize over different lives only if they are like parts of a single life.

When presented with this argument, Utilitarians would deny its premise. They might claim: "What justifies maximization is not the unity of a life. Suffering is bad, and happiness is good. It is better if there is less of what is bad, and more of what is good. This is enough to justify maximization. Since it is not the unity of a life that, within this life, justifies maximization, this can be justified over different lives without the assumption that mankind is a super-person."

One connection with the Reductionist View is this. It is on this, rather than the Non-Reductionist View, that the premise of Gauthier's argument is more plausibly denied. If the unity of a life is less deep, it is more plausible to claim that this unity is not what justifies maximization. This is one of the ways in which the Reductionist View provides some support for the Utilitarian View.

I shall expand these remarks. There are two kinds of distribution: within lives, and between lives. And there are two ways of treating these alike. We can apply distributive principles to both, or to neither.

Utilitarians apply them to neither. I suggest that this may be, in part, because they accept the Reductionist View. An incompatible suggestion is that they accept the reverse view, believing that mankind is a super-person.

My suggestion may seem clearly wrong if we overlook the fact that there are two routes to the abandonment of distributive principles. We may give them no scope, or instead give them no weight.

Suppose we assume that the only route is the change in scope. This is suggested by Rawls's claim that "the utilitarian extends to society the principle of choice for one man." The assumption here is that the route to Utilitarianism is a change in the scope, not of distributive principles, but of its correlative: our freedom to ignore these principles. If we assume that the only route is a change in scope, it may indeed seem that Utilitarians must either be assuming that any group of people is like a single person (Gauthier's suggestion), or at least be forgetting that it is not (Rawls's suggestion).

I shall describe the other route. Utilitarians may not be denying that distributive principles have scope. They may be denying that they have weight. This denial may be given some support by the Reductionist View.

More exactly, my suggestion is this. The Reductionist View does support a change in the scope of distributive principles. It supports giving these principles *more* scope. It supports applying these principles even within a single life. This is what I claimed in the case of the Child's Burden. A Reductionist is more likely to regard this child's relation to his adult self as being like a relation to a different person. He is thus more likely to claim that it is unfair to impose burdens on this child merely to benefit his adult self. It is on the Non-Reductionist View that we can more plausibly reply, "This cannot be unfair, since it will be just as much *he* who will later benefit." As we shall later see, there is another argument which, on the Reductionist View, supports a greater widening in the scope of distributive principles. Though in these two ways the Reductionist View supports widening the scope of distributive principles, it also supports giving these principles less weight. And, if we give these principles *no* weight, it will make no difference that we have given them wider scope. This is how the net effect might be the Utilitarian View.

This suggestion differs from the others in the following way. Rawls remarks that the Utilitarian View seems to involve "conflating all persons into one." Nagel similarly claims that a Utilitarian 'treats the desires . . . of distinct persons as if they were the desires . . . of a mass person.' And I have quoted Gauthier's similar claim. On my suggestion, the Utilitarian View may be supported by, not the conflation of persons, but their partial disintegration. It may rest upon the view that a person's life is less deeply integrated than most of us assume. Utilitarians may be treating benefits and burdens, not as if they all came within the same life, but as if it made no moral difference where they came. And this belief may be partly supported by the view that the unity of each life, and hence the difference between lives, is in its nature less deep.

In ignoring principles of distribution between different people, the Utilitarian View is *impersonal*. Rawls suggests that it "mistakes impersonality for impartiality." This would be so if the way in which Utilitarians try to be impartial leads them to overlook the difference between persons. And this may be claimed for the few Utilitarians whose method of moral reasoning does have this effect. It may be claimed about an *identifying* Impartial Observer, whose method of reasoning leads him to imagine that he will himself be all of the affected people. But few Utilitarians have reasoned in this way. And, on my suggestion, they do not mistake impersonality for impartiality. The impersonality of their view is partly supported by the Reductionist View about the nature of persons. As Rawls writes, 'the correct regulative principle for anything depends upon the nature of that thing.'

Can It Be Right to Burden Someone Merely to Benefit Someone Else?

I shall now develop my suggestion. Utilitarians believe that benefits and burdens can be freely weighed against each other, even if they come to different people. This is frequently denied.

We can first distinguish two kinds of weighing. The claim that a certain burden *factually outweighs* another is the claim that it is greater. The claim that it *morally outweighs* another is the claim that we ought to relieve it even at the cost of failing to relieve the other. Similar remarks apply to the weighing of different burdens, and to the weighing of burdens against benefits. It is worth explaining how a benefit can be greater than, or factually outweigh, a burden. This would be most clearly true if, when offered the choice of having either both or neither, everyone would choose to have both. Everyone would here believe that it is worth undergoing this burden for the sake of this benefit. For this to be a good test, people must be equally concerned about the parts of their lives in which they would receive these benefits and burdens. Since most people care less about the further future, the test is best applied by asking people whether they would choose to undergo this burden before receiving the benefit. If they believe that this would be worth doing, we can claim that, in their case, this benefit factually outweighs this burden.

Certain people claim that one burden cannot be factually outweighed by another, if they come within different lives. These people claim that such interpersonal comparisons make no sense. If I lose my finger, and you lose your life, it makes no sense to claim that your loss may be greater than mine. I shall here ignore this view.

Others claim that burdens and benefits in different lives cannot be *morally* weighed. I shall consider one part of this claim. This is the claim that someone's burden cannot be morally outweighed by mere benefits to someone else. I say *mere* benefits, because the claim is not intended to deny that it can be right to burden someone so as to benefit someone else. This might be required by distributive justice. We can rightly tax the rich to benefit the poor. What the claim denies is that such acts can be justified solely upon the utilitarian ground that the benefit is greater than the burden. It denies that one person's burden can be morally outweighed by mere benefits to someone else.

This claim often takes qualified forms. It can be restricted to great burdens, or be made to claim that, to outweigh one person's burden, the benefit to others must be much greater. I shall here discuss this claim in its simplest form, for most of my remarks could be applied to the other forms. Rawls puts the claim as follows: 'The reasoning which balances the gains and losses of different persons . . . is excluded'. I call this the *Objection to Balancing*.

This objection rests in part on a different claim. This is that someone's burden cannot be *compensated* by benefits to someone else. I call this the *Claim about Compensation*. This claim is, with one qualification, clearly true. Our burdens can be compensated by benefits to those we love. But they cannot be compensated by benefits to total strangers.

We cannot deny the Claim about Compensation. If becoming Reductionist affects our view about this claim, the effects would be these. We might, first, extend the claim even within single lives. We might claim, in the example that I gave, that the child's burden cannot be compensated by benefits to his adult self. Or we might claim that there cannot here be *full* compensation. This might support the claim that the child's burden would be morally outweighed only if the benefit to his adult self is *much* greater. These claims would be like the claims that, when the psychological connections have been markedly reduced, we deserve less punishment for, and are less committed by, the actions of our earlier selves. These claims treat weakly connected parts of one life as, in some respects, or to some degree, like different lives. The claims therefore change the scope of our principles. If we believe that, between some parts of the same life, there can be either no or less compensation, we are changing the scope of the Claim about Compensation. Given the content of the Reductionist View, this is a change of scope in the right direction.

We might, next, give this claim less weight. Our ground would be the one that I earlier suggested. Compensation presupposes personal identity. On the Reductionist View, we believe that the fact of personal identity over time is less deep, or involves less. We may therefore claim that this fact has less moral importance. Since this fact is presupposed by compensation, we may claim that the fact of compensation is itself morally less important. Though it cannot be denied, the claim about compensation may thus be given less weight. (Here is another example of this distinction. That it is unjust to punish the innocent cannot be denied. But the claim can be given no weight. Our inability to deny this claim does not force us to believe in desert. If we do not believe in desert, perhaps because we are determinists, we can claim, "Though it is bad to punish the innocent, punishing the guilty is just as bad."

Return now to the Objection to Balancing. Unlike compensation, the concept of *greater moral weight than* does not presuppose personal identity. The Objection to Balancing can therefore be denied.

The denial might be put like this: 'Our burdens cannot be compensated by mere benefits to someone else. But they may be morally outweighed by such benefits. It may still be right to give the benefits rather than relieve the burdens. Burdens are morally outweighed by benefits if they are factually outweighed by these benefits. All that is needed is that the benefits be greater than the burdens. It is unimportant, in itself, to whom both come.'

This is the Utilitarian's reply. It would be his reply to the many arguments in which the Objection to Balancing seems not to be distinguished from the Claim about Compensation. Thus Rawls uses the phrase, 'cannot be justified by, or compensated for by'. And Perry writes, 'The happiness of a million somehow fails utterly to compensate or to even to mitigate the torture of one'. This undeniable claim Perry seems to equate with the Objection to Balancing. This is a mistake.

The Reductionist View gives some support to the Utilitarian's reply. The Objection to Balancing rests, in part, on the Claim about Compensation. The Reductionist View supports both the claim that there is less scope for compensation, and the claim that compensation has less moral weight. Compensation has less scope and less weight than it would have had if the Non-Reductionist View had been true. Since compensation is, in these two ways, morally less important, there is less support for the Objection to Balancing. We can therefore claim that the Utilitarian's reply is more plausible than it would be if the Non-Reductionist View was true. But this claim does not imply that we must accept the Utilitarian View. This is why this claim gives only *some* support to this view.

These claims can be explained in a different way. Even those who object to balancing think that it can be justified to impose burdens on a child for his own greater benefit later in his life. Their claim is that a person's burden, while it can be morally outweighed by benefits to him, cannot *ever* be outweighed by mere benefits to others. This is held to be so even if the benefits are far greater than the burden. The claim thus gives to the boundaries between lives — or to the fact of non-identity — overwhelming significance. It allows within the same life what, over different lives, it totally forbids.

This claim would be more plausible on the Non-Reductionist View. Since the fact of identity is, here, thought to be deeper, the fact of non-identity could more plausibly seem to have such importance. On this view, it is a deep truth that all of a person's life is as much his life. If we are impressed by this truth — by the unity of each life — the boundaries between lives will seem to be deeper. This supports the claim that, in the moral calculus, these boundaries cannot be crossed. On the Reductionist View, we are less impressed by this truth. We regard the unity of each life as, in its nature, less deep, and as a matter of degree. We may therefore think the boundaries between lives to be less like those between, say, the squares on a chessboard, dividing what is all pure white from what is all jet black. We may think these boundaries to be more like those between different countries. They may then seem less morally important.

It may be objected: The Reductionist claims that the parts of each life are less deeply unified. But he does not claim that there is more unity between different lives. The boundaries between lives are, on his view, just as deep.

We could answer: If some unity is less deep, so is the corresponding disunity. The fact that we live different lives is the fact that we are not the same person. If the fact of personal identity is less deep, so is the fact of non-identity. There are not two different facts here, one of which is less deep on the Reductionist View, while the other remains as deep. There is merely one fact, and this fact's denial. The separateness of persons is the denial that we are all the same person. If the fact of personal identity is less deep, so is this fact's denial.

RONALD DWORKIN*

The "Double Counting" Objection

THE UTILITARIAN ARGUMENT, that a policy is justified if it satisfies more preferences overall, seems at first sight to be an egalitarian argument. It seems to observe strict impartiality. If the community has only enough medicine to treat some of those who are sick, the argument seems to recommend that those who are sickest be treated first. If the community can afford a swimming pool or a new theater, but not both, and more people want the pool, then it recommends that the community build the pool, unless those who want the theater can show that their preferences are so much more intense that they have more weight in spite of the numbers. One sick man is not to be preferred to another because he is worthier of official concern; the tastes of the theater audience are not to be preferred because they are more admirable. In Bentham's phrase, each man is to count as one and no man is to count as more than one.

These simple examples suggest that the utilitarian argument not only respects, but embodies, the right of each citizen to be treated as the equal of any other. The chance that each individual's preferences have to succeed, in the competition for social policy, will depend upon how important his preference is to him, and how many others share it, compared to the intensity and number of competing preferences. His chance will not be affected by the esteem or contempt of either officials or fellow citizens, and he will therefore not be subservient or beholden to them.

*From Ronald Dworkin, *Taking Rights Seriously*, Chapter 9.

But if we examine the range of preferences that individuals in fact have, we shall see that the apparent egalitarian character of a utilitarian argument is often deceptive. Preference utilitarianism asks officials to attempt to satisfy people's preferences so far as this is possible. But the preferences of an individual for the consequences of a particular policy may be seen to reflect, on further analysis, either a *personal* preference for his own enjoyment of some goods or opportunities, or an *external* preference for the assignment of goods and opportunities to others, or both. A white law school candidate might have a personal preference for the consequences of segregation, for example, because the policy improves his own chances of success, or an external preference for those consequences because he has contempt for blacks and disapproves social situations in which the races mix.

The distinction between personal and external preferences is of great importance for this reason. If a utilitarian argument counts external preferences along with personal preferences, then the egalitarian character of that argument is corrupted, because the chance that anyone's preferences have to succeed will then depend, not only on the demands that the personal preferences of others make on scarce resources, but on the respect or affection they have for him or for his way of life. If external preferences tip the balance, then the fact that a policy makes the community better off in a utilitarian sense would *not* provide a justification compatible with the right of those it disadvantages to be treated as equals.

This corruption of utilitarianism is plain when some people have external preferences because they hold political theories that are themselves contrary to utilitarianism. Suppose many citizens, who are not themselves sick, are racists in political theory, and therefore prefer that scarce medicine be given to a white man who needs it rather than a black man who needs it more. If utilitarianism counts these political preferences at face value, then it will be, from the standpoint of personal preferences, self-defeating, because the distribution of medicine will then not be, from that standpoint, utilitarian at all. In any case, self-defeating or not, the distribution will not be egalitarian in the sense defined. Blacks will suffer, to a degree that depends upon the strength of the racist preference, from the fact that others think them less worthy of respect and concern.

This is a similar corruption when the external preferences that are counted are altruistic or moralistic. Suppose many citizens, who themselves do not swim, prefer the pool to the theater because they approve of sports and admire athletes, or because they think that the theater is immoral and ought to be repressed. If the altruistic preferences are counted, so as to reinforce the personal preferences of swimmers, the result will be a form of double counting: each swimmer will have the benefit not only of his own preference, but also of the preference of someone else who takes pleasure in his success. If the moralistic preferences are counted, the effect will be the same: actors and audiences will suffer because their preferences are held in lower respect by citizens whose personal preferences are not themselves engaged.

In these examples, external preferences are independent of personal preferences. But of course political, altruistic, and moralistic preferences are often not independent, but grafted on to the personal preferences they reinforce. If I am white and sick, I may also hold a racist political theory. If I want a swimming pool for my own enjoyment I may also be altruistic in favor of my fellow athlete, or I may also think that the theater is immoral. The consequences of counting these external preferences will be as grave for equality as if they were independent of personal preference, because those against whom the external preferences run might be unable or unwilling to develop reciprocal external preferences that would right the balance.

External preferences therefore present a great difficulty for utilitarianism. That theory owes much of its popularity to the assumption that it embodies the right of citizens to be treated as equals. But if external preferences are counted in overall preferences, then this assumption is jeopardized. That is, in itself, an important and neglected point in political theory; it bears, for example, on the liberal thesis, first made prominent by Mill, that the government has no right to enforce popular morality by law. It is often said that this liberal thesis is inconsistent with utilitarianism, because if the preferences of the majority that homosexuality should be repressed, for example, are sufficiently strong, utilitarianism must give way to their wishes. But the preference against homosexuality is an external preference, and the present argument provides a general reason why utilitarians should not count external preferences of any form. If utilitarianism is suitably reconstituted so as to count only personal preferences, then the liberal thesis is a consequence, not an enemy, of that theory.

It is not always possible, however, to reconstitute a utilitarian argument so as to count only personal preferences. Sometimes personal and external preferences are so inextricably tied together, and so mutually dependent, that no practical test for measuring preferences will be able to discriminate the personal and external elements in any individual's overall preference. That is especially true when preferences are affected by prejudice. Consider, for example, the associational preference of a white law student for white classmates. This may be said to be a personal preference for an association with one kind of colleague rather than another. But it is a personal preference that is parasitic upon external preferences: except in very rare cases a white student prefers the company of other whites because he has racist, social, and political convictions, or because he has contempt for blacks as a group. If these associational preferences are counted in a utilitarian argument used to justify segregation, then the egalitarian character of the argument is destroyed just as if the underlying external preferences were counted directly. Blacks would be denied their right to be treated as equals because the chance that their preferences would prevail in the design of admissions policy would be crippled by the low esteem in which others hold them. In any community in which prejudice against a particular minority is strong, then the personal preferences upon which a utilitarian argument must fix will be saturated with that prejudice; it follows that in such a community no utilitarian argument purporting to justify a disadvantage to that minority can be fair.[1]

[1] The argument of this paragraph is powerful, but it is not, in itself, sufficient to disqualify all utilitarian arguments that produce substantial disadvantages to minorities who suffer from prejudice. Suppose the government decides, on a utilitarian argument, to allow unemployment to increase because the loss to those who lose their jobs is outweighed by the gain to those who would otherwise suffer from inflation. The burden of this policy will fall disproportionately on blacks, who will be fired first because prejudice runs against them. But though prejudice in this way affects the consequences of the policy of unemployment, it does not figure, even indirectly, in the utilitarian argument that supports that policy. (It figures, if at all, as a utilitarian argument against it.) We cannot say, therefore, that the special damage blacks suffer from a high unemployment policy is unjust for the reasons described in this essay. It may well be unjust for other reasons; if John Rawls is right, for example, it is unjust because the policy improves the condition of the majority at the expense of those already worse off.

H.L.A. HART*

Comments on the "Double Counting" Objection

IN CONSTRUCTING HIS anti-utilitarian right-based theory Dworkin has sought to derive too much from the idea of equal concern and respect for persons, just as Nozick in constructing his theory sought to derive too much from the idea of the separateness of persons. Both of course appear to offer something comfortably firm and uncontroversial as a foundation for a theory of basic rights. But this appearance is deceptive: that it is so becomes clear if we press the question why, as Dworkin argues, does a utilitarian decision procedure or democratic vote which counts both personal and external preferences *for that reason* fail to treat persons as equals, so that when as he says it is "antecedently likely" that external preferences may tip the balance against some individual's specific liberty, that liberty becomes clothed with the status of a moral right not to be overridden by such procedures. Dworkin's argument is that counting external preferences corrupts the utilitarian argument or a majority vote as a decision procedure, and this of course must be distinguished from any further independent moral objection there may be to the actual decision resulting from the procedure. An obvious example of such a vice in utilitarian argument or in a majority vote procedure would of course be double counting, e.g. counting one individual's (a Brahmin's or a white man's) vote or preference twice while counting another's (an Untouchable's or a black man's) only once. This is, of course, the very vice excluded by the

*From H.L.A. Hart: "Between Utility and Rights," in Alan Ryan (ed.): *The Idea of Freedom*.

maxim "everybody to count for one, nobody for more than one" which Mill thought made utilitarianism so splendid. Of course an Untouchable denied some liberty, say liberty to worship, or a black student denied access to higher education as a result of such double counting would not have been treated as an equal, but the right needed to protect him against this is not a right to any specific liberty but simply a right to have his vote or preference count equally with the Brahmin's. And of course the decision to deprive him of the liberty in question might also be morally objectionable for reasons quite independent of the unfairness in the procedure by which it was reached: if freedom of religion or access to education is something of which no one should be deprived whatever decision procedure, fair or unfair, is used, then a right to that freedom would be necessary for its protection. But it is vital to distinguish the specific alleged vice of unrefined utilitarianism or a democratic vote in failing, e.g. through double counting, to treat persons as equals, from any independent objection to a particular decision reached through such arguments. It is necessary to bear this in mind in considering Dworkin's argument.

So, finally, why is counting external preferences thought to be, like the double counting of the Brahmin's or white man's preference, a vice of utilitarian argument or a majority vote? Dworkin actually says that the inclusion of external preference *is* a "form of double counting."[1] To understand this we must distinguish cases where the external preference is *favourable* to, and so supports, some personal preference or want for some good or advantage or liberty from cases where the external preference is hostile. Dworkin's simple example of the former is where one person wants the construction of a swimming-pool[2] for his use and other non-swimmers support this. But why is this a "form of double counting?" No one's preference is counted twice as the Brahmin's is; it is only the case that the proposal for the allocation of some good to the swimmer is supported by the preferences both of the swimmer and (say) his disinterested non-swimmer neighbour. Each of the two preferences is counted only as one; and surely *not* to count the neighbour's disinterested preference on this issue would be to fail to treat the two as equals. It would be 'undercounting' and presumably as bad as double counting. Suppose — to widen the illustration — the issue is freedom for homosexual relationships, and suppose that (as may well have been the case at least in England when the old law was reformed in 1967)[3] it was the disinterested external preferences of liberal heterosexual persons that homosexuals should have this freedom that tipped the balance against the external preferences of other het-

[1]Dworkin, previous extract, p. 146.
[2]ibid.
[3]Sexual Offences Act 1967.

erosexuals who would deny this freedom. How in this situation could the defeated opponents of freedom or any one else complain that the procedure, through counting external preferences (both those supporting the freedom for others and those denying it) as well as the personal preferences of homosexuals wanting it for themselves, had failed to treat persons as equals?

It is clear that where the external preferences are hostile to the assignment of some liberty wanted by others, the phenomenon of one person's preferences being supported by those of another, which, as I think, Dworkin misdescribes as a "form of double counting," is altogether absent. Why then, since the charge of double counting is irrelevant, does counting such hostile external preferences mean that the procedure does not treat persons as equals? Dworkin's answer seems to be that if, as a result of such preferences tipping the balance, persons are denied some liberty, say to form certain sexual relations, those so deprived suffer because by this result their conception of a proper or desirable form of life is despised by others, and this is tantamount to treating them as inferior to or of less worth than others, or not deserving equal concern or respect. So every denial of freedom on the basis of external preferences implies that those denied are not entitled to equal concern and respect, are not to be considered as equals. But even if we allow this most questionable interpretation of denials of freedom, still for Dworkin to argue in this way is altogether to change the argument. The objection is no longer that the utilitarian argument or a majority vote is, like double counting, unfair as a procedure because it counts in "external preference," but that a particular *upshot* of the procedure where the balance is tipped by a *particular kind* of external preference, one which denies liberty and is assumed to express contempt, fails to treat persons as equals. But this is a vice not of the mere externality of the preferences that have tipped the balance but of their content: that is, their liberty-denying and respect-denying content. Yet this is no longer to assign certain liberties the status of ("anti-utilitarian") rights simply as a response to the specific defects of utilitarianism as Dworkin claims to do. But that is not the main weakness in his ingenious argument. What is fundamentally wrong is the suggested interpretation of denials of freedom as denials of equal concern or respect. This surely is mistaken. It is indeed least credible where the denial of the liberty is the upshot of a utilitarian decision procedure or majority vote in which the defeated minority's preference or vote for the liberty has been weighed equally with others and outweighed by numbers. Then the message need not be, as Dworkin interprets it, "You and your views are inferior, not entitled to equal consideration, concern or respect," but "You and your supporters are too few. You, like everyone else, are counted as one but no more than one. Increase your numbers and then your views may win out." Where those who are denied by a majority vote the liberty they seek are able, as they are in a fairly working democracy, to continue to press their views in public argument and to attempt to change their opponents' minds, as they in fact with success did after several defeats when the law relating to homosexuality was changed in England, it seems quite impossible to construe every denial of liberty by a majority vote based on external preferences as a judgement that the minority whom it defeats are of inferior worth, not entitled to be treated as equals or with equal concern and respect. What is true is something different and quite familiar but no support for Dworkin's argument: namely that the procedural fairness of a voting system or utilitarian argument which weighs votes and preferences equally is no guarantee that all the requirements of fairness will be met in the actual working of the system in given social conditions. This is so because majority views may be, though they are not always, ill-informed and impervious to argument: a majority of theoretically independent voters may be consolidated by prejudice into a self-deafened or self-perpetuating block which affords no fair opportunities to a despised minority to publicise and argue its case. All that is possible and has sometimes been actual. But the moral unacceptability of the results in such cases is not traceable to the inherent vice of the decision procedure in counting external preferences, as if this was analogous to double counting. That, of course, would mean that every denial of liberty secured by the doubly counted votes or preferences would necessarily not only be a denial of liberty but also an instance of failing to treat those denied as equals.

AMARTYA SEN*

Rights Consequentialism

I. Welfarist Consequentialism and Constraint-based Deontology

IN THE INSTRUMENTAL view rights are not valuable in themselves, but right-based rules, conventions, institutions, etc., are useful in pursuing other — right-independent — goals. The most commonly identified goals in the instrumental approach tend to be "welfarist" goals,[1] with the goodness of states of affairs being judged entirely by the personal utility features of the respective states. One special case of welfarist evaluation is by far more common than others, and that is the case of utilitarian evaluation in which the goodness of a state of affairs is judged simply by the sum total of personal utilities in that state.[2] But other welfarist approaches exist, for example, judging states by the utility level of the worst-off individual in that state, as under a variant of

---

*From Amartya Sen: "Rights and Agency," *Philosophy and Public Affairs*, 1982.

[1]For a discussion of the distinguishing features of welfarism, and a critique, see my "Utilitarianism and Welfarism," *Journal of Philosophy* 76 (September 1979).

[2]When the population is a variable, one has to make the further distinction between "classical" and "average" utilitarianism. In this paper I shall not go into that issue.

Rawls's "Difference Principle,"[3] or by some other method of distribution-sensitive aggregation of personal utilities.[4]

In contrast, in the constraint-based deontological view rights are treated as constraints on actions. These constraints must not be violated *even if* such violation would lead to better states of affairs. Violating rights is simply wrong. Unlike in the instrumental view, rights *are* given intrinsic importance, but unlike in "goal rights systems," to be presented later in this paper, rights *directly* affect judgments of actions — and only of actions — rather than being embedded first in the evaluation of states of affairs and then affecting the evaluation of actions through consequential links between actions and states. As Robert Nozick puts it, "Individuals have rights, and there are things no person or group may do to them (without violating their rights)."[5] Further, "Rights do not determine a social ordering but instead set the constraints within which a social choice is to be made, by excluding certain alternatives, fixing others, and so on."[6]

I shall now argue that both the welfarist instrumental approach (including, inter alia, the traditional utilitarian approach) and the deontological constraint-based approach are inadequate in important ways. Furthermore their respective inadequacies are related to a common ground shared by the two, despite sharp differences in other respects. The particular common ground is the *denial* that realization and failure of rights should enter into the evaluation of states of affairs themselves and could be used for consequential analysis of actions. Nozick's view that "rights do not determine a social ordering" is shared fully by welfarists in general and utilitarians in particular. Their ways part there, however, with the welfarist instrumentalist viewing rights in terms of their consequences for *right-independent* goals and the constraint-based deontologist reflecting rights *without consequential justification* as constraints on actions. State-evaluation independent of rights leaves a gap that cannot be adequately closed by either of these approaches.

[3]John Rawls, *A Theory of Justice* (Cambridge, MA: Harvard University Press, 1971). Rawls himself repudiates this *variant*, but it is nevertheless much used. See E.S. Phelps. ed., *Economic Justice* (Harmondsworth: Penguin Books, 1973); P.J. Hammond, "Equity, Arrow's Conditions and Rawls's Difference Principle," *Econometrica* 42 (1976); and C. d'Aspremont and L. Gevers, "Equity and Information Basis of Collective Choice," *Review of Economic Studies* 46 (1977).

[4]See my *On Economic Inequality* (Oxford: Basil Blackwell, 1973). Kevin Roberts has provided an axiomatization of the class of distribution-sensitive, utility-based social welfare functionals, satisfying symmetry, homotheticity, and additive separability; see his "Interpersonal Comparability and Social Choice Theory," *Review of Economic Studies* 47 (1980). See also C. Blackorby and D. Donaldson, "Utility vs. Equity: Some Plausible Quasi-orderings," *Journal of Public Economics* 7 (1977).

[5]R. Nozick, *Anarchy, State and Utopia* (Oxford: Basil Blackwell, 1974), p. ix.

[6]Nozick, *Anarchy, State and Utopia*, p. 166.

Consider the constraint-based deontological approach first. It is of course obvious that this approach can hardly do justice to those rights associated with the so-called positive freedom.[7] But the problem is not confined to that, and is present even when the intrinsic value of positive freedom is disputed and the focus is chosen to be entirely on noncoercion and related issues of negative freedom. Even with negative freedom, *multilateral* interdependences can arise and undermine the rationale of the constraint-based deontological approach. The only way of stopping the violation of a very important liberty of one person by another may be for a third to violate some other, less important liberty of a fourth. To take a crude example, the only way of saving A from rape by B could be for C to arrive speedily at the spot in a car stolen from D, who is not a party to the rape but who does not want his car to be used for this purpose. The justification of C's action will require consequential analysis trading off the badness of violating D's right to the disposal of his own car against the badness of letting the rape occur. Since the constraint-based deontological view does not permit violation or realization of rights "to determine the social ordering,"[8] it is particularly inadequate in dealing with such cases of *multilateral* interdependences, which can be easily accommodated however in a system of consequential evaluation.

The instrumental welfarist approach is well-armed with a consequential framework of moral evaluation. But since the evaluation of consequences is based ultimately on utility information only (non-utility information being valued just as a causal influence on — or as a surrogate for — utility information[9]), mental features (such as pleasures, happiness, desires, etc., depending on the particular interpretation of utility) rule the roost entirely. The losses of the victim and other

---

[7]For the classic statement of the distinction between "positive" and "negative" freedom, see Isaiah Berlin, "Two Concepts of Liberty," in his *Four Essays on Liberty* (Oxford: Clarendon Press, 1969).

[8]Nozick, p. 166. It is, however, possible to respond to problems of this kind by making the so-called "constraints" nonconstraining under particular circumstances, though there is obviously a danger here of resorting to *ad hoc* solutions. (For an illuminating critique of some possible reasons for overriding right-based constraints, see Judith Jarvis Thomson, *Self-defense and Rights: The Lindley Lecture*, University of Kansas, 1976.) For example, it can be specified that if the badness of the state of affairs resulting from obeying the constraint exceeds some "threshold," then the constraint may be overridden. Such a threshold-based "constraint" system must rest ultimately on consequential analysis, comparing one set of consequences (badness resulting from obeying the constraint) with another (badness of violating the constraint itself, given by the threshold), and its distinguishing feature will be the particular *form* of the consequence-evaluation function. Compromises of this kind raise other problems, which I do not pursue here, but I should emphasize that I do not include such consequential analysis in the category of "constraint-based deontological approach," against which my criticism here is directed.

[9]See my "On Weights and Measures: Informational Constraints in Social Welfare Analysis," *Econometrica* 43 (1977), and "Personal Utilities and Public Judgments: Or What's Wrong with Welfare Economics?" *Economic Journal* 89 (1979).

sufferers are contrasted with the gains of the violators and other gainers entirely in terms of relative utility features. There might have been good utilitarian reasons for forcing men to fight wild animals in the Colosseum with the utility gain of the thousands of spectators outweighing the utility loss of the few forced men.

I shall return to these general issues later. In the next section, I illustrate the difficulties created by the two traditional approaches by taking up a particular example of a moral problem.

II. An Illustrative Moral Problem

Ali is a successful shopkeeper, who has quickly built up a good business in London since immigrating from East Africa. He is, however, hated by a small group of local racists, and a particular gang of them — I shall call them bashers — are, it happens, planning to bash Ali that evening in some secluded spot to which Ali will go alone. Donna, a West Indian friend of Ali, has just come to know of the bashers' plan, and wants to warn Ali about it. But Ali has gone away for the day, and will go to that secluded spot without returning home. Donna does not know where Ali has gone nor the location of the planned bashing, but she does know that Ali has left a message on the desk of his business contact Charles about his movement. However, Charles is away for the day also, and cannot be contacted. Hence the only way of getting Ali's message is by breaking into Charles's room. Donna asked for the help of the police, who dismissed Donna's story as a piece of paranoiac fantasy. Donna knows that she can certainly frustrate the planned bashing by breaking into Charles's room, recovering the message, and warning Ali during the day. But she cannot do this without violating the privacy of Charles, who is, Donna also knows, a secretive man who will feel rather embarrassed at the thought of someone looking through his personal papers to find the message. Indeed, Donna also knows Charles, a self-centered egoist, well enough to be sure that he will be more disturbed by the violation of his own privacy than by the bashing of Ali. What should Donna do?

The long-term utilities of Ali and the ten people in the gang of bashers are given in Table 1.

Table 1
Long-term Utilities

State of Affairs	Ali's Utility	Each Basher's Utility (10 Bashers)	Utility Sum Total	Minimum Utility	Inequality of Utilities
No bashing	15	5	65	5	more
Bashing	10	6	70	6	less

Notice that Ali will suffer a good deal more than any of the bashers will gain in utility terms, but the aggregate utility gain of the bashers exceeds the utility loss of Ali. In terms of these utilities, however, Ali remains better off than the gang of poor, unemployed bashers, even though his suffering is large enough to make a substantial impact on his long-term utility total.[10]

Donna considers the utility information in viewing the problem first from the welfarist angle. In terms of the utilitarian objective, it is clear that the bashing up is doing more good than harm. There could be indirect effects, of course, but Donna finds that they won't be very serious in this case. There is so much fear of racial violence in that locality anyway, that one incident will not *add* significantly to the general sense of insecurity. Also, whether or not the bashing is pre-vented by warning Ali, the bashers will continue to go about their business as usual, and there will certainly not be any better chance of making the police take some action if Ali is *not* actually bashed up. Thus, there is nothing in these considerations to weaken the utility argument for the incident. Of course, there is Charles's utility also, but that will strengthen the case for no action by Donna, since breaking into his room to stop the bashing will reduce his utility.

Donna turns next to the welfarist version of Rawlsian difference principle. She finds that the utility level of the worst-off individuals will go up rather than down as a consequence of the bashing up. So this "maximin" view also favors doing nothing to stop the bashing up. Indeed, so will every welfarist criterion that responds positively to a *larger utility total, more equally distributed*. So Donna moves to indirect utilitarian (and more generally, indirect welfarist) reasoning. She can well believe that among the class of 'uniform' rules dealing with bash-ing up, the rule of not treating anyone thus, in any situation whatever, may receive much support from the point of view of utilitarian evalua-tion of outcomes. But clearly from the same point of view that is, at most, a second best if choices are not necessarily confined to such uniform rules. Better still will be compliance with the no-bashing rule *except* in cases like this, in view of the net utility gain from this particu-lar incident. Why should utilitarianism settle for such a second best by arbitrarily restricting choices to the class of rigid rules only?[11] Will it not be better from the utilitarian point of view to have a more flexible

---

[10]Cardinal interpersonal comparability of utility is assumed in the table. None of the arguments will change if the numbers are all altered by applying some positive linear (affine) transformation, for example, multiplying each number by 10, or adding 100 to each. On the framework for measurability and comparability assumptions, see my *Collective Choice and Social Welfare* (San Francisco: Holden-Day, 1970; distribution taken over by North Holland, Amsterdam); and L. Gevers, "On Interpersonal Comparability and Social Welfare Orderings," *Econometrica* 45 (1979). Also K. Basu, *Revealed Preference of Governments* (Cambridge: Cambridge University Press, 1979).

[11]Cf. David Lyons, "Utility and Rights," mimeographed (Cornell University, 1979); forthcoming in *Nomos* 24 (1982).

rule that permits bashing up in cases of the type described, thereby avoiding unnecessary sacrifice of utility? The justification of any policy —be it a rule, or an act, or something else—must rest ultimately on the ability to produce the best outcomes, judged by "outcomes utilitarianism."[12]

However, it is possible that following such flexible rules is not feasible, and this is quite possibly a case when we should deal with 'disposition' as a variable. Henry Sidgwick[13] had seen in this an argument for going against act utilitarian reasoning, and recently this aspect of the problem has been thoroughly investigated from different perspectives in the works of Richard Hare, Robert Adams, John Harsanyi, and others.[14] Even if a particular act of bashing, or raping, or torturing improves the utility picture, given other things, this does not imply a utilitarian endorsement of that act if that act must go with a certain disposition that will typically cause harm.[15] The eschewal of that act will then be a necessary part of the suppression of that bad disposition.

Donna ponders over this indirect utilitarian reasoning, and becomes convinced that if she were to advise *the bashers* on what to do, from the utilitarian point of view, she would indeed argue for the removal of the disposition to bash up innocent people (including Ali). But Donna also recognizes that advising the bashers on what to do is not the exercise in which she is currently engaged, and her actions, whatever they are, are most unlikely to have any significant effect on the disposition of the bashers. Her moral problem concerns the issue of whether to break into Charles's room to collect the information that will permit her to warn Ali. There is no direct utilitarian case for her to break in, and it is not clear how bringing in the choice of dispositions is going to provide an argument for her to break in. Of course, if a disposition "to break into other people's rooms" were found to be a good disposition to cultivate, this would give her, in terms of disposition utilitarianism, a reason to break in. But she can hardly believe that it is likely that such a general disposition to break in, or even a disposition to break in for a perceived excellent cause, will be a good one to cultivate in terms of utilitarian evaluation of consequences. Clearly, what is needed in this particular case and in cases like this is a *discriminating* defense of breaking in that balances pros and cons, rather than a general disposition to break down

[12]Cf. my "Utilitarianism and Welfarism," pp. 464–67.

[13]Henry Sidgwick, *The Method of Ethics*, 7th ed. (London: Macmillan, 1907).

[14]See especially R. M. Hare, "Ethical Theory and Utilitarianism," in *Contemporary British Philosophy*, ed. H. D. Lewis (London: Allen & Unwin, 1976); R. M. Adams, "Motive Utilitarianism," *Journal of Philosophy* 73 (August 1976); J. Harsanyi, "Rule Utilarianism and Decision Theory," in *Decision Theory and Social Ethics*, ed. H. W. Gottinger and W. Leinfellner (Dordrecht: Reidel, 1978).

[15]For a discussion of some of the difficulties with this general approach, see the "Introduction" to *Utilitarianism and Beyond*, ed. A. Sen and B. Williams (Cambridge: Cambridge University Press, forthcoming).

the door. And in this case such a calculating defense of the act of breaking in is yet to be found within the utilitarian (and more generally, welfarist) approach.

Of course, a strong argument for breaking into Charles's room could have emerged if the violation of Ali's bodily integrity were given a force strong enough for it not to be outweighed by the countervailing utility advantage of the bashers. But the utilitarian and other welfarist methods of outcome evaluation do not permit this, as they insist on judging the strength of claims exclusively in terms of utility information only.

Despite this failure of welfarism (including utilitarianism) to give Donna a good ground for doing what her moral conviction tells her she should do, to wit, break into Charles's room and save Ali, she decides that she must stick by her conviction. How can a person's bodily integrity, his freedom to move about without harm, be outweighed by mere pleasure or desire-fulfillment of the bashers? By not stopping the bashers, she would rob Ali of one of his most elementary rights. With this thought in mind, Donna decides to turn now to constraint-based deontological approaches. And yes, she sees that there is indeed an inflexible "side constraint," in Nozick's terms, which is morally imposed on the bashers not to bash up Ali. However, this constraint does not affect Donna directly since she is not one of the bashers! There is nothing in that constraint-based deontological perspective that would require Donna to do anything at all.

The more Donna thinks about it, however, the more she feels convinced that she must really break into Charles's room and save Ali from bodily injury. Maybe she is not *required* to do anything, but surely she is *free* to? But, no, she isn't free to break into Charles's room since that deontological perspective also imposes a side constraint against the violation of *Charles's* rights. Since right violations and realizations do not enter the evaluation of states of affairs ("do not," as Nozick puts it, "determine a social ordering") and the violation of Ali's more important right cannot be used for consequential justification of infringing Charles's less important right, Donna's hands are tied. Indeed, Nozick repudiates such trade-offs (what he calls "utilitarianism of rights")[16], and the constraint-based deontological approach, free from consequential analysis, offers nothing else.

To summarize the position, at the risk of some oversimplification, Donna can have a good case for breaking into Charles's room to save Ali if she can use a consequential analysis with nonwelfarist evaluation of consequences. Constraint-based deontology does not permit the former (namely, consequential analysis), while welfarist instrumenta-

[16]Nozick, *Anarchy*, pp. 28–29. On this question see Herbert Hart, "Between Utility and Rights," *Columbia Law Review* 79 (1979): 828–46.

lism does not permit the latter (namely, nonwelfarist evaluation of consequences). It appears that to make room for her deeply held and resilient conviction that she must save Ali by breaking into Charles's room, Donna must reject both these traditional approaches and look for a new approach that is at once consequentialist and nonwelfarist.

PART FOUR
LIFE AND DEATH

WHAT IS WRONG with killing people? It is generally thought that the wrongness of killing is so obvious that it seems to need no further justification. But difficult cases may lead to deeper questioning. Is killing *always* wrong? What about killing in war? Or abortion? Or suicide? Are we justified in killing animals for food, or do the reasons why killing people is wrong apply equally to them? It is hard to give answers to these questions without going into the reasons why killing people is in general wrong. Views that decisions about death belong to the person whose life it is give different answers about suicide from views that killing is wrong because God has forbidden it. The belief that killing people is wrong because life is sacred has unwelcome consequences for the use of sprays against mosquitoes.

Utilitarians think killing is wrong because it decreases happiness. The person who is killed will be missed by family and friends. There will be the loss of whatever contribution to society he or she would have made. And, most important, there will be the loss of that person's own happiness in the years that would have been lived if life had not been cut short.

"Happiness" here may be interpreted as a mental state, or in terms of the satisfaction of desires. On the desire interpretation, there are problems about how much it matters whether you know if your desire is satisfied. Desire-utilitarians give great weight to the (usually very strong) desire not to be killed. But if you are killed in your sleep, you will not know that your desire has not been satisfied. On the other hand, if you are not killed, you *will* be aware of this. There is a family of

119

mental state and desire versions of utilitarianism. They give rather different accounts of the wrongness of killing. (The differences are most notable where someone wants to die despite having a good chance of a happy life.) But their shared consequentialist approach sharply separates all utilitarians from believers in the sanctity of life.

One strong and persistent criticism stresses cases where the happiness of other people supports a utilitarian case for killing someone. In *Crime and Punishment*, Dostoyevsky gives Raskolnikov's reasons for murdering an old moneylender. Among these are that she is a blight on the lives of others and that she is not particularly happy herself. When reading the novel (or when thinking in real life), few of us can be comfortable with the apparently utilitarian view that such considerations may make it permissible (or even obligatory) to kill someone.

A similar question about the utilitarian view of killing is raised by the "survival lottery" devised by John Harris. Suppose two people are in danger of dying through organ failure, and donors are not available. Would it be right to kill a healthy person whose organs could be used to save the two? We can imagine a system in which the person whose number came up in the lottery would be killed and used as a donor. Utilitarians, like other people, show little enthusiasm for this proposal. But there is a question whether their theory gives adequate reasons for opposing it. There would, of course, be horrors associated with such a survival lottery. But would *no* number of lives saved outweigh this in the utilitarian calculation?

Another issue for utilitarians concerns creating life. Should utilitarians increase total happiness by creating extra happy people?

Imagine a family where the parents are utilitarians: "When we had the three children, we were all *very* happy. Of course, Adam, Benjamin and Rebecca sometimes had problems, but we had lots of time to talk and do things together, and there was plenty of room in the house. Now things are much more of a squash, and Adam, Benjamin, and Rebecca do not have as good a life as they used to. And we are often exhausted from looking after Adam, Benjamin, Rebecca, Ann, Dale, Toby, Derek, Janet, Jeff, Sally, William, Sophie, Richard, Mary, Aaron, and Colin. But look at the total. We must be a happier family now."

What has gone wrong here? Some say that the remedy is to make sure that utilitarianism takes a "personal" rather than an "impersonal" form. Jan Narveson argues that utilitarians should be concerned to make people happy rather than to make happy people. For a "personal" utilitarian, acts are only good if there are people who are made happier by them, and only bad if there are people who are made less happy. No one is made happier than they were by being brought into existence, so creating extra people has no particular merit for the "personal" utilitarian.

One problem for this view is the difficulty (which Narveson considers) of explaining why it is wrong to bring into existence someone whose life will be miserable. Another problem is that, for the "personal" utilitarian, it does not seem to matter whether there are people at all. If we all took a drug that made us blissful but sterile, we would be the last generation of people. To some of us, this seems almost the worst thing we could do. But personal utilitarianism has to accept it, as no one is made less happy than they were.

Another diagnosis of what the utilitarian parents did wrong is that they aimed at the largest *total* happiness. A popular alternative goal is the highest *average* happiness. This rules out creating extra people if the result will be a drop in the general level. Quantity is not allowed to compensate for quality. But, as Derek Parfit points out, the average view is also paradoxical. Suppose we discover a group of people whose existence was previously unknown. They have happy lives, but are not quite as happy as the average person among the rest of us. On the average view, the world is, because of their existence, a less good place than we had supposed. In other words, it would have been better if they had not been born. This seems absurd. Now suppose that we find our previous calculations of the average level of happiness in the original population were mistaken. It is lower than we had thought. The additional group turn out to be just above the average rather than just below. Now it turns out to be a good thing that they were born. There must be something wrong with a theory according to which someone's existence being a good or bad thing depends on these calculations about the happiness of other unconnected people. These are just the start of the paradoxes in the ethics of population size, as Derek Parfit's article shows.

The population problem is one of the greatest we face. Until recently, the problem seemed entirely one of means: of how best to slow the frightening growth in numbers. This is still the most urgent problem. But we are starting to see deep intellectual problems in working out what the ideal population size would be. It is a problem fairly natural to pose in utilitarian terms, but where none of the obvious forms of utilitarianism seems adequate. And we have no coherently worked out non-utilitarian alternative. It is alarming that such an important issue is one filled with paradox, where plausible premises lead to absurd conclusions, and where most of the thinking has still to be done. This should be a major challenge to moral philosophers, utilitarians as well as their opponents.

JOHN HARRIS*

The Survival Lottery

LET US SUPPOSE that organ transplant procedures have been perfected; in such circumstances if two dying patients could be saved by organ transplants then, if surgeons have the requisite organs in stock and no other needy patients, but nevertheless allow their patients to die, we would be inclined to say, and be justified in saying, that the patients died because the doctors refused to save them. But if there are no spare organs in stock and none otherwise available, the doctors have no choice, they cannot save their patients and so must let them die. In this case we would be disinclined to say that the doctors are in any sense the cause of their patients' deaths. But let us further suppose that the two dying patients, Y and Z, are not happy about being left to die. They might argue that it is not strictly true that there are no organs which could be used to save them. Y needs a new heart and Z new lungs. They point out that if just one healthy person were to be killed his organs could be removed and both of them be saved. We and the doctors would probably be alike in thinking that such a step, while technically possible, would be out of the question. We would not say that the doctors were killing their patients if they refused to prey upon the healthy to save the sick. And because this sort of surgical Robin Hood-ery is out of the question we can tell Y and Z that they cannot be saved, and that when they die they will have died of natural causes and not of the neglect of their doctors. Y and Z do not however agree, they insist

*From John Harris, "The Survival Lottery," *Philosophy*, 1975.

that if the doctors fail to kill a healthy man and use his organs to save them, then the doctors will be responsible for their deaths.

Many philosophers have for various reasons believed that we must not kill even if by doing so we could save life. They believe that there is a moral difference between killing and letting die. On this view, to kill A so that Y and Z might live is ruled out because we have a strict obligation not to kill but a duty of some lesser kind to save life. A. H. Clough's dictum "Thou shalt not kill but need'st not strive officiously to keep alive" expresses bluntly this point of view. The dying Y and Z may be excused for not being much impressed by Clough's dictum. They agree that it is wrong to kill the innocent and are prepared to agree to an absolute prohibition against so doing. They do not agree, however, that A is more innocent than they are. Y and Z might go on to point out that the currently acknowledged right of the innocent not to be killed, even where their deaths might give life to others, is just a decision to prefer the lives of the fortunate to those of the unfortunate. A is innocent in the sense that he has done nothing to deserve death, but Y and Z are also innocent in this sense. Why should they be the ones to die simply because they are so unlucky as to have diseased organs? Why, they might argue, should their living or dying be left to chance when in so many others areas of human life we believe that we have an obligation to ensure the survival of the maximum number of lives possible?

Y and Z argue that if a doctor refuses to treat a patient, with the result that the patient dies, he has killed that patient as sure as shooting, and that, in exactly the same way, if the doctors refuse Y and Z the transplants that they need, then their refusal will kill Y and Z, again as sure as shooting. The doctors, and indeed the society which supports their inaction, cannot defend themselves by arguing that they are neither expected, nor required by law or convention, to kill so that lives may be saved (indeed, quite the reverse) since this is just an appeal to custom or authority. A man who does his own moral thinking must decide whether, in these circumstances, he ought to save two lives at the cost of one, or one life at the cost of two. The fact that so called "third parties" have never before been brought into such calculations, have never before been thought of as being involved, is not an argument against their now becoming so. There are of course, good arguments against allowing doctors simply to haul passers-by off the streets whenever they have a couple of patients in need of new organs. And the harmful side-effects of such a practice in terms of terror and distress to the victims, the witnesses and society generally, would give us further reasons for dismissing the idea. Y and Z realize this and have a proposal, which they will shortly produce, which would largely meet objections to placing such power in the hands of doctors and eliminate at least some of the harmful side-effects.

In the unlikely event of their feeling obliged to reply to the re-
proaches of Y and Z, the doctors might offer the following argument:
they might maintain that a man is only responsible for the death of
someone whose life he might have saved, if, in all the circumstances of
the case, he ought to have saved the man by the means available. This is
why a doctor might be a murderer if he simply refused or neglected to
treat a patient who would die without treatment, but not if he could
only save the patient by doing something he ought in no circumstances
to do — kill the innocent. Y and Z readily agree that a man ought not to
do what he ought not to do, but they point out that if the doctors, and
for that matter society at large, ought on balance to kill one man if two
can thereby be saved, then failure to do so will involve responsibility
for the consequent deaths. The fact that Y's and Z's proposal involves
killing the innocent cannot be a reason for refusing to consider their
proposal, for this would just be a refusal to face the question at issue
and so avoid having to make a decision as to what ought to be done in
circumstances like these. It is Y's and Z's claim that failure to adopt
their plan will also involve killing the innocent, rather more of the
innocent than the proposed alternative.

To back up this last point, to remove the arbitrariness of permitting
doctors to select their donors from among the chance passers-by outside hospitals, and the tremendous power this would place in doctors'
hands, to mitigate worries about side-effects and lastly to appease those
who wonder why poor old A should be singled out for sacrifice, Y and Z
put forward the following scheme: they propose that everyone be given
a sort of lottery number. Whenever doctors have two or more dying
patients who could be saved by transplants, and no suitable organs have
come to hand through "natural" deaths, they can ask a central computer to supply a suitable donor. The computer will then pick the
number of a suitable donor at random and he will be killed so that the
lives of two or more others may be saved. No doubt if the scheme were
ever to be implemented a suitable euphemism for "killed" would be
employed. Perhaps we would begin to talk about citizens being called
upon to "give life" to others. With the refinement of transplant procedures such a scheme could offer the chance of saving large numbers of
lives that are now lost. Indeed, even taking into account the loss of the
lives of donors, the numbers of untimely deaths each year might be
dramatically reduced, so much so that everyone's chance of living to a
ripe old age might be increased. If this were to be the consequence of
the adoption of such a scheme, and it might well be, it could not be
dismissed lightly. It might of course be objected that it is likely that
more old people will need transplants to prolong their lives than will
the young, and so the scheme would inevitably lead to a society dominated by the old. But if such a society is thought objectionable, there is
no reason to suppose that a program could not be designed for the

computer that would ensure the maintenance of whatever is considered to be an optimum age distribution throughout the population.

Suppose that inter-planetary travel revealed a world of people like ourselves, but who organized their society according to this scheme. No one was considered to have an absolute right to life or freedom from interference, but everything was always done to ensure that as many people as possible would enjoy long and happy lives. In such a world a man who attempted to escape when his number was up or who resisted on the grounds that no one had a right to take his life, might well be regarded as a murderer. We might or might not prefer to live in such a world, but the morality of its inhabitants would surely be one that we could respect. It would not be obviously more barbaric or cruel or immoral than our own.

Y and Z are willing to concede one exception to the universal application of their scheme. They realize that it would be unfair to allow people who have brought their misfortune on themselves to benefit from the lottery. There would clearly be something unjust about killing the abstemious B so that W (whose heavy smoking has given him lung cancer) and X (whose drinking has destroyed his liver) should be preserved to over-indulge again.

What objections could be made to the lottery scheme? A first straw to clutch at would be the desire for security. Under such a scheme we would never know when we would hear *them* knocking at the door. Every post might bring a sentence of death, every sound in the night might be the sound of boots on the stairs. But, as we have seen, the chances of actually being called upon to make the ultimate sacrifice might be slimmer than is the present risk of being killed on the roads, and most of us do not lie trembling a-bed, appalled at the prospect of being dispatched on the morrow. The truth is that lives might well be more secure under such a scheme.

If we respect individuality and see every human being as unique in his own way, we might want to reject a society in which it appeared that individuals were seen merely as interchangeable units in a structure, the value of which lies in its having as many healthy units as possible. But of course Y and Z would want to know why A's individuality was more worthy of respect than theirs.

Another plausible objection is the natural reluctance to play God with men's lives, the feeling that it is wrong to make any attempt to re-allot the life opportunities that fate has determined, that the deaths of Y and Z would be "natural," whereas the death of anyone killed to save them would have been perpetrated by men. But if we are able to change things, then to elect not to do so is also to determine what will happen in the world.

Neither does the alleged moral differences between killing and letting die afford a respectable way of rejecting the claims of Y and Z. For if we really want to counter proponents of the lottery, if we really want to answer Y and Z and not just put them off, we cannot do so by saying that the lottery involves killing and object to it for that reason, because to do so would, as we have seen, just beg the question as to whether the failure to save as many people as possible might not also amount to killing.

To opt for the society which Y and Z propose would be then to adopt a society in which saintliness would be mandatory. Each of us would have to recognize a binding obligation to give up his own life for others when called upon to do so. In such a society anyone who reneged upon this duty would be a murderer. The most promising objection to such a society, and indeed to any principle which required us to kill A in order to save Y and Z, is, I suspect, that we are committed to the right of self-defence. If I can kill A to save Y and Z then he can kill me to save P and Q, and it is only if I am prepared to agree to this that I will opt for the lottery or be prepared to agree to a man's being killed if doing so would save the lives of more than one other man. Of course there is something paradoxical about basing objections to the lottery scheme on the right of self-defence since, *ex hyposthesi*, each person would have a better chance of living to a ripe old age if the lottery scheme were to be implemented. None the less, the feeling that no man should be required to lay down his life for others makes many people shy away from such a scheme, even though it might be rational to accept it on prudential grounds, and perhaps even mandatory on utilitarian grounds. Again, Y and Z would reply that the right of self-defence must extend to them as much as to anyone else; and while it is true that they can only live if another man is killed, they would claim that it is also true that if they are left to die, then someone who lives on does so over their dead bodies.

It might be argued that the institution of the survival lottery has not gone far to mitigate the harmful side-effects in terms of terror and distress to victims, witnesses and society generally, that would be occasioned by doctors simply snatching passers-by off the streets and disorganizing them for the benefit of the unfortunate. Donors would after all still have to be procured, and this process, however it was carried out, would still be likely to prove distressing to all concerned. The lottery scheme would eliminate the arbitrariness of leaving the life and death decisions to the doctors, and remove the possibility of such terrible power falling into the hands of any individuals, but the terror and distress would remain. The effect of having to apprehend presumably unwilling victims would give us pause. Perhaps only a long period of education or propaganda could remove our abhorrence. What this abhorrence reveals about the rights and wrongs of the situation is however more difficult to assess. We might be inclined to say that only monsters could ignore the promptings of conscience so far as to operate the lottery scheme. But the promptings of conscience are not necessarily the most reliable guide. In the present case Y and Z would argue that such promptings are mere squeamishness, an over-nice self-indulgence that costs lives. Death, Y and Z would remind us, is a distressing experience whenever and to whomever it occurs, so the less it occurs the better. Fewer victims and witnesses will be distressed as part of the side-effects of the lottery scheme than would suffer as part of the side-effects of not instituting it.

Lastly, a more limited objection might be made, not to the idea of killing to save lives, but to the involvement of "third parties." Why, so the objection goes, should we not give X's heart to Y or Y's lungs to X, the same number of lives being thereby preserved and no one else's life set at risk? Y's and Z's reply to this objection differs from their previous line of argument. To amend their plan so that the involvement of so called "third parties" is ruled out would, Y and Z claim, violate their right to equal concern and respect with the rest of society. They argue that such a proposal would amount to treating the unfortunate who need new organs as a class within society whose lives are considered to be of less value than those of its more fortunate members. What possible justification could there be for singling out one group of people whom we would be justified in using as donors but not another? The idea in the mind of those who would propose such a step must be something like the following: since Y and Z cannot survive, since they are going to die in any event, there is no harm in putting their names into the lottery, for the chances of their dying cannot thereby be increased and will in fact almost certainly be reduced. But this is just to ignore everything that Y and Z have been saying. For if their lottery scheme is adopted they are not going to die anyway — their chances of dying are no greater and no less than those of any other participant in the lottery whose number may come up. This ground for confining selection of donors to the unfortunate therefore disappears. Any other ground must discriminate against Y and Z as members of a class whose lives are less worthy of respect than those of the rest of society.

It might more plausibly be argued that the dying who cannot themselves be saved by transplants, or by any other means at all, should be the priority selection group for the computer programme. But how far off must death be for a man to be classified as "dying"? Those so classified might argue that their last few days or weeks of life are as valuable to them (if not more valuable) than the possibly longer span remaining to others. The problem of narowing down the class of possible donors without discriminating unfairly against some sub-class of society is, I suspect, insoluble.

Such is the case for the survival lottery. Utilitarians ought to be in favour of it, and absolutists cannot object to it on the ground that it involves killing the innocent, for it is Y's and Z's case that any alternative must also involve killing the innocent. If the absolutist wishes to maintain his objection he must point to some morally relevant difference between positive and negative killing. This challenge opens the door to a large topic with a whole library of literature, but Y and Z are dying and do not have time to explore it exhaustively. In their own case the most likely candidate for some feature which might make this moral difference is the malevolent intent of Y and Z themselves. An absolutist might well argue that while no one intends the deaths of Y and Z, no one necessarily wishes them dead, or aims at their demise for any reason, they do mean to kill A (or have him killed). But Y and Z can reply that the death of A is no part of their plan, they merely wish to use a couple of his organs, and if he cannot live without them . . . *tant pis!* None would be more delighted than Y and Z if artificial organs would do as well, and so render the lottery scheme otiose.

One form of absolutist argument perhaps remains. This involves taking an Orwellian stand on some principle of common decency. The argument would then be that even to enter into the sort of "macabre" calculations that Y and Z propose displays a blunted sensibility, a corrupted and vitiated mind. Forms of this argument have recently been advanced by Noam Chomsky (*American Power and the New Mandarins*) and Stuart Hampshire (*Morality and Pessimism*). The indefatigable Y and Z would of course deny that their calculations are in any sense "macabre," and would present them as the most humane course available in the circumstances. Moreover they would claim that the Orwellian stand on decency is the product of a closed mind, and not susceptible to rational argument. Any reasoned defence of such a principle must appeal to notions like respect for human life, as Hampshire's argument in fact does, and these Y and Z could make conformable to their own position.

Can Y and Z be answered? Perhaps only by relying on moral intuition, on the insistence that we do feel there is something wrong with the survival lottery and our confidence that this feeling is prompted by some morally relevant difference between our bringing about the death of A and our bringing about the deaths of Y and Z. Whether we could retain this confidence in our intuitions if we were to be confronted by a society in which the survival lottery operated, was accepted by all, and was seen to save many lives that would otherwise have been lost, it would be interesting to know.

There would of course be great practical difficulties in the way of implementing the lottery. In so many cases it would be agonizingly difficult to decide whether or not a person had brought his misfortune on himself. There are numerous ways in which a person may contribute to his predicament, and the task of deciding how far, or how decisively, a person is himself responsible for his fate would be formidable. And in those cases where we can be confident that a person is innocent of responsibility for his predicament, can we acquire this confidence in time to save him? The lottery scheme would be a powerful weapon in the hands of someone willing and able to misuse it. Could we ever feel certain the lottery was safe from unscrupulous computer programmers? Perhaps we should be thankful that such practical difficulties make the survival lottery an unlikely consequence of the perfection of transplants. Or perhaps we should be appalled.

It may be that we would want to tell Y and Z that the difficulties and dangers of their scheme would be too great a price to pay for its benefits. It is as well to be clear, however, that there is also a high, perhaps an even higher, price to be paid for the rejection of the scheme. That price is the lives of Y and Z and many like them, and we delude ourselves if we suppose that the reason why we reject their plan is that we accept the sixth commandment.[1]

[1]Thanks are due to Ronald Dworkin, Jonathan Glover, M. J. Inwood and Anne Seller for helpful comments.

JAN NARVESON*

Utilitarianism and New Generations

ONE OF THE STOCK objections to utilitarianism goes like this: "If utilitarianism is correct, then we must be obliged to produce as many children as possible, so long as their happiness would exceed their misery." It has always seemed to me that there is a certain air of sophistry about this argument, and in this paper, I shall endeavor to demonstrate this by exposing the fallacies upon which it is founded.

In order to show that the general happiness would be increased by our having a child, the argument would have to go as follows. Imagine that the total number of people is N, and that the total happiness is H, the average happiness therefore being $N/H = 1$. Now suppose that we have good evidence that any child produced by us would be twice as happy as that, giving him a value of 2. Then the average happiness after he is born will be $(N + 2)/(H + 1)$, which would be somewhat larger, therefore, than before. Does this give us a moral reason to produce children? No. We have committed a fallacy.

Suppose that we live in a certain country, say, Fervia, and we are told by our king that something is about to happen which will greatly increase the general happiness of the Fervians: namely that a certain city on Mars, populated by extremely happy Martians will shortly become a part of Fervia. Since these new Fervians are very happy, the average happiness, hence the "general happiness" of the Fervians will be greatly increased. Balderdash. If you were a Fervian, would you be impressed by this reasoning? Obviously not. What has happened, of

*From Jan Narveson, "Utilitarianism and New Generations," *Mind*, 1967.

course, is simply that the base upon which the average was calculated has been shifted. When the Fervians are told that their happiness will be affected by something, they assume that the happiness of those presently understood by them as being Fervians will be increased. The king has pulled the wool over their eyes by using, in effect, a fallacy of four terms: "Fervians" refers to one group of people on one occasion —"The general happiness of the Fervians will be increased", — and another on another occasion — "Hence, the general happiness of the Fervians has been increased." Because the Fervians$_2$ are a different group from the Fervians, although including the latter, it is a mere piece of sophistry to say that an increase in the happiness of the Fervians has come about as a result of this new acquisition of Martian citizenry. The fraud lies in the fact that no *particular* Fervian's happiness has been increased; whereas the principle of utility requires that before we have a moral reason for doing something, it must be because of a change in the happiness of some of the affected persons.

The argument that an increase in the general happiness will result from our having a happy child involves precisely the same fallacy. If you ask, "Whose happiness has been increased as a result of his being born?" the answer is that nobody's has. Of course, his being born might have indirect effects on the general happiness, but that is quite another matter. The "general populace" is just as happy as it was before; now, what of our new personnel? Remember that the question we must ask about *him* is not whether he is happy, but whether he is happier as a result of being born. And if put this way, we see that again we have a piece of nonsense on our hands if we suppose that the answer is either "yes" or "no." For if it is, then with whom, or with what, are we comparing his new state of bliss? Is the child, perhaps, happier than he used to be before he was born? Or happier, perhaps, than his alter ego? Obviously, there can be no sensible answer here. The child cannot be happi*er* as a result of being born, since we would then have a relative term lacking on relatum. The child's happiness has not been increased, in any intelligible sense, as a result of his being born; and since nobody else's has either, directly, there is no moral reason for bringing him into existence.

On the other hand, however, I now wish to argue that it does follow from utilitarian principles that, if we could predict that a child would be miserable if born, then it is our duty *not* to have it. This result, I admit, will look rather peculiar in view of my preceding argument; but the peculiarity can be overcome if we consider certain logical points about duty-fulfilling and duty-transgressing.

As is generally accepted today, every statement describing a particular duty on a particular occasion must be backed up by a general principle of some kind, from which the particular one follows by application. Such is certainly the case with utilitarianism, at any rate. Now let us suppose, as is plausible, that two of our utilitarian duties are to avoid inflicting misery on people, and to reduce misery where it exists.

Now let us suppose that we are contemplating having a child, who would, we know, be miserable. For example, suppose that, we know he would have a hereditarily-acquired painful disease all his life; or that we are poverty-stricken unemployables living in a slum. In both these cases, we can reasonably predict that any child of ours would be miserable. Now, these miseries will be unavoidable if we produce the child; and consequently, a counter-instance to a duty statement will be true, namely: "a child of Smith's is miserable and the Smiths could have prevented this." This would violate the second duty. But quite likely it would violate the first too, for although one does not inflict pain on someone by giving birth to him even though he is in pain ever after, since if you cannot make someone happy by bearing him, you also cannot make him miserable by doing so, nevertheless in many such cases, *e.g.* the slum-dwelling case, you will actually have inflicted misery on the child, by underfeeding him, exposing him to disease, filth, and ugliness, making him associate with equally wretched persons, and so forth, and thus you will also have transgressed the first duty. And in both cases, you could have avoided these evils by not having the child in question.

If, therefore, it is our duty to prevent suffering and relieve it, it is also our duty not to bring children into the world if we know that they would suffer or that we would inflict suffering upon them. And incidentally, I think this also is a strong argument against those who think that it is our *duty* to make everyone as happy as possible. For this is a duty we could infringe by having a child who we know would not be as happy as possible. And of how many people can't *this* be foreseen? Frankly, I do not think there is any such duty on utilitarian principles, but it is something to think about for those who do.

DEREK PARFIT*

Overpopulation and the Quality of Life

HOW MANY PEOPLE should there be? Can there be *overpopulation*: too many people living? I shall present a puzzling argument about these questions, show how this argument can be strengthened, then sketch a possible reply.

1 Quality and Quantity

Consider the outcomes that might be produced, in some part of the world, by two rates of population growth. Suppose that, if there is faster growth, there would later be more people, who would all be worse off. These outcomes are shown in Fig. 1. The width of the block shows the number of people living; the height shows how well off these people are. Compared with outcome A, outcome B would have twice as many people, who would all be worse off. To avoid irrelevant complications, I assume that in each outcome there would be no inequality: no one would be worse off than anyone else. I also assume that everyone's life would be well worth living.

*Derek Parfit, "Overpopulation and the Quality of Life." © 1986 Derek Parfit. Printed by permission of the author.

*The first half of this essay summarizes a longer discussion in my *Reasons and Persons* (Oxford, 1984). I have been greatly helped by J. McMahan, J. R. Richards, L. Temkin, K. Kalafski, and R. Jones. For further reading on this subject, see *Obligations to Future Generations*, ed. R. I. Sikora and B. Barry (Philadelphia, 1978) and McMahan's long review of this anthology in *Ethics* 92, No. 1, 1981.

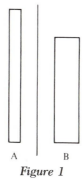

Figure 1

There are various ways in which, because there would be twice as many people in outcome B, these people might be all worse off than the people in A. There might be worse housing, overcrowded schools, more pollution, less unspoilt countryside, fewer opportunities, and a smaller share per person of various other kinds of resources. I shall say, for short, that in B there is *a lower quality of life*.

Except for the absence of inequality, these two outcomes could be the real alternatives for some country, or mankind, given two rates of population growth over many years. Would one of these outcomes be worse than the other? I do not mean "morally worse" in the sense that applies only to agents and to acts. But one of two outcomes can be worse in another sense that has moral relevance. It would be worse, in this sense, if more people suffer, or die young.

Would it be worse, in this sense, if the outcome was B rather than A? Part of the answer is clear. We would all agree that B would be, in one way, worse than A: it would be bad that everyone would be worse off.

On one view, this is all that matters, and it makes B worse than A. This view is expressed in

The Average Principle: If other things are equal, it is better if people's lives go, on average, better.

The *Hedonistic* version of this principle substitutes, for "go better," "contain more happiness."[1]

On the other main view about this question, it is good if any extra life is lived, that is worth living. On this view B might be better than A. B would be in one way worse, because everyone would be worse off. But

---

[1]Of the many economists who appeal to the Average Principle, some make it true by definition. See, for example, P. A. Samuelson, *Economics* (New York, 1970), p. 551. Certain writers state this principle so that it covers only the lives that are, at any time, being lived. This makes the principle imply that it would have been better if all but the best-off people had just dropped dead. My versions of the Average Principle do not imply this absurd conclusion. If anyone with a life worth living dies earlier, this causes people's lives to go, on average, worse, and to contain a smaller average sum of happiness.

in another way B would be better, because there would be more people living, all of whose lives would be worth living. And the fact that people would be worse off might be less important than — or *outweighed* by — the fact that there would be more people living.

Which of these views should we accept? Could a loss in the *quality* of people's lives be outweighed by a sufficient increase in the *quantity* of worthwhile life lived? If this is so, what are the relative values of quality and quantity? These are the central questions about overpopulation.[2]

The Average Principle implies that only quality matters. At the other extreme is

The Hedonistic Total Principle: If other things are equal, it is better if there is a greater total sum of happiness.

This principle implies that only quantity matters. Its non-Hedonistic version substitutes, for "happiness," "whatever makes life worth living."

On the Hedonistic Total Principle, B would be better than A because each life in B would be *more than half* as happy as each life in A. Though the people in B would each be less happy than the people in A, they *together* would have more happiness — just as two bottles more than half-full hold more than a bottleful. On the non-Hedonistic version of this principle, B would be better than A because, compared with lives in A, lives in B would be *more than half* as much worth living.

These claims may seem implausibly precise. But lives in B would be more than half as much worth living if, though a move from the level in A to that in B would be a decline in the quality of life, it would take much more than another similarly large decline before people's lives ceased to be worth living. There are many actual cases in which such a claim would be true.[3]

2   The Repugnant Conclusion

Consider Fig. 2. On the Total Principle, just as B would be better than A, C would be better than B, D better than C, and so on.

Best of all would be Z. This is an enormous population all of whom have lives that are not much above the level where they would cease to be worth living. A life could be like this either because its ecstasies

---

[2]These remarks assume that the quality of life is higher if people's lives go better, and that each life goes better if it contains a greater quantity either of happiness or of whatever else makes life worth living. "Quality" thus means "quantity, per life lived." In Section 5 below I drop this assumption, thereby simplifying the contrast between quality and quantity. (If this note is puzzling, ignore it.)

[3]In what follows I assume, for convenience, that there can be precise differences between the quality of life of different groups. I believe that there could not really be such precise differences. All that my arguments require is that some people can be worse off than others, in morally significant ways, and by more or less.

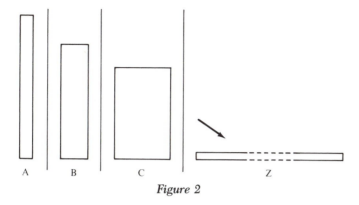

Figure 2

make its agonies seem just worth enduring, or because it is painless but drab. Let us imagine lives in Z to be of this second kind. There is nothing bad in each of these lives; but there is little happiness, and little else that is good. The people in Z never suffer; but all they have is muzak and potatoes. Though there is little happiness in each life in Z, because there are so many of these lives Z is the outcome in which there would be the greatest total sum of happiness. Similarly, Z is the outcome in which there would be the greatest quantity of whatever makes life worth living. (The greatest mass of milk might be in a vast heap of bottles each containing only one drop.)

It is worth comparing Z with Nozick's imagined *Utility Monster*. This is someone who would gain more happiness than we would lose whenever he is given any of our resources. Some Utilitarians believe that the Hedonistic Total Principle should be our only moral principle. Nozick claims that, on this Utilitarian theory, it would be best if all our resources were taken away and given to his Utility Monster, since this would produce the greatest total sum of happiness. As he writes, "unacceptably, the theory seems to require that we all be sacrificed in the monster's maw."[4]

How could it be true that, if all mankind's resources were given to Nozick's Monster, this would produce the greatest total sum of happiness? For this to be true, this Monster's life must, compared with other people's lives, be *millions* of times as much worth living. We cannot imagine, even in the dimmest way, what such a life would be like. Nozick's appeal to his Monster is therefore not a good objection to the Total Principle. We cannot test a moral principle by applying it to a case which we cannot even imagine.

Return now to the population in outcome Z. This is another Utility Monster. The difference is that the greater sum of happiness would

[4]R. Nozick, *Anarchy, State, and Utopia* (Oxford, 1974), p. 41.

come from a vast increase, not in the quality of one person's life, but in the number of lives lived. And *this* Utility Monster can be imagined. We can imagine what it would be for someone's life to be barely worth living — containing only muzak and potatoes. And we can imagine what it would be for there to be many people with such lives. In order to imagine Z, we merely have to imagine that there would be *very* many.

We could not in practice face a choice between A and Z. Given the limits to the world's resources, we could not in fact produce the greatest possible sum of happiness, or the greatest amount of whatever makes life worth living, by producing an enormous population whose lives were barely worth living.[5] But this would be merely *technically* impossible. In order to suppose it possible, we merely need to add some assumptions about the nature and availability of resources. We can therefore test our moral principles by applying them to A and Z.[6]

The Total Principle implies that Z would be better than A. More generally, the principle implies

The Repugnant Conclusion: Compared with the existence of very many people — say, ten billion — all of whom have a very high quality of life, there must be some much larger number of people whose existence, if other things are equal, would be *better*, even though these people would have lives that are barely worth living.[7]

As its name suggests, most of us find this conclusion hard to accept. Most of us believe that Z would be much worse than A. To keep this

---

[5]According to some versions of the widely assumed *Law of Diminishing Marginal Utility*, we could do this. The point can be made most easily in Hedonistic terms. It is assumed that, because resources produce more happiness if they are given to people who are worse off, they would produce most happiness if they are all given to people whose lives are barely worth living. There is here an obvious oversight. Many resources are needed to make each person's life even reach a level where it begins to be worth living. Such resources do not help to produce the greatest possible quantity of happiness, since they are merely being used to raise people to the level where their happiness begins to outweigh their suffering.

[6]It may help to give this illustration. Suppose that, as a *Negative Utilitarian*, I believe that all that matters morally is the relief or prevention of suffering. It is pointed out to me that, on my view, it would be best if all life on Earth was painlessly destroyed, since only this would ensure that there would be no more suffering. And suppose I agreed that this would be a very bad outcome. Could I say: "It is true that this very bad outcome would, according to my moral view, be the best outcome. But there is no objection to my view, since we are not in fact able to bring about this outcome." This would be no defence. On my view, I ought to *regret* our inability to bring about this outcome. Whether my view is plausible cannot depend on what is technically possible. Since this view implies that the destruction of all life on Earth would be the best outcome, if I firmly believe that this outcome would be very bad, I should reject this view.

[7]The phrase "if other things are equal" allows for the possibility that the existence of the larger population might, in some other way, be worse. It might, for instance, involve injustice. What the Repugnant Conclusion claims is that, though the lower quality of life would make Z in one way worse than A, this bad feature could be less important than, or be outweighed by, Z's good feature: the existence of enough extra people whose lives are — even if only barely — worth living.

belief, we must reject the Total Principle. We must also reject the broader view that any loss in the quality of life could be outweighed by a sufficient increase in the total quantity of whatever makes life worth living. Unless we reject this view, we cannot avoid the Repugnant Conclusion.

When the stakes are lower, as in the comparison between A and B, most of us believe that B would be worse. We believe that, compared with the existence of ten billion people whose lives are very well worth living, it would be worse if instead there were twice as many people who were all worse off. To keep this belief, we must again reject the Total Principle.

Suppose that we do reject this principle. Unfortunately, this is not enough. As I shall now argue, it is hard to defend the belief that B would be worse than A, and it is also hard to avoid the Repugnant Conclusion.

3   The Mere Addition Paradox

Consider the alternatives shown in Fig. 3. There is here a new outcome, A+. This differs from A only by the addition of an extra group of people, whose lives are well worth living, though they are worse off than the original group.

The inequality in A+ is *natural*: not the result of any kind of social injustice. Take my waves to show the Atlantic Ocean, and assume that we are considering possible outcomes in some past century, before the Atlantic had been crossed. In A+ there was one group of people living in Europe, Asia, and Africa, and another group, who were worse off, living in the Americas. A is a different possible outcome at this time, in which the Americas were uninhabited. Perhaps the Bering Straits had opened before the land was crossed.

Is A+ worse than A? Note that I am not asking whether it is *better*. If we do not believe that the existence of extra people is in itself good, we

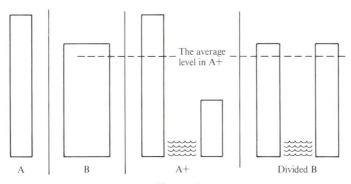

Figure 3

shall deny that the extra group in A+ makes A+ better than A. But is A+ *worse* than A? Would it have been better if the extra group had never existed? This is hard to believe. It may seem a bad feature that there is natural inequality in A+—that the extra group are, through no fault of theirs, worse off than the original group. But the inequality in A+ does not seem to justify the view that the extra group should never have existed. Why are they such a blot on the Universe?

You may think that you have no view about whether it would have been better if the extra group had never existed. It may help to consider another outcome: A + Hell. In this outcome the extra group are innocent people who all have lives which are much worse than nothing. They would all kill themselves if they could, but their torturers prevent this. We would all agree that A + Hell *is* worse than A. It would have been better if *this* extra group, as they all passionately wish, had never existed. Since we believe that A + Hell is worse than A, we must be able to compare A+ and A. Unlike the extra group in Hell, the extra people in A+ have lives that are well worth living; and their existence is not bad for anyone. Most of us could not honestly claim to believe that it would have been better if these people had never existed. Most of us would therefore believe that A+ is not worse than A.

Now suppose that, as a result of changes in the environment, A+ turned into Divided B. In both these outcomes the same number of people would exist, so we are not making one of the unfamiliar comparisons which involve different numbers of people in existence. Since the numbers are the same in A+ and Divided B, our ordinary moral principles apply.

On the principles which most of us accept, Divided B would be better than A+. On the Principle of Utility it is better if there is a greater net sum of benefits—a greater sum of benefits minus losses. Divided B would be better than A+ in utilitarian terms, since the benefits to the people who gain would be greater than the losses to the people who lose. On the Principle of Equality it is better if there is less inequality between different people. Divided B would be better than A+ in egalitarian terms, since the benefits would all go to the people who are worse off.

It might be objected that the Principle of Equality does not apply to people who cannot even communicate. But suppose that I know about two such people, one of whom is, through mere bad luck, worse off. Call these people *Poor* and *Rich*. I could either benefit Rich, or give a greater benefit to Poor. Most of us would believe that it would be better if I do the second. And we would believe that this would make the outcome better, not only because I would give Poor a greater benefit, but also because he is worse off than Rich. Most of us would believe this even though Poor and Rich cannot (except through me) communicate.

How could we deny that a change from A+ to Divided B would be a change for the better? We would have to claim that the loss to the best-off people in A+ matters more than the greater gain to the equally numerous worst-off people. This seems to commit us to the *Élitist* view that what matters most is the condition of the best-off people. This is the opposite of Rawls's famous view that what matters most is the condition of the worst-off people.[8] Most of us would reject this Élitist View. Most of us would therefore agree that Divided B would be better than A+.

Suppose finally that the Atlantic is crossed, turning Divided B into B. These two outcomes are clearly equally good. Since Divided B would be better than A+, B must be better than A+.

Let us now combine the conclusions we have reached. Most of us believe both that A+ is not worse than A, and that B is better than A+. These beliefs together imply that B is not worse than A. B cannot be worse than A if it is *better* than something—A+—which is *not worse* than A. In the same way, you cannot be taller than me if you are shorter than someone who is not taller than me. But, as I earlier claimed, most of us also believe that B *is* worse than A. We therefore have three beliefs which are inconsistent, and imply a contradiction. These beliefs imply that B both is and is not worse than A. I call this *the Mere Addition Paradox*.

This is not just a conflict between different moral principles. Suppose that we accept both the Principle of Equality and the Principle of Utility. There can be cases where these principles conflict—where greater equality would reduce the sum of benefits. But such a case does not reveal any inconsistency in our moral view. We would merely have to ask whether, given the details of the case, the gain in equality would be more important than the loss of benefits. We would here be trying to decide what, after considering all the details, we believe would be the better outcome.

In the Mere Addition Paradox, things are different. Most of us here believe, *all thing considered*, that B is worse than A, though B is better than A+, which is not worse than A. If we continue to hold these three beliefs, we must conclude that B both is and is not worse than A. But we cannot possibly accept this conclusion, any more than we could accept that you both are and are not taller than me. Since we cannot possibly accept what these three beliefs imply, at least one belief must go.

Which should go? Suppose that we keep our belief that B is better than A+, because we cannot persuade ourselves that what matters most is the condition of the best-off people. Suppose that we also keep our belief that A+ is not worse than A, because we cannot persuade our-selves that it would have been better if the extra group had never

[8]J. Rawls, *A Theory of Justice* (Cambridge, Mass., 1971).

existed. We must then reject our belief that B is worse than A. We must conclude that, if these were two possible futures for some society or the world, it would *not* be worse if what comes about is B: twice the population, who are all worse off.

The Mere Addition Paradox does not force us to this conclusion. We can avoid the conclusion if we reject one of our other two beliefs. Some people reject the belief that A+ is not worse than A, because they think that the inequality in A+ is enough to make A+ worse. These people can keep their belief that B is worse than A. Note, however, that we cannot simply claim that A+ must be worse than A, since it is worse than something—B—which is worse than A. We would here be re-jecting one of our three inconsistent beliefs simply on the ground that it is not consistent with the other two. This could be said against *each* belief. To avoid the paradox we must believe, without considering the rest of the argument, that A+ is worse than A. We must believe that it was bad in itself that the extra people ever lived, even though these people had lives that were well worth living, and their existence was bad for no one. To the extent that we find this hard to believe, we still face a paradox.

It may be objected: "Your argument involves a kind of trick. When you compare A and A+, you claim that the extra group's existence was bad for no one. But by the time we have moved to B the original group have become worse off. The addition of the extra group *was* bad for the original group."

The argument can be restated. Suppose that A+ was the actual state of the world in some past century. A is a different state of the world which was merely possible. We can ask, "Would A have been better? Would it have been better if the worse-off group had never existed?" As I have said, most of us could not answer Yes. Suppose next that A+ did *not* in fact later change into either Divided B or B. We can ask, "*If* this change had occurred, would it have been a change for the better?" It is hard to answer No. On this version of the argument, the last objection has been met. The better-off group in A+ was not an origi-nally existing group, to which the worse-off group was added. And the existence of the worse-off group was not bad for the better-off group.

It is worth giving another version of the argument. To ensure that there was no social injustice, we assumed that the two groups in A+ did not know of each other's existence. We could assume instead that both these groups live in the same society, and that the people in one group are worse off, not because of social injustice, but because they all have some handicap which cannot be cured. Suppose, for example, that they are deaf. If this is so, would it have been better even though these people's lives are worth living, their existence is not bad for anyone, and if they had never existed no one else would have existed in their place? It is hard to believe that these deaf people should never have existed. On this version of the argument, it again seems that A+ is not worse than A.

Suppose next that these deaf people could be cured, at some lesser cost to the other group. This would be like the change from A+ to B. It is again hard to deny that this change would make the outcome better. In this version of the argument, with the groups in one society, we seem again driven to conclude that, since B would be better than A+, which is not worse than A, B cannot be worse than A.

There are some other possible objections to this argument. But rather than discussing these I shall turn to another argument. This is harder to answer, and it also leads to the Repugnant Conclusion.

4   The Second Paradox

Consider the first three outcomes shown in Fig. 4. Though this argument involves many outcomes, we need to make only two comparisons.

One is between A+ and the much more populated Alpha. Suppose that Alpha will be the actual outcome at some time far in the future, after humans have colonized thousands of planets in this Galaxy. A+ is a different possible outcome at this time, in which humans have colonized only one other planet, near a distant star. As before, in neither Alpha nor A+ would the inequality between different people be the result of social injustice. Because of the difficulties of trans-Galactic travel, those who are better off could not raise the quality of life of those who are worse off.

The comparison between A+ and Alpha replaces the comparison, in the old argument, between A and A+. On one view, the natural inequality in A+ makes it worse than A. If I held this view, I would now say:

> The inequality in Alpha is in one way worse than the inequality in A+, since the gap between the better-off and worse-off people is slightly greater. But in another way the inequality is less bad. This is a matter of the relative numbers of, or the *ratio* between, those who are better-off and those who are worse-off. Half of the people in A+ are better off than the other half. This is a worse inequality than a situation in which almost everyone is equally well off, and those who are better off are only a fraction of one per cent. And this is the difference between A+ and Alpha. Because there are so many groups at level 45 (most of them not shown in the diagram), the better-off people in Alpha are only a fraction of one per cent.
>
> To put these claims together: The inequality in Alpha is in one way slightly worse than the inequality in A+, but in another way much better. There is a slightly greater gap between the better-off and

[9]If you believe that the inequality is worse in Alpha than it is in A+, read (when you reach it) footnote 11.

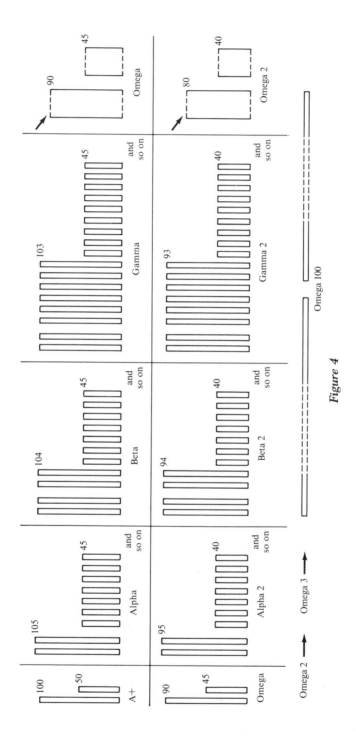

Figure 4

144

worse-off groups, but a much better ratio between these groups. All things considered, the natural inequality in Alpha is not worse than the natural inequality in A+.[9]

It may be objected that Alpha is worse than A+ because the worst-off groups in Alpha are worse off than the worst-off group in A+. Many people accept Rawls's view that what matters most is the condition of the worst-off group. But there are two quite different ways in which any worst-off group might have been better off. This group might have existed, and been better off. This is the ordinary case, which Rawls discusses. Things would have been quite different if the worst-off group had never existed. This would have provided another sense in which the "worst-off" group would have been better off, since some other group would then have *been* those who are worst off. Would this have made the outcome better? If we answer Yes, we must agree that it would have been even better if the second worst-off group had also never existed, and the third worst-off group, and the fourth worst-off group, and so on. It would have been best if everyone except the best-off group had never existed. Similarly, it might be best if in future only the best-off nation — such as the Norwegians — have children. Even if this would be worse for them, it might cause it to be true that, after the rest of us have died, the "worst-off" people in the world are as well off as possible. This way of raising the level of "the worst-off group" has no moral merit. The non-existence of all but the best-off group would not, in the morally relevant sense, make the worst-off group better off.

The inequality in Alpha is not worse than the inequality in A+; nor is Alpha worse than A+ because the worst-off groups are worse off. Nor is there any other way in which Alpha is worse than A+.[10] And, in one way, Alpha is *better* than A+. Alpha does not differ from A+ merely by involving the existence of the very many groups at level 45. All of the people in A+ are in one of two groups, and both these groups are, in Alpha, better off. (These are the groups at level 105.) I conclude that, since Alpha is in this way better than A+, and is in no way worse, Alpha is better than A+. We are assuming that the actual outcome at some future time is Alpha. If the outcome had been A+, this would have been worse.

[10]Alpha is worse than A+ according to the Average Principle. But this is one of the cases which show that we should reject this principle. The Average Principle could also imply that it would be best if in future all except the Norwegians have no children. For further objections to this principle, see my *Reasons and Persons*, Section 143, and J. A. McMahan, "Problems of Population Theory," *Ethics*, Vol. 92 no. 1, Oct. 1981. It may also be claimed, "Alpha is worse than A+ because, if we had to choose in which outcome we would prefer to exist — without knowing who we would be — it would be rational to choose A+." For objections to this claim, see my *Reasons and Persons*, Section 133.

Could we honestly deny this conclusion? Could we honestly claim that A+ would not have been worse than Alpha? This is the claim that it would not have been worse if the worst-off people in Alpha had never existed, even though their lives are worth living, and if they had never existed, so that the outcome had been A+, the inequality would have been no better, and *everyone who did exist would have been worse off*. That this would *not* have been worse is hard to believe.[11]

Consider next whether Beta would be better than Alpha. In a change from Alpha to Beta, the best-off group in Alpha would lose a little, but an equally large worse-off group would gain very much more. If this is all we know about this change, it would need extreme Élitism to deny that it would be a change for the better.

The rest of the argument merely involves repetition. Gamma would be better than Beta in the same way in which Beta would be better than Alpha. Delta would be better than Gamma in the same way, Epsilon better than Delta, and so on down to Omega. We then run through the argument again, on the second line of the diagram, from Omega to Omega 2. (Omega is thinner on this second line only because, to make room, all widths are reduced.) Similar steps take us to Omega 3, Omega 4, and all the way to Omega 100. Every step would be a change for the better, so Omega 100 must be the best of all these outcomes.

Since this argument implies that Omega 100 would be better than A+, it leads us to the Repugnant Conclusion. A+ might be a world with ten billion people, of whom even the worse-off half have an *extremely high* quality of life. According to this argument it would be *better* if instead there were vastly many more people, all of whose lives were *barely worth living*.

What is wrong with this argument? To avoid its conclusion, we must either deny that A+ would have been worse than Alpha, or deny that Beta would be better than Alpha. Unless we deny one of these claims, we cannot plausibly deny the similar claims which carry us down to Omega 100. But how can we deny that A+ would have been worse than Alpha? If the outcome had been A+, everyone who existed would have been worse off. And how can we deny that Beta would be better than

---

[11]Suppose you believe that the inequality in Alpha is worse than the inequality in A+. Is this enough to justify the claim that it would *not* have been worse if the actual outcome had been A+ rather than Alpha? Which would have mattered more: (1) that the inequality would have been less bad, or (2) that everyone who did exist would have been worse off? It is hard to deny that (2) would have mattered more.

[12]It may be objected that my argument is like what are called *Sorites Arguments*, which are known to lead to false conclusions. Suppose we assume that removing any single grain of sand cannot turn a heap of sand into something that is not a heap. It can then be argued that, even if we remove every single grain, we must still have a heap. Or suppose we assume that the loss of any single hair cannot cause someone who is not bald to be bald. There is a similar argument for the conclusion that, even if someone loses all his hair, this cannot make him bald. If my argument was like this, it could be referred to those who work on what is wrong with Sorites Arguments. But my argument is not like this. A

Alpha? In a change to Beta some people would lose a little, but as many people who are much worse off would gain much more.

While we consider these outcomes in these simple terms, it is hard to answer this argument. There is little room for manoeuvre. To find an answer we must consider other features of these outcomes.[12]

5 The Quality of Single Lives

Consider first the analogue, within one life, of the Repugnant Conclusion.[13] Suppose that I can choose between two futures. I could live for another 100 years, all of an extremely high quality. Call this *the Century of Ecstasy*. I could instead live for ever, with a life that would always be barely worth living. Though there would be nothing bad in this life, the only good things would be muzak and potatoes. Call this *the Drab Eternity*.

I believe that, of these two, the Century of Ecstasy would give me a better future. And this is the future that I would prefer. Many people would have the same belief, and preference.

On one view about what makes our lives go best, we would be making a mistake. On this view, though the Century of Ecstasy would have great value for me, this value would be finite, or have an upper limit. In contrast, since each day in the Drab Eternity would have the same small value for me, there would be no limit to the total value for me of this second life. This value must, in the end, be greater than the limited value of the Century of Ecstasy.

I reject this view. I claim that, though each day of the Drab Eternity would be worth living, the Century of Ecstasy would give me a better life. This is like Mill's claim about the "difference in quality" between human and pig-like pleasures.[14] It is often said that Mill's "higher pleasures" are merely *greater* pleasures: pleasures with more value. As Sidgwick wrote, "all qualitative comparison of pleasures must really resolve itself in quantitative [comparison.]"[15] This would be so if the value of all pleasures lay on the same scale. But this is what I have just denied. The Century of Ecstasy would be better for me in an essentially qualitative way. Though each day of the Drab Eternity would have some value for me, *no* amount of this value could be as good for me as the Century of Ecstasy.

Sorites Argument appeals to a series of steps, each of which is assumed to *make no difference*. My argument would be like this if it claimed that Alpha is *not worse* than A+, Beta is not worse than Alpha, Gamma is not worse than Beta, and so on. But the argument claims that Alpha is *better* than A+, Beta is better than Alpha, Gamma is better than Beta, and so on. The objections to Sorites Arguments are therefore irrelevant.

[13]This section is partly based on an unpublished paper by J. McMahan.

[14]J. S. Mill, *Utilitarianism* (London, 1863), Chapter II.

[15]H. Sidgwick, *The Methods of Ethics* (London, 1907), p. 94.

6 *Perfectionism*

Return to the argument about overpopulation. Should we make a similar claim, not about the value for one person of different possible futures, but about the relative goodness of different outcomes? Cardinal Newman made such a claim about pain and sin. He believed that both of these were bad, but that no amount of pain could be as bad as the least amount of sin. He therefore wrote that, "if all mankind suffered extremest agony, this would be less bad than if one venial sin was committed."[16] Can we make such a claim about what is good in my outcomes A and Z?

Consider what I shall call *the best things in life*. These are the best kinds of creative activity and aesthetic experience, the best relationships between different people, and the other things which do most to make life worth living. Return next to A and B. Suppose that all of the best things in life are, in B, *better*. The people in B are all worse off than the people in A only because they each have many fewer of these things. In B, for example, people can hear good music only a few times in their lives; in A they can often hear music that is nearly as good. If this was the difference between A and B, I would cease to believe that B would be worse.

A similar claim applies to the Repugnant Conclusion. Why is it so hard to believe that my imagined world Z — or Omega 100 — would be better than a world of ten billion people, all of whom have an extremely high quality of life? This is hard to believe because in Z two things are true: people's lives are barely worth living, and most of the good things in life are lost.

Suppose that only the first of these was true. Suppose that, in Z, all of the best things in life remain. People's lives are barely worth living because these best things are so thinly spread. The people in Z do each, once in their lives, have or engage in one of the best experiences or activities. But all the rest is muzak and potatoes. If this is what Z involves, it is still hard to believe that Z would be better than a world of ten billion people, each of whose lives is very well worth living. But, if Z retains all of the best things in life, this belief is less repugnant.

Now restore the assumption that in Z, and Omega 100, most of the good things in life are lost. There is only muzak and potatoes. By appealing to the value of the best things in life, we can try to answer the argument.

The argument involves two kinds of steps. One is the claim that Alpha is better than A+, Alpha 2 is better than Omega, and similar later claims. A+ contains two groups of people, all of whom are better off in

---

[16]J. H. Newman, *Certain Difficulties Felt by Anglicans in Catholic Teaching* (London, 1885), Vol. I, p. 204.

Alpha. We can add the assumption that these people are better off because, in Alpha, the best things in life are even better. Appealing to the value of these best things cannot help us to reject the claim that Alpha is better than A+. And, as I argued, there seems to be no other way to reject this claim. If the actual outcome had been A+, the inequality would have been no better, and everyone who existed would have been worse off. How can we deny that this would have been worse? There seems to be little hope of answering these steps in the argument.

The other steps are all redistributive. In each step the best-off people would lose a little, but an equally large worse-off group would gain much more. Can we claim that at least one of these steps would not be a change for the better? This cannot be plausibly claimed if what we appeal to is the Élitist View. We cannot plausibly claim that it is the best-off people whose condition matters most.

What we might appeal to is not Élitism, but *Perfectionism.* In the move from Alpha to Omega 100, the best things in life must have disappeared. Suppose for instance that, in the move from Alpha to Beta, Mozart's music would be lost, in the move to Gamma, Haydn's. In the move to Delta, Venice would be destroyed, in the move to Epsilon, Verona.[17] We might claim that, even if some change brings a great net benefit to those who are affected, it is a change for the worse if it involves the loss of one of the best things in life.

When should we make this claim? It would not be plausible when we are considering outcomes that are close to Omega 100. Suppose that, in one such outcome, the best thing left is a bad performance of Ravel's Bolero; in the next outcome, it is an even worse performance of Ravel's Bolero. We cannot claim that great benefits to those who are worst-off would not make the outcome better if they involved the loss of a bad performance of Ravel's Bolero. If such a claim is to have any plausibility, it must be made at the start. We must reject the change in which the music of Mozart is lost.

Has such a claim any plausibility? I believe that it has. It expresses one of our two main reasons for wanting to avoid the Repugnant Conclusion. When we are most concerned about overpopulation, our concern is only partly about the value that each life will have for the person whose life it is. We are also concerned about the disappearance from the world of the kinds of experience and activity which do most to make life worth living.

---

[17]If, in the move from Alpha to Beta, the best-off people lose Mozart, it may seem that their quality of life cannot, as my argument assumes, fall by only a little. But I have explained how this might be so. The loss of a few performances of Mozart could for these people be nearly outweighed by many extra performances of Haydn.

Perfectionism faces many objections. One is raised by the moral importance of relieving or preventing great suffering. We should reject the Nietzschean view that the prevention of great suffering can be ranked wholly below the preservation of creation of the best things in life. What should Perfectionists claim about great suffering? But this problem is irrelevant here, since we can assume that in the various outcomes we are considering there would be no such suffering.

Another problem is raised by the fact that the good things in life do not come in quite different categories. It is because pain and sin are in such different categories that Newman believed sin to be infinitely worse. If we merely compare Mozart and muzak, these two may also seem to be in quite different categories. But there is a fairly smooth continuum between these two. Though Haydn is not as good as Mozart, he is very good. And there is other music which is not far below Haydn's, other music not far below this, and so on. Similar claims apply to the other best experiences, activities, and personal relationships, and to the other things which give most to the value of life. Most of these things are on fairly smooth continua, ranging from the best to the least good. Since this is so, it may be hard to defend the view that what is best has more value — or does more to make the outcome better — than any amount of what is nearly as good. This view conflicts with the preferences that most of us would have about our own futures. But, unless we can defend this view, any loss of quality could be outweighed by a sufficient gain in the quantity of lesser goods.

These are only two of the objections facing this view. It seems to me, at times, crazy. But at least, unlike the Élitist View, it is not morally monstrous. And without Perfectionism how can we avoid the Repugnant Conclusion?[18]

[18]I would be grateful for any comments on this essay, which could be sent to me at All Souls College, Oxford.

PART FIVE
CONSEQUENCES AND CHARACTER

IN ONE OF the Nazi concentration camps, some doctors imprisoned there were presented with an appalling dilemma. The authorities wanted them to carry out medically unnecessary operations, without anaesthetic, on the testicles of other prisoners. The doctors, whose first thought was naturally to refuse, were told that their refusal would not stop the operations: they would instead be carried out by a medically unskilled army corporal.

Under this pressure, one of the doctors carried out the operation. He reasoned that, whereas this was in itself an appalling thing to do, it would be the lesser evil for the victims.

Another doctor refused. She perhaps thought that, if any acts at all are utterly evil, to be repudiated whatever the consequences, this operation must be one of them. She may also have hoped that the threat might be a bluff.

The threat did turn out to be a bluff, and the corporal did not carry out the operation. What should we think of the ethics of the different decisions by the two doctors?

Perhaps for most of us, any reaction we have will be mingled with relief that we do not ourselves have to face such a choice, and with a reluctance to condemn anyone who found themselves in that nightmare. Our strongest response may be relief that the second doctor decided as she did. She avoided doing something unspeakable, *and* the consequences for the prisoners were better.

But what should we think of the first doctor's choice? With the benefit of hindsight, we, of course, wish it had been different. But the

151

doctor had to reach his decision without the knowledge we have. He believed, wrongly, that the threat about the corporal would be carried out. *Given that belief*, was his decision wrong?

In answering this question, people disagree very deeply. Some say that the end does not justify the means and that here the means are such that nothing whatever could possibly justify them. This view, often called deontological, is that some acts are absolutely prohibited, regardless of consequences. Only a monster, it is thought, could perform such an act. To abandon absolute prohibitions leaves morality based only on the shifting sands of consequences and lets any enormity on to the possible agenda. Others say that the deontological view is too self-centered. If a doctor refused to do the operation and the threat about the corporal was carried out, he would have kept his own hands clean, but at an appalling additional cost to the victims. Those who think this way often think that no acts are absolutely forbidden, taking instead a consequentialist view. The doctor may find it terrible to live with himself after performing the operation, but his psychological state should not be put before minimizing the horror for the victims.

This is one of the deepest divides in moral philosophy. And, in thinking about real cases like this one, many of us are divided within ourselves.

The clash between absolute prohibitions and consequentialist moralities such as utilitarianism was historically often a clash between religious and secular views. How do we decide which acts are on the "absolutely prohibited" list? On one view they are those acts forbidden by God. Religious believers (despite the problems about whether God exists, how they know what morality He favors, and why we should give such weight to His opinions) have an answer to the question. Not all deontologists base their position on appeals to authority. For those who do not, there is a problem about what the alternative basis for absolute prohibitions can be.

One influential recent line of thought starts from the character of the agent. A mistake of consequentialists, it is suggested, is to treat actions as though they can somehow be isolated from the people performing them. An action does not come about impersonally: it flows from a person with a particular character and outlook. In judging actions, we should not just focus on their effects, but should also see them as expressing a character of a certain kind. As Stuart Hampshire argues, moral reflection may be about a whole way of life, with its distinctive picture of what things are virtues or vices, as well as about the consequences of particular actions.

A utilitarian or consequentialist reply to this line of thought is to grant a certain degree of importance to personal ideals. Most of us, partly consciously and partly unconsciously, have a picture or set of pictures of what a good life is like, or of the kind of person we hope to be. Such pictures are often central to what makes our lives seem worthwhile. So any utilitarian who understands this is likely to give great weight to people following their own ideals. The world would not be a happier place if these ideals were systematically stifled. But the consequentialist will give the pursuit of a chosen way of life *great* weight rather than *absolute* weight. A doctor could be right to obey the order to commit the atrocity where the price to others of keeping his own hands clean is simply too high. Pursuit of personal ideals on this view is a large but bounded part of morality, and in desperate cases the right action can be the one that most revolts you. The cultivation of your own character is something that should sometimes take second place to the plight of others.

Bernard Williams raises a problem for this consequentialist view. He describes a case (similar in structure to that of the concentration camp doctors) where a man is told that twenty people are to be shot, but that if *he* shoots one, the others will go free. The man feels appalled at the thought of shooting one of the victims, but, if he takes the utilitarian view, "he will regard these feelings just as unpleasant experiences of his." But this, Williams suggests, is a morally disastrous view of them. "Because our moral relation to the world is partly given by such feelings, and by a sense of what we can or cannot "live with," to come to regard those feelings from a purely utilitarian point of view, that is to say, as happenings outside one's moral self, is to lose a sense of one's moral identity, to lose, in the most literal way, one's integrity."

One reply to this is that given by J. J. C. Smart, that it is right for the utilitarian to sacrifice the harmony of his own mind to others. Another possible reply is to doubt that the utilitarian approach need involve any loss of integrity. Perhaps the utilitarian need not see his or her feelings of revulsion *just* as unpleasant personal experiences, or as something outside his or her moral self. The utilitarian may recognize that his or her morality is rooted in such feelings, and so that there is a real loss in overriding them. Unlike cruder utilitarians, this person will not see these feelings as analogous to a headache, to be wiped out by a "guilt pill" if one is ever developed. The utilitarian differs from Williams in a less crude way: the question at issue is not whether feelings of moral revulsion are on a par with a headache, but whether giving them due weight means giving them absolute trumping power over any disaster to others.

There are three kinds of psychological or moral attitude someone could bring to a dilemma like that of the concentration camp. One would be that of an uncomplicated deontologist. "This kind of act is absolutely forbidden, and I shall have no moral regrets in refusing." The second would be that of an uncomplicated consequentialist: "I believe the consequences will be far worse if I refuse, and so I shall have no moral regrets in doing the act." The third attitude (perhaps that of most of us) is to be aghast at either prospect and to be sure we will feel some sense of being appalled by whichever choice we make.

Those with either of the first two views will act with no threat to their integrity. The simple deontologist and the simple consequentialist will both act in harmony with their deepest feelings and beliefs. But what of the rest of us, whose feelings pull us both ways? *Whichever* choice we make is to betray part of ourselves, and we can see this. And perhaps it is right to betray the part of ourselves that stands in the way of doing the best we can for others. What is missing from the debate so far is the argument that would be needed to show that, for the person pulled both ways, the consequentialist choice involves a loss of integrity, whereas the other choice does not.

These divisions between consequentialism and deontology have always permeated the hardest questions in personal morality. Now they are turning out to be fundamental to the political debate over nuclear deterrence. There are well-known consequentialist arguments that to use nuclear weapons would be one of the worst things we could do. There are similar deontological arguments based on the prohibition on intentionally killing innocent people. On one interpretation, this prohibition on the *use* of nuclear weapons also rules out effective nuclear deterrence. Some argue that effective deterrence cannot be based on bluff: it will work only if we *intend* to retaliate. And, on one version of deontology, if an act is prohibited, it is also wrong to form even the conditional intention to carry it out.

Gregory Kavka sees nuclear deterrence as a field of paradoxes. Perhaps forming the intention to use nuclear retaliation if attacked may both be the best way to avoid the catastrophe of nuclear war and at the same time be morally corrupting. Can it be that the best thing to do is to turn yourself into a morally worse person? We may hope that statesmen have motives for refraining from nuclear attack other than the fear of retaliation. We may hope for a world in which we have outgrown the quarrels that create these dilemmas. But if nuclear deterrence does help keep the peace and if a bluffing threat is ineffective (both questionable assumptions), Kavka's problems are with us now. There seems a large gap between being the morally best sort of person and being able to adopt the morally best policy.

The deepest dilemma of personal morality now shapes our thinking about the most important political question in the world.

STUART HAMPSHIRE*

"The Mainspring of Morality Has Been Taken Away"

EACH MORAL PHILOSOPHY singles out some ultimate ground or grounds for unconditional praise of persons, and prescribes the ultimate grounds for preferring one way of life to another. This is no less true of a utilitarian ethics than of any other; the effectively beneficent and happy man is accounted by a utilitarian more praiseworthy and admirable than any other type of man, and his useful life is thought the best kind of life that anyone could have, merely in virtue of its usefulness, and apart from any other characteristics it may have. The utilitarian philosophy picks out its own essential virtues, very clearly, and the duties of a utilitarian are not hard to discern, even though they may on occasion involve difficult computations.

But there is one feature of familiar moralities which utilitarian ethics famously repudiates, or at least makes little of. There are a number of different moral prohibitions, apparent barriers to action, which a man acknowledges and which he thinks of as more or less insurmountable, except in abnormal, painful and improbable circumstances. One expects to meet these prohibitions, barriers to action, in certain quite distinct and clearly marked areas of action; these are the taking of human life, sexual relations, family duties and obligations, and the administration of justice according to the laws and customs of a given

*From Stuart Hampshire: *Morality and Pessimism*.

society. There are other areas in which strong barriers are to be expected; but these are, I think, the central and obvious ones. A morality is, at the very least, the regulation of the taking of life and the regulation of sexual relations, and it also includes rules of distributive and corrective justice: family duties: almost always duties of friendship: also rights and duties in respect of money and property. When specific prohibitions in these areas are probed and challenged by reflection, and the rational grounds for them looked for, the questioner will think that he is questioning a particular morality specified by particular prohibitions. But if he were to question the validity of any prohibitions in these areas, he would think of himself as challenging the claims of morality itself; for the notion of morality requires that there be some strong barriers against the taking of life, against some varieties of sexual and family relations, against some forms of trial and punishment, some taking of property, and against some distributions of rewards and benefits.

Moral theories of the philosophical kind are differentiated in part by the different accounts that they give of these prohibitions: whether the prohibitions are to be thought of as systematically connected or not: whether they are absolute prohibitions or to be thought of as conditional. Utilitarians always had, and still have, very definite answers: first, they *are* systematically connected, and, secondly, they are to be thought of as not absolute, but conditional, being dependent for their validity as prohibitions upon the beneficial consequences of observing them. Plainly there is no possibility of proof here, since this is a question in ethics, and not in logic or in the experimental sciences. But various reasons for rejecting the utilitarian position can be given.

All of us sometimes speak of things that cannot be done, or that must not be done, and that are ruled out as impossible by the nature of the case: also there are things that one must do, that one cannot not do, because of the nature of the case. The signs of necessity in such contexts mark the unqualified, unweakened, barrier to action, while the word "ought," too much discussed in philosophical writing, conveys a weakened prohibition or instruction. The same contrast appears in the context of empirical statements, as in the judgments "The inflation ought to stop soon" and "The inflation must stop soon." The modal words "must" and "ought" preserve a constant relation in a number of different types of discourse, of which moral discourse is only one, not particularly conspicuous, example: he who in a shop says to the salesman "The coat must cover my knees," alternatively, "The coat ought to cover my knees," speaks of a need or requirement and of something less: he who, looking at the mathematical puzzle, says "This must be the way to solve it," alternatively "This ought to be the way to solve it," speaks of a kind of rational necessity, and of something less: examples of "ought" as the weaker variant of "must" could be indefinitely prolonged into other types of contexts. So "He must help him" is the basic, unmodified judgment in the context of moral discussion or reflection, and "He ought to help him" is its weakened variant, as it is in all other contexts. To learn what a man's moral beliefs are entails learning what he thinks that he must not do, at any cost or at almost any cost.

Social anthropologists may record fairly wide variations in the range of the morally impossible, and also, I believe, some barriers that are very general, though not quite universal; and historians similarly. For example, in addition to certain fairly specific types of killing, certain fairly specific types of sexual promiscuity, certain takings of property, there are also types of disloyalty and of cowardice, particularly disloyalty to friends, which are very generally, almost universally, forbidden and forbidden absolutely: they are forbidden as being intrinsically disgraceful and unworthy, and as being, just for these reasons, ruled out: ruled out because they would be disgusting, or disgraceful, or shameful, or brutal, or inhuman, or base, or an outrage.

In arguing against utilitarians I must dwell a little on these epithets usually associated with morally impossible action, on a sense of disgrace, of outrage, of horror, of baseness, of brutality, and, most important, a sense that a barrier, assumed to be firm and almost insurmountable, has been knocked over, and a feeling that, if this horrible, or outrageous, or squalid, or brutal, action is possible, then anything is possible and nothing is forbidden, and all restraints are threatened. Evidently these ideas have often been associated with impiety, and with a belief that God, or the Gods, have been defied, and with a fear of divine anger. But they need not have these associations with the supernatural, and they may have, and often have had, a secular setting. In the face of the doing of something that must not be done, and that is categorically excluded and forbidden morally, the fear that one may feel is fear of human nature. A relapse into a state of nature seems a real possibility: or perhaps seems actually to have occurred, unless an alternative morality with new restraints is clearly implied when the old barrier is crossed. This fear of human nature, and sense of outrage, when a barrier is broken down, is an aspect of respect for morality itself rather than for any particular morality, and for any particular set of prohibitions.

The notion of the morally impossible — "I cannot leave him now: it would be quite impossible." "Surely you understand that I *must* help him" — is distinct. A course of conduct is ruled out ("You cannot do that"), because it would be inexcusably unjust, or dishonest, or humiliating, or treacherous, or cruel, or ungenerous, or harsh. These epithets, specifying why the conduct is impossible, mark the vices characteristically recognised in a particular morality. In other societies, at other places and times, other specific epithets might be more usually associated with outrage and morally impossible conduct; but the outrage or shock, and the recognition of impossibility, will be the same in cases where the type of conduct rejected, and the reasons for the rejection, are rather different.

The utilitarian will not deny these facts, but he will interpret them differently. Shock, he will say, is the primitive, pre-rational reaction; after rational reflection the strength of feeling associated with a prohibition can be, and ought to be, proportional to the estimated harm of the immediate and remote consequences; and he will find no more in the signs of necessity and impossibility than an emphasis on the moral rules which have proved to be necessary protections against evil effects. The signs of necessity are signs that there is a rule. But the rational justification of there being a rule is to be found in the full consequences of its observance, and not in nonrational reactions of horror, disgust, shame, and other emotional repugnances.

But I believe that critical reflection may leave the notion of absolutely forbidden, because absolutely repugnant, conduct untouched. There may in many cases be good reflective reasons why doing such things, assuming such a character, may be abhorrent, and excluded from the range of possible conduct; there may be reflective reasons, in the sense that one is able to say why the conduct is impossible as destroying the ideal of a way of life that one aspires to and respects, as being, for example, utterly unjust or cruel or treacherous or corruptly dishonest. To show that these vices are vices, and unconditionally to be avoided, would take one back to the criteria for the assessment of persons as persons, and therefore to the whole way of life that one aspires to as the best way of life. A reflective, critical scrutiny of moral claims is compatible, both logically and psychologically, with an overriding concern for a record of unmonstrous and respectworthy conduct, and of action that has never been mean or inhuman; and it may follow an assessment of the worth of persons which is not to be identified only with a computation of consequences and effects.

There is a model of rational reflection which depends upon a contrast between the primitive moral response of an uneducated man, and of an uneducated society, and the comparatively detached arguments of the sophisticated moralist, who discounts his intuitive responses as being prejudices inherited from an uncritical past. Conspicuous in the philosophical radicals, in John Stuart Mill, and in the Victorian free-thinkers generally, this model in turn depended upon the idea that primitive, pre-scientific men are usually governed by strict moral taboos, and that in future intellectually evolved, and scientifically trained, men will be emancipated from these bonds, and will start again with clear reasoning about consequences. The word 'taboo,' so often used in these contexts, shows the assumption of moral progress from primitive beginnings, and suggests a rather naive contrast between older moralities and the open morality of the future; empirical calculation succeeds a priori prejudice, and the calculation of consequences is reason.

But reflection may discover a plurality of clear and definite moral injunctions; injunctions about the taking of life, about sexual relations, about the conduct of parents towards children and of children towards parents, about one's duties in times of war, about the conditions under which truth must be told and under which it may be concealed, about rights to property, about duties of friendship, and so on over the various aspects and phases of a normal span of life. Such injunctions need not be inferrable from a few basic principles, corresponding to the axioms of a theory. The pattern that they form can have a different type of unity. Taken together, a full set of such injunctions, prohibiting types of conduct in types of circumstance, describes in rough and indeterminate outline, an attainable and recognisable way of life, aspired to, respected and admired: or at least the minimum general features of a respectworthy way of life. And a way of life is not identified and characterised by one distinct purpose, such as the increase of general happiness, or even by a set of such distinct purposes. The connection between the injunctions, the connection upon which a reasonable man reflects, is to be found in the coherence of a single way of life, distinguished by the characteristic virtues and vices recognised within it.

A way of life is a complicated thing, marked out by many details of style and manner, and also by particular activities and interests, which a group of people of similar dispositions in a similar social situation may share; so that the group may become an imitable human type who transmit many of their habits and ideals to their descendants, provided that social change is not too rapid.

In rational reflection one may justify an intuitively accepted and unconditional prohibition, as a common, expected feature of a recognisable way of life which on other grounds one values and finds admirable: or as a necessary preliminary condition of this way of life. There are rather precise grounds in experience and in history for the reasonable man to expect that certain virtues, which he admires and values, can only be attained at the cost of certain others, and that the virtues typical of several different ways of life cannot be freely combined, as he might wish. Therefore a reasonable and reflective person will review the separate moral injunctions, which intuitively present themselves as having force and authority, as making a skeleton of an attainable, respectworthy and preferred way of life. He will reject those that seem likely in practice to conflict with others that seem more closely part of, or conditions of, the way of life that he values and admires, or that seem irrelevant to this way of life.

One must not exaggerate the degree of connectedness that can be claimed for the set of injunctions that constitute the skeleton of a man's morality. For example, it is a loose, empirical connection that reasonably associates certain sexual customs with the observation of certain family duties, and certain loyalties to the state or country with the recognition of certain duties in respect of property, and in time of war. The phrase "way of life" is vague and is chosen for its vagueness. The unity of a single way of life, and the compatibility in practice of different habits and dispositions, are learnt from observation, direct experience and from psychology and history: we know that human nature naturally varies, and is deliberately variable, only within limits: and that not all theoretically compatible achievements and enjoyments are compatible in normal circumstances. A reasonable man may envisage a way of life, which excludes various kinds of conduct as impossible, without excluding a great variety of morally tolerable ways of life within this minimum framework. The moral prohibitions constitute a kind of grammar of conduct, showing the elements out of which any fully respectworthy conduct, as one conceives it, must be built.

The plurality of absolute prohibitions, and the looseness of their association with any one way of life, which stresses a certain set of virtues, is to be contrasted with the unity and simplicity of utilitarian ethics. One might interpret the contrast in this way: to the utilitarian it is certain that all reasonable purposes are parts of a single purpose in a creature known to be governed by the pleasure principle or by a variant of it. The anti-utilitarian replies: nothing is certain in the *theory* of morality: but, at a pretheoretical level, some human virtues fit together as virtues to form a way of life aspired to, and some monstrous and brutal acts are certainly vicious in the sense that they undermine and corrupt this way of life; and we can explain why they are, and what makes them so, provided that we do not insist upon either precision or certainty or simplicity in the explanation.

The absolute moral prohibitions, which I am defending, are not to be identified with Kant's categorical moral injunctions; for they are not to be picked out by the logical feature of being universal in form. Nor are they prescriptions that must be affirmed, and that cannot be questioned or denied, just because they are principles of rationality, and because any contrary principles would involve a form of contradiction. They are indeed judgments of unconditional necessity, in the sense that they imply that what must be done is not necessary because it is a means to some independently valued end, but because the action is a necessary part of a way of life and ideal of conduct. The necessity resides in the nature of the action itself, as specified in the fully explicit moral judgment. The principal and proximate grounds for claiming that the action must, or must not, be performed are to be found in the characterisation of the action offered within the prescription; and if the argument is pressed further, first a virtue or vice, and then a whole way of life will have to be described.

But still a number of distinctions are needed to avoid misunderstand-ings. First, he who says, for example, "You must not give a judgment about this until you have heard the evidence," or "I must stand by my friend in this crisis," claiming an absolute, and unconditional, necessity to act just so on this occasion, is not claiming an overriding necessity so to act in all circumstances and situations. He has so far not generalised at all, as he would have generalised if he were to add "always" or "in all circumstances." The immediate grounds for the necessity of the action or abstention are indicated in the judgment itself. These particular actions, which are cases of the general type "respecting evidence" and "standing by friends," are said to be necessary on this occasion in virtue of having just this character, and in virtue of their being this type of action. In other painful circumstances, and on other occasions, other unconditional necessities, with other grounds, might be judged to have overriding claims.

In a situation of conflict, the necessities may be felt to be stringent, and even generally inescapable, and the agent's further reflection may confirm his first feeling of their stringency. Yet in the circumstances of conflict he has to make a choice, and to bring himself to do one of the normally forbidden things, in order to avoid doing the other. He may finally recognise one overriding necessity, even though he would not be ready to generalise it to other circumstances. The necessity that is associated with types of action — e.g. not to betray one's friends — is absolute and unconditional, in the sense that it is not relative to, or conditional upon, some desirable external end: but it is liable occasion-ally to conflict with other necessities.

A second distinction must be drawn: from the fact that a man thinks that there is nothing other than X which he can do in a particular situation it does not follow that it is intuitively obvious to him that he must do X. Certainly he may have reached the conclusion immediately and without reflection; but he might also have reached the very same conclusion after weighing a number of arguments for and against. A person's belief that so-and-so must be done, and that he must not act in any other way, may be the outcome of the calculation of the conse-quences of not doing the necessary thing: always provided that he sees the avoidance of bringing about these consequences as something that is imposed on him as a necessity in virtue of the character of the action. The reason for the necessity of the action sometimes is to be found in its later consequences, rather than in the nature and quality of the action evident at the time of action. In every case there will be a description of the action that shows the immediate ground for the necessity, usually by indicating the virtue or vice involved.

Different men, and different social groups, recognise rather different moral necessities in the same essential areas of moral concern. This is no more surprising, or philosophically disquieting, than the fact that

different men, and different social groups, will order the primary virtues of men, and the features of an admirable way of life, differently.
That the poverty stricken and the destitute must be helped, just because they suffer, and that a great wrong does not demand a great
punishment as retribution, are typical modern opinions about what
must be done. Reasoning is associated with these opinions, as it is also
with the different orderings of essential virtues; there are no conclusive
proofs, or infallible intuitions, which put a stop to the adducing of new
considerations. One does not expect that everyone should recognise
the same moral necessities; but rather that everyone should recognise
some moral necessities, and similar and overlapping ones, in the same,
or almost the same areas, of moral concern.

A man's morality, and the morality of a social group, can properly be
seen as falling into two parts, first, a picture of the activities necessary
to an ideal way of life which is aspired to, and, second, the unavoidable
duties and necessities without which even the elements of human
worth, and of a respectworthy way of life, are lacking. The two parts
are not rationally unconnected. To take the obvious classical examples:
a betrayal of friends in a moment of danger, and for the sake of one's
own safety, is excluded from the calculation of possibilities; one may
lose perhaps everything else, but this cannot be done; the stain would
be too great. And one may take public examples: an outrage of cruelty
perpetrated upon undefended civilians in war would constitute a stain
that would not be erased and would not be balanced against political
success.

How would a sceptical, utilitarian friend of Stephen's, a philosophical
friend of the utilitarians, respond to these suggestions? Among other
objections he would certainly say that I was turning the clock back,
suggesting a return to the moral philosophies of the past: absolute
prohibitions, elementary decencies, the recognition of a plurality of
prohibitions which do not all serve a single purpose: and with nothing
more definite behind them than a form of life aspired to; this is the
outline of an Aristotelian ethics: ancient doctrine. Modern utilitarians
thought that men have the possibility of indefinite improvement in
their moral thinking, and that they were confined and confused by their
innate endowments of moral repugnances and emotional admirations.
There was a sense of the open future in all their writing. But hope of
continuing improvement, if it survives at all now, is now largely without
evidence. Lowering the barriers of prohibition, and making rational
calculation of consequences the sole foundation of public policies, have
so far favoured, and are still favouring, a new callousness in policy, a
dullness of sensibility, and sometimes moral despair, at least in respect
of public affairs. When the generally respected barriers of impermissi-
ble conduct are once crossed, and when no different unconditional
barriers, within the same areas of conduct, are put in their place, then

the special, apparently superstitious value attached to the preservation of human life will be questioned. This particular value will no longer be distinguished by an exceptionally solemn prohibition; rather it will be assessed on a common scale alongside other desirable things. Yet it is not clear that the taking of lives can be marked and evaluated on a common scale on which increases of pleasure and diminutions of suffering are also measured. This is the suggested discontinuity which a utilitarian must deny.

Moral prohibitions in general, and particularly those that govern the taking of life, the celebration of the dead, and that govern sexual relations and family relations, are artifices that give human lives some distinctive, peculiar, even arbitrary human shape and pattern. They humanise the natural phases of experience, and lend them a distinguishing sense and direction, one among many possible ones. It is natural for men to expect these artificialities, without which their lives would seen to them inhuman. Largely for this reason a purely naturalistic and utilitarian interpretation of duties and obligations, permissions and prohibitions, in these areas, and particularly in the taking of human life, leaves uneasiness. The idea of morality is connected with the idea that taking human life is a terrible act, which has to be regulated by some set of overriding constraints that constitute a morality; and the connection of ideas alleged here is not a vague one. If there were a people who did not recoil from killing, and, what is a distinguishable matter, who seemed to attach no exceptional value to human life, they would be accounted a community of the subhuman; or, more probably, we would doubt whether their words and practices had been rightly interpreted and whether their way of life had been understood. Yet the taking of life does not have any exceptional importance in utilitarian ethics, that is, in an ethics that is founded exclusively on the actual, ascertained desires and sentiments of men (unlike J. S. Mill's); the taking of life is morally significant in so far as it brings other losses with it. For a strict utilitarian (which J. S. Mill was not) the horror of killing is only the horror of causing other losses, principally of possible happiness; in cases where there are evidently no such losses, the horror of killing becomes superstition. And such a conclusion of naturalism, pressed to its limits, does produce a certain vertigo after reflection. It seems that the mainspring of morality has been taken away.

This vertigo is not principally the result of looking across a century of cool political massacres, undertaken with rational aims; it is also a sentiment with a philosophical thought behind it. A consistent naturalism displaces the pre-reflective moral emphasis upon respect for life, and for the preservation of life, on to an exclusive concern for one or other of the expected future products of being alive — happiness, pleasure, the satisfaction of desires. Respect for human life, independent of the use made of it, may seem to utilitarians a survival of a sacramental consciousness, or at least a survival of a doctrine of the soul's destiny, or of the unique relation between God and man. It had been natural to speak of the moral prohibitions against the taking of life as being respect for the sacredness of an individual life; and this phrase has no proper place, it is very reasonably assumed, in the thought of anyone who has rejected belief in supernatural sanctions.

But the situation may be more complicated. The sacredness of life, so called, and the absolute prohibitions against the taking of life, except under strictly defined conditions, may be admitted to be human inventions. Once the human origin of the prohibitions has been recognised, the prohibition against the taking of life, and respect for human life as such, may still be reaffirmed as absolute. They are reaffirmed as complementary to a set of customs, habits and observances, which are understood by reference to their function, and which are sustained, partly because of, partly in spite of, this understanding: I mean sexual customs, family observances, ceremonial treatment of the dead, gentle treatment of those who are diseased and useless, and of the old and senile, customs of war and treatment of prisoners, treatment of convicted criminals, political and legal safeguards for the rights of individuals, and the customary rituals of respect and gentleness in personal dealings. This complex of habits, and the rituals associated with them, are carried over into a secular morality which makes no existential claims that a naturalist would dispute, and which still rejects the utilitarian morality associated with naturalism. The error of the optimistic utilitarian is that he carries the deritualisation of transactions between men to a point at which men not only can, but ought to, use and exploit each other as they use and exploit any other natural objects, as far as this is compatible with general happiness. And at this point, when the mere existence of an individual person by itself has no value, apart from the by-products and uses of the individual in producing and enjoying desirable states of mind, there is no theoretical barrier against social surgery of all kinds. Not only is there no such barrier in theory: but, more important, the non-existence of the barriers is explicitly recognised. The draining of moral significance from ceremonies, rituals, manners and observances, which imaginatively express moral attitudes and prohibitions, leaves morality incorporated only in a set of propositions and computations: thin and uninteresting propositions, when so isolated from their base in the observances, and manners, which govern ordinary relations with people, and which always manifest implicit moral attitudes and opinions. The computational morality, on which optimists rely, dismisses the non-propositional and unprogrammed elements in morality altogether, falsely confident that these elements can all be ticketed and brought into the computations.

BERNARD WILLIAMS*

Utilitarianism and Integrity

(I) GEORGE, WHO HAS just taken his Ph.D. in chemistry, finds it extremely difficult to get a job. He is not very robust in health, which cuts down the number of jobs he might be able to do satisfactorily. His wife has to go out to work to keep them, which itself causes a great deal of strain, since they have small children and there are severe problems about looking after them. The results of all this, especially on the children, are damaging. An older chemist, who knows about this situation, says that he can get George a decently paid job in a certain laboratory, which pursues research into chemical and biological warfare. George says that he cannot accept this, since he is opposed to chemical and biological warfare. The older man replies that he is not too keen on it himself, come to that, but after all George's refusal is not going to make the job or the laboratory go away; what is more, he happens to know that if George refuses the job, it will certainly go to a contemporary of George's who is not inhibited by any such scruples and is likely if appointed to push along the research with greater zeal than George would. Indeed, it is not merely concern for George and his family, but (to speak frankly and in confidence) some alarm about this other man's excess of zeal, which has led the older man to offer to use his influence to get George the job . . . George's wife, to whom he is deeply attached, has views (the details of which need not concern us) from which

*From Bernard Williams, "A Critique of Utilitarianism," in J. J. C. Smart and Bernard Williams: *Utilitarianism, For and Against.*

165

it follows that at least there is nothing particularly wrong with research into CBW. What should he do?

(2) Jim finds himself in the central square of a small South American town. Tied up against the wall are a row of twenty Indians, most terrified, a few defiant, in front of them several armed men in uniform. A heavy man in a sweat-stained khaki shirt turns out to be the captain in charge and, after a good deal of questioning of Jim which establishes that he got there by accident while on a botanical expedition, explains that the Indians are a random group of the inhabitants who, after recent acts of protest against the government, are just about to be killed to remind other possible protestors of the advantages of not protesting. However, since Jim is an honoured visitor from another land, the captain is happy to offer him a guest's privilege of killing one of the Indians himself. If Jim accepts, then as a special mark of the occasion, the other Indians will be let off. Of course, if Jim refuses, then there is no special occasion, and Pedro here will do what he was about to do when Jim arrived, and kill them all. Jim, with some desperate recollection of schoolboy fiction, wonders whether if he got hold of a gun, he could hold the captain, Pedro, and the rest of the soldiers to threat, but it is quite clear from the set-up that nothing of that kind is going to work: any attempt at that sort of thing will mean that all the Indians will be killed, and himself. The men against the wall, and the other villagers, understand the situation, and are obviously begging him to accept. What should he do?

To these dilemmas, it seems to me that utilitarianism replies, in the first case, that George should accept the job, and in the second, that Jim should kill the Indian. Not only does utilitarianism give these answers but, if the situations are essentially as described and there are no further special factors, it regards them, it seems to me, as *obviously* the right answers. But many of us would certainly wonder whether, in (1), that could possibly be the right answer at all; and in the case of (2), even one who came to think that perhaps that was the answer, might well wonder whether it was obviously the answer. Nor is it just a question of the rightness or obviousness of these answers. It is also a question of what sort of considerations come into finding the answer. A feature of utilitarianism is that it cuts out a kind of consideration which for some others makes a difference to what they feel about such cases: a consideration involving the idea, as we might first and very simply put it, that each of us is specially responsible for what *he* does, rather than for what other people do. This is an idea closely connected with the value of integrity. It is often suspected that utilitarianism, at least in its direct forms, makes integrity as a value more or less unintelligible. I shall try to show that this suspicion is correct. Of course, even if that is correct, it would not necessarily follow that we should reject utilitarianism; perhaps, as utilitarians sometimes suggest, we should just forget about integrity, in favour of such things as a concern for the general good. However, if I am right, we cannot merely do that, since the reason why utilitarianism cannot understand integrity is that it cannot coherently describe the relations between a man's projects and his actions.

Two Kinds of Remoter Effect

A lot of what we have to say about this question will be about the relations between my projects and other people's projects. But before we get on to that, we should first ask whether we are assuming too hastily what the utilitarian answers to the dilemmas will be. In terms of more direct effects of the possible decisions, there does not indeed seem much doubt about the answer in either case; but it might be said that in terms of more remote or less evident effects counterweights might be found to enter the utilitarian scales. Thus the effect on George of a decision to take the job might be invoked, or its effect on others who might know of his decision. The possibility of there being more beneficent labours in the future from which he might be barred or disqualified, might be mentioned; and so forth. Such effects — in particular, possible effects on the agent's character, and effects on the public at large — are often invoked by utilitarian writers dealing with problems about lying or promise-breaking, and some similar considerations might be invoked here.

There is one very general remark that is worth making about arguments of this sort. The certainty that attaches to these hypotheses about possible effects is usually pretty low; in some cases, indeed, the hypothesis invoked is so implausible that it would scarcely pass if it were not being used to deliver the respectable moral answer, as in the standard fantasy that one of the effects of one's telling a particular lie is to weaken the disposition of the world at large to tell the truth. The demands on the certainty or probability of these beliefs as beliefs about particular actions are much milder than they would be on beliefs favouring the unconventional course. It may be said that this is as it should be, since the presumption must be in favour of the conventional course: but that scarcely seems a *utilitarian* answer, unless utilitarianism has already taken off in the direction of not applying the consequences to the particular act at all.

Leaving aside that very general point, I want to consider now two types of effect that are often invoked by utilitarians, and which might be invoked in connexion with these imaginary cases. The attitude or tone involved in invoking these effects may sometimes seem peculiar; but that sort of peculiarity soon becomes familiar in utilitarian discussions, and indeed it can be something of an achievement to retain a sense of it.

First, there is the psychological effect on the agent. Our descriptions of these situations have not so far taken account of how George or Jim will be after they have taken the one course or the other; and it might be said that if they take the course which seemed at first the utilitarian one, the effects on them will be in fact bad enough and extensive enough to cancel out the initial utilitarian advantages of that course. Now there is one version of this effect in which, for a utilitarian, some confusion must be involved, namely that in which the agent feels bad, his subsequent conduct and relations are crippled and so on, *because he thinks that he has done the wrong thing*—for if the balance of outcomes was as it appeared to be *before* invoking this effect, then he has not (from the utilitarian point of view) done the wrong thing. So that version of the effect, for a rational and utilitarian agent, could not possibly make any difference to the assessment of right and wrong. However, perhaps he is not a thoroughly rational agent, and is disposed to have bad feelings, whichever he decided to do. Now such feelings, which are from a strictly utilitarian point of view irrational—nothing, a utilitarian can point out, is advanced by having them—cannot, consistently, have any great weight in a utilitarian calculation. I shall consider in a moment an argument to suggest that they should have no weight at all in it. But short of that, the utilitarian could reasonably say that such feelings should not be encouraged, even if we accept their existence, and that to give them a lot of weight is to encourage them. Or, at the very best, even if they are straightforwardly and without any discount to be put into the calculation, their weight must be small: they are after all (and at best) one man's feelings.

That consideration might seem to have particular force in Jim's case. In George's case, his feelings represent a larger proportion of what is to be weighed, and are more commensurate in character with other items in the calculations. In Jim's case, however, his feelings might seem to be of very little weight compared with other things that are at stake. There is a powerful and recognizable appeal that can be made on this point: as that a refusal by Jim to do what he has been invited to do would be a kind of self-indulgent squeamishness. That is an appeal which can be made by other than utilitarians—indeed, there are some uses of it which cannot be consistently made by utilitarians, as when it essentially involves the idea that there is something dishonourable about such self-indulgence. But in some versions it is a familiar, and it must be said a powerful, weapon of utilitarianism. One must be clear, though, about what it can and cannot accomplish. The most it can do, so far as I can see, is to invite one to consider how seriously, and for what reasons, one feels that one is invited to do is (in these circumstances) wrong, and in particular, to consider that question from the utilitarian point of view. When the agent is not seeing the situation from a utilitarian point of view, the appeal cannot force him to do so; and if he does come round to seeing it from a utilitarian point of view, there is virtually nothing left for the appeal to do. If he does not see it from a utilitarian point of view, he will not see his resistance to the invitation, and the unpleasant feelings he associates with accepting it, *just* as disagreeable experiences of his; they figure rather as emotional expressions of a thought that to accept would be wrong. He may be asked, as by the appeal, to consider whether he is right, and indeed whether he is fully serious, in thinking that. But the assertion of the appeal, that he is being self-indulgently squeamish, will not itself answer that question, or even help to answer it, since it essentially tells him to regard his feelings just as unpleasant experiences of his, and he cannot, by doing that, answer the question they pose when they are precisely not so regarded, but are regarded as indications[1] of what he thinks is right and wrong. If he does come round fully to the utilitarian point of view then of course he will regard these feelings just as unpleasant experiences of his. And once Jim — at least — has come to see them in that light, there is nothing left for the appeal to do, since *of course* his feelings, so regarded, are of virtually no weight at all in relation to the other things at stake. The "squeamishness" appeal is not an argument which adds in a hitherto neglected consideration. Rather, it is an invitation to consider the situation, and one's own feelings, from a utilitarian point of view.

The reason why the squeamishness appeal can be very unsettling, and one can be unnerved by the suggestion of self-indulgence in going against utilitarian considerations, is not that we are utilitarians who are uncertain what utilitarian value to attach to our moral feelings, but that we are partially at least not utilitarians, and cannot regard our moral feelings merely as objects of utilitarian value. Because our moral relation to the world is partly given by such feelings, and by a sense of what we can or cannot "live with," to come to regard those feelings from a purely utilitarian point of view, that is to say, as happenings outside one's moral self, is to lose a sense of one's moral identity; to lose, in the most literal way, one's integrity.

---

[1]On the non-cognitivist meta-ethic in terms of which Smart presents his utilitarianism, the term "indications" here would represent an understatement.

J. J. C. SMART*

❧

Integrity and Squeamishness

❧

SUPPOSE THAT AN innocent man is sentenced to imprisonment or a stupid student is given a prize for outstanding excellence. In such cases it can be held that an injustice has been done and that this injustice is of a non-comparative kind. If all innocent men were to be punished or all stupid students given a prize this would only compound the injustice. The most poignant sort of case, of course, is that of the punishment of an innocent man. Suppose that in order to prevent a riot in which thousands would certainly be killed a sheriff were to frame and execute an innocent man.[1] On utilitarian principles would not the sacrifice of one life in order to save thousands be justified? The usual utilitarian reply is that if such a thing were to be done it would probably be detected, or would leak out, that an innocent man had been punished, and the resulting destruction of faith in the law would lead to more harm than would result even from thousands of people being killed in the riot. If faith in the due processes of the law is destroyed the very foundations of society are shaken. If a potential criminal thinks that innocent people may be punished, he will be less likely to be deterred

---

*From J. J. C. Smart, "Utilitarianism and Justice," *Journal of Chinese Philosophy*, 1978.

[1]This sort of case is discussed by H. J. McCloskey in his paper "An Examination of Restricted Utilitarianism," *Philosophical Review* 66 (1957), 466–485, reprinted in Michael D. Bayles (ed.) *Contemporary Utilitarianism* (Garden City, New York: Doubleday, 1968). See also H. J. McCloskey "A Non-Utilitarian Approach to Punishment," *Inquiry* 8 (1965), 249–263, reprinted in Michael D. Bayles (ed.) *Contemporary Utilitarianism*, and H. J. McCloskey, "A Note on Utilitarian Punishment," *Mind* 72 (1963), 599.

by the threat of punishment, since he may reasonably enough think that
he might as well be hanged for a sheep as for a goat. Nevertheless, this
sort of reply will not do, because the case can be made a very strong
one: we may assume that detection of the sheriff's deceit is almost
impossible. If need be the story can also be altered so as to make the
likely harm done in the riot even greater than it was in the original
story. There must come a time at which it will be agreed on all sides
that the harm done by punishing the innocent man would be less (even
much less) than that which would be done by the riot. Moreover, it is
not relevant to object that it is merely probable that there would be a
riot if the innocent man were not punished, whereas the harm done by
executing the innocent man would be quite certain to occur. We must
in a utilitarian calculation (in which probabilities are relevant) take the
harm done to be the total probable harm, and the objector to utilitarianism can always state the case so that the harm caused by doing the
injustice to the innocent man is much less than the total probable harm
which is prevented.

Certainly it is cases such as this one which make me wonder whether
after all I really am a utilitarian. To do a serious injustice to someone is
a terrible thing. How terrible it must be for a man to know that he is
about to be executed, or that he must stay in prison for many years.
How much worse it must be for the man if he knows that he is innocent:
to all the usual pains and penalties is added the anguish of his believing
himself to be disgraced and held in contempt because people had false
beliefs about him. It really is distressing even to think about such a
case, let alone to be the victim oneself. And yet one can argue that our
feelings of distress are (at least partly) due to looking at only one aspect
of the situation. If the harm done to the victim really is (as on the
hypothesis) much less than the harm that would have been caused by
the riot, with the thousands of deaths, the fatherless and motherless
children, and so on, then it ought to give us even more anguish if we
contemplate this side of the story.

Certainly the utilitarian is entitled to assert that such cases in which it
would be right to do an injustice must be very rare indeed. In nearly all
empirically likely situations there are almost certainly better ways of
dealing with the situation.[2] It is therefore highly improbable that any
utilitarian will find himself called upon by his own principles to commit
a flagrant act of injustice of the sort which we have been considering.
Moreover, the sort of man who is most likely to behave in the most
optimific way in normal circumstances is one who will find it hard and
distasteful to do the act of injustice which is postulated in the case

---

[2]For a very perceptive discussion of the issues involved in such cases, see T. L. S.
Sprigge, "A Utilitarian Reply to Dr. McCloskey," *Inquiry* 8 (1963), 264–291, reprinted
in Michael D. Bayles (ed.) *Contemporary Utilitarianism.*

which we have been considering: he will have a lively and sorrowful sympathy with the man who has to be sacrificed for the good of others. After all, if he is not sympathetic in particular instances he is unlikely to have the strong feeling of generalized benevolence which is the basis of utilitarianism.[3]

There will therefore be fearful conflicts in the mind of a utilitarian who has to do an act of injustice of the sort which we have been considering. Injustice of this sort does harm to someone and no benevolent person can like this. There will therefore be a sort of conflict in the mind of a utilitarian which contributes to what Bernard Williams has described as a lack of integrity. I think that the utilitarian must be prepared to sacrifice the harmony of his own mind for the good of others. If, to use Williams's example,[4] the only way in which I can save twenty men from being wrongfully executed in the field by an army captain is to myself shoot the twentieth (who is to be executed anyway) then I must do it. No doubt I shall feel bad about it, and perhaps I shall not be able to bring myself to do it. But in this case the nineteen men who will otherwise be shot are unlikely to thank me for it (as Williams recognizes).[5] The case is analogous to one in which I might have the knowledge to perform a life saving operation, but in which I just could not bring myself to cut into human flesh. This would be weakness of will, however laudable (because generally optimific) a squeamishness about cutting into human flesh would be in normal circumstances (supposing of course that I am not a medical person, who must learn to overcome such squeamishness). The man who is most likely to do the utilitarian thing in normal circumstances may not be the one who is likely to do the utilitarian thing in very out of the way circumstances. We must however distinguish between what a utilitarian may in fact be most likely to do and what he, on his own principles, ought to do. What he ought to do may be to sacrifice his own inner harmony. To be solicitous for one's own integrity when it conflicts with the general good would be thought by the utilitarian to be too self-regarding. (Williams is aware of this sort of objection. He seems from his point of view to regard the objection as question begging.[6]) I do not suppose that there are any surgeons who fail to overcome their initial distaste as medical students for cutting into human flesh and for the sight of blood. But let us suppose that all or most surgeons were like this. Then surely

---

[3] I say this in spite of the fact that we do come across people who worry a lot (or profess to worry a lot) about the fate of humanity in general, but who show little tenderness or sympathy in their personal relationships.

[4] See J. J. C. Smart and Bernard Williams, *Utilitarianism: For and Against*, p. 98.

[5] *Op. cit.* p. 99, near top.

[6] *Op. cit.* p. 120. See also Bernard Williams, "Utilitarianism and Moral Self-Indulgence," in H. D. Lewis (ed.) *Contemporary British Philosophy* (London: Allen and Unwin, 1976).

it would be better for mankind that they should continue to work at surgery, despite their inner conflicts and messily unintegrated selves, than that they should give up surgery for other pursuits. Similarly if non-comparative justice flagrantly conflicts with the utilitarian principle, the utilitarian will find himself in a similar position to these surgeons. One may reasonably hope, however, that very extreme situations of this sort will almost never occur.

It should be noticed that I have been assuming that our particular feelings (e.g. for justice) have to be criticized in the light of our most general feeling of universal benevolence. In ethics the situation seems to be disanalogous to that in science. In science we test our theories by means of particular observations. (This is a bit of an over-simplification, but near enough the truth for present purposes.) However, in ethics (so I have been assuming) we are concerned with expressions of feelings rather than with statements of what is the case in the universe. It seems reasonable (or not unreasonable) to trust our most general feelings and to test our particular feelings by reference to them. That is, because of the non-cognitivist nature of ethics, the situation seems to be the opposite to that in science.[7]

Consider now the case in which as a utilitarian I over-rule my feelings against doing an injustice, let us say a breach of non-comparative justice. These feelings may be simply due to the dislike of doing harm to someone, even though the desire to do good to others may outweigh this. However, the dislike of doing harm may in the circumstances be more powerful than strict utilitarian calculations will warrant. Furthermore I may have feelings against doing the injustice which derive from my traditional, non-utilitarian, moral training in the past. When these things are so, can I be said really to subscribe to the utilitarian principle (at least if the non-cognitivist meta-ethical position is accepted)? Would I not be an adherent of some compromise position, like that of Sir David Ross or of H. J. McCloskey?[8] Such a position would be deontological but would have its utilitarian aspect, in so far as beneficence would be one prima-facie duty among others. I have suggested earlier in this paper that the situation may be better understood as a case where one does not have a compromise ethics, but rather one in which in some moods one is a utilitarian and in some moods one is not. However, I should like now to put forward yet another possible account of the situation. I have suggested that if the utilitarian can not

[7] I have discussed this issue more fully in my paper "The Methods of Ethics and the Methods of Science," *Journal of Philosophy* 62 (1965), 344–349. Peter Singer has defended a rather similar view to mine about the methodology of ethics, though he bases it on a cognitivist meta-ethics, in his interesting paper "Sidgwick and Reflective Equilibrium," *Monist* 58 (1974), 490–517.

[8] Sir David Ross, *Foundations of Ethics* (London: Oxford University Press, 1939). H. J. McCloskey, *Meta-Ethics and Normative Ethics* (The Hague: Martinus Nijhoff, 1969).

bring himself to act as a utilitarian he may put this down to weakness of will. Weakness of will may occur whatever one's ethical system: for example through partiality to a friend a man may act unjustly. One needs some sort of account according to which our desires and attitudes belong to a hierarchy. Thus second order attitudes are dispositions to modify our first order attitudes, and third order attitudes are dispositions to modify our second order attitudes. Our moral attitudes will be those which are highest in the hierarchy and will be our "over-riding" wants, as D. H. Monro has called them,[9] and in the case of the utilitarian will be the sentiment of generalized benevolence. It may well be that the utilitarian will have dispositions to behave according to the tenets of traditional morality. Since these are lower in the hierarchy, if the utilitarian acts according to them he will act in accordance with weakness of will, no less than he would if he ate (through hunger) on an occasion when he knew that it was not in his own interests to eat. One can, through weakness of will, act against one's prudence, and similarly, the fact that a utilitarian might not be able to do an act which is traditionally classified as unjust need not prove that he is not really a utilitarian.[10]

[9]D. H. Monro, *Empiricism and Ethics* (London: Cambridge University Press, 1967). See chapter 17.
[10]I am grateful to Peter Singer and Robert Young for helpfully commenting on an earlier draft of this article.

GREGORY S. KAVKA*

Some Paradoxes of Deterrence*

DETERRENCE IS A parent of paradox. Conflict theorists, notably Thomas Schelling, have pointed out several paradoxes of deterrence: that it may be to the advantage of someone who is trying to deter another to be irrational, to have fewer available options, or to lack relevant information.[1] I shall describe certain new paradoxes that emerge when one attempts to analyze deterrence from a moral rather than a strategic perspective. These paradoxes are presented in the form of statements that appear absurd or incredible on first inspection, but can be supported by quite convincing arguments.

Consider a typical situation involving deterrence. A potential wrongdoer is about to commit an offense that would unjustly harm someone. A defender intends, and threatens, to retaliate should the wrongdoer commit the offense. Carrying out retaliation, if the offense is committed, could well be morally wrong. (The wrongdoer could be insane, or the retaliation could be out of proportion with the offense, or could seriously harm others besides the wrongdoer.) The moral paradoxes of deterrence arise out of the attempt to determine the moral status of the defender's *intention* to retaliate in such cases. If the defender knows

*From Gregory S. Kavka: Some Paradoxes of Deterrence, *Journal of Philosophy*, 1978.

*An earlier version of this paper was presented at Stanford University. I am grateful to several, especially Robert Merrihew Adams, Tyler Burge, Warren Quinn, and Virginia Warren, for helpful comments on previous drafts. My work was supported, in part, by a Regents' Faculty Research Fellowship from the University of California.

[1]*The Strategy of Conflict* (New York: Oxford, 1960), Chaps. 1–2; and *Arms and Influence* (New Haven, Conn.: Yale, 1966), chap 2.

175

retaliation to be wrong, it would appear that this intention is evil. Yet such "evil" intentions may pave the road to heaven, by preventing serious offenses and by doing so without actually harming anyone.

Scrutiny of such morally ambiguous retaliatory intentions reveals paradoxes that call into question certain significant and widely accepted moral doctrines. These doctrines are what I call *bridge principles*. They attempt to link together the moral evaluation of actions and the moral evaluation of agents (and their states) in certain simple and apparently natural ways. The general acceptance, and intuitive appeal, of such principles, lends credibility to the project of constructing a consistent moral system that accurately reflects our firmest moral beliefs about both agents and actions. By raising doubts about the validity of certain popular bridge principles, the paradoxes presented here pose new difficulties for this important project.

I

In this section, a certain class of situations involving deterrence is characterized, and a plausible normative assumption is presented. In the following three sections, we shall see how application of this assumption to these situations yields paradoxes.

The class of paradox-producing situations is best introduced by means of an example. Consider the balance of nuclear terror as viewed from the perspective of one of its superpower participants, nation N. N sees the threat of nuclear retaliation as its only reliable means of preventing nuclear attack (or nuclear blackmail leading to world domination) by its superpower rival. N is confident such a threat will succeed in deterring its adversary, provided it really intends to carry out that threat. (N fears that, if it bluffs, its adversary is likely to learn this through leaks or espionage.) Finally, N recognizes it would have conclusive moral reasons *not* to carry out the threatened retaliation, if its opponent were to obliterate N with a surprise attack. For although retaliation would punish the leaders who committed this unprecedented crime and would prevent them from dominating the postwar world, N knows it would also destroy many millions of innocent civilians in the attacking nation (and in other nations), would set back postwar economic recovery for the world immeasurably, and might add enough fallout to the atmosphere to destroy the human race.

Let us call situations of the sort that nation N perceives itself as being in, *Special Deterrent Situations* (SDSs). More precisely, an agent is in an SDS when he reasonably and correctly believes that the following conditions hold. First, it is likely he must intend (conditionally) to apply a harmful sanction to innocent people, if an extremely harmful and unjust offense is to be prevented. Second, such an intention would very likely deter the offense. Third, the amounts of harm involved in the offense and the threatened sanction are very large and of roughly similar quantity (or the latter amount is smaller than the former). Finally, he would have conclusive moral reasons not to apply the sanction if the offense were to occur.

The first condition in this definition requires some comment. Deterrence depends only on the potential wrongdoer's *beliefs* about the prospects of the sanction being applied. Hence, the first condition will be satisfied only if attempts by the defender to bluff would likely be perceived as such by the wrongdoer. This may be the case if the defender is an unconvincing liar, or is a group with a collective decision procedure, or if the wrongdoer is shrewd and knows the defender quite well. Generally, however, bluffing will be a promising course of action. Hence, although it is surely logically and physically possible for an SDS to occur, there will be few actual SDSs. It may be noted, though, that writers on strategic policy frequently assert that nuclear deterrence will be effective only if the defending nation really intends to retaliate.[2] If this is so, the balance of terror may fit the definition of an SDS, and the paradoxes developed here could have significant practical implications.[3] Further, were there no actual SDSs, these paradoxes would still be of considerable theoretical interest. For they indicate that the validity of some widely accepted moral doctrines rests on the presupposition that certain situations that could arise (i.e., SDSs) will not.

Turning to our normative assumption, we begin by noting that any reasonable system of ethics must have substantial utilitarian elements. The assumption that produces the paradoxes of deterrence concerns the role of utilitarian considerations in determining one's moral duty in a narrowly limited class of situations. Let the *most useful* act in a given choice situation be that with the highest expected utility. Our assumption says that the most useful act should be performed whenever a very great deal of utility is at stake. This means that, if the difference in expected utility between the most useful act and its alternatives is extremely large (e.g., equivalent to the difference between life and death for a very large number of people), other moral considerations are overridden by utilitarian considerations.

This assumption may be substantially weakened by restricting in various ways its range of application. I restrict the assumption to apply only when (i) a great deal of *negative* utility is at stake, and (ii) people will likely suffer serious injustices if the agent fails to perform the most useful act. This makes the assumption more plausible, since the propriety of doing one person a serious injustice, in order to produce positive

---

[2]See, e.g., Herman Kahn, *On Thermonuclear War*, 2nd ed. (Princeton, N.J.: University Press, 1960), p. 185; and Anthony Kenny, "Counterforce and Countervalue," in Walter Stein, ed., *Nuclear Weapons: A Catholic Response* (London: Merlin Press, 1965), pp. 162–164.

[3]See, e.g., n. 9, below.

benefits for others, is highly questionable. The justifiability of doing the same injustice to prevent a utilitarian disaster which itself involves grave injustices, seems more in accordance with our moral intuitions.

The above restrictions appear to bring our assumption into line with the views of philosophers such as Robert Nozick, Thomas Nagel, and Richard Brandt, who portray moral rules as "absolutely" forbidding certain kinds of acts, but acknowledge that exceptions might have to be allowed in cases in which such acts are necessary to prevent catastrophe.[4] Even with these restrictions, however, the proposed assumption would be rejected by supporters of genuine Absolutism, the doctrine that there are certain acts (such as vicarious punishment and deliberate killing of the innocent) that are always wrong, whatever the consequences of not performing them. (Call such acts *inherently evil*.) We can, though, accommodate the Absolutists. To do so, let us further qualify our assumption by limiting its application to cases in which (iii) performing the most useful act involves, at most, a small *risk* of performing an inherently evil act. With this restriction, the assumption still leads to paradoxes, yet is consistent with Absolutism (unless that doctrine is extended to include absolute prohibitions on something other than doing acts of the sort usually regarded as inherently evil).[5] The triply qualified assumption is quite plausible; so the fact that it produces paradoxes is both interesting and disturbing.

II

The first moral paradox of deterrence is:

(P1) There are cases in which, although it would be wrong for an agent to perform a certain act in a certain situation, it would nonetheless be right for him, knowing this, to form the intention to perform that act in that situation.

At first, this strikes one as absurd. If it is wrong and he is aware that it is wrong, how could it be right for him to form the intention to do it? (P1) is the direct denial of a simple moral thesis, the Wrongful Intentions Principle (WIP): *To intend to do what one knows to be wrong is itself wrong.*[6] WIP seems so obvious that, although philosophers never call it

---

[4]Nozick, *Anarchy, State, and Utopia* (New York: Basic Books, 1974), pp. 30/1 n; Nagel, "War and Massacre," *Philosophy and Public Affairs*, I, 2 (Winter 1972): 123–144, p. 126; Brandt, "Utilitarianism and the Rules of War," *ibid.*, 145–165, p. 147, especially n. 3.

[5]Extensions of Absolutism that would block some or all of the paradoxes include those which forbid intending to do what is wrong, deliberately making oneself less virtuous, or intentionally risking performing an inherently evil act. (An explanation of the relevant sense of 'risking performing an act' will be offered in section iv.)

[6]I assume henceforth that, if it would be wrong to do something, the agent knows this. (The agent, discussed in section iv, who has become corrupt may be an exception.) This keeps the discussion of the paradoxes from getting tangled up with the separate problem of whether an agent's duty is to do what is actually right, or what he believes is right.

into question, they rarely bother to assert it or argue for it. Nevertheless, it appears that Abelard, Aquinas, Butler, Bentham, Kant, and Sidgwick, as well as recent writers such as Anthony Kenny and Jan Narveson, have accepted the principle, at least implicitly.[7]

Why does WIP seem so obviously true? First, we regard the man who fully intends to perform a wrongful act and is prevented from doing so solely by external circumstances (e.g., a man whose murder plan is interrupted by the victim's fatal heart attack) as being just as bad as the man who performs a like wrongful act. Second, we view the man who intends to do what is wrong, and then changes his mind, as having corrected a moral failing or error. Third, it is convenient, for many purposes, to treat a prior intention to perform an act, as the beginning of the act itself. Hence, we are inclined to view intentions as parts of actions and to ascribe to each intention the moral status ascribed to the act "containing" it.

It is essential to note the WIP appears to apply to conditional intentions in the same manner as it applies to nonconditional ones. Suppose I form the intention to kill my neighbor if he insults me again, and fail to kill him only because, fortuitously, he refrains from doing so. I am as bad, or nearly as bad, as if he had insulted me and I had killed him. My failure to perform the act no more erases the wrongness of my intention, than my neighbor's dropping dead as I load my gun would negate the wrongness of the simple intention to kill him. Thus the same considerations adduced above in support of WIP seem to support the formulation: If it would be wrong to perform an act in certain circumstances, then it is wrong to intend to perform that act on the condition that those circumstances arise.

Having noted the source of the strong feeling that (P1) should be rejected, we must consider an instantiation of (P1):

> (P1′) In an SDS, it would be wrong for the defender to apply the sanction if the wrongdoer were to commit the offense, but it is right for the defender to form the (conditional) intention to apply the sanction if the wrongdoer commits the offense.

The first half of (P1′), the wrongness of applying the sanction, follows directly from the last part of the definition of an SDS, which says that the defender would have conclusive moral reasons not to apply the sanction. The latter half of (P1′), which asserts the rightness of forming

[7]See *Peter Abelard's Ethics*, D. E. Luscombe, trans. (New York: Oxford, 1971), pp. 5–37; Thomas Aquinas, *Summa Theologica*, 1a2ae, 18–20; Joseph Butler, "A Dissertation on the Nature of Virtue," in *Five Sermons* (Indianapolis: Bobbs-Merrill, 1950), p. 83; Immanuel Kant, *Foundations of the Metaphysics of Morals*, first section; Jeremy Bentham, *An Introduction to the Principles of Morals and Legislation*, chap. 9, secs. 13–16; Henry Sidgwick, *The Methods of Ethics* (New York: Dover, 1907), pp. 60/1, 201–204; Kenny, pp. 159, 162; and Jan Narveson, *Morality and Utility* (Baltimore: Johns Hopkins, 1967), pp. 106–108.

the intention to apply the sanction, follows from the definition of an SDS and our normative assumption. According to the definition, the defender's forming this intention is likely necessary, and very likely sufficient, to prevent a seriously harmful and unjust offense. Further, the offense and the sanction would each produce very large and roughly commensurate amounts of negative utility (or the latter would produce a smaller amount). It follows that utilitarian considerations heavily favor forming the intention to apply the sanction, and that doing so involves only a small risk of performing an inherently evil act.[8] Applying our normative assumption yields the conclusion that it is right for the defender to form the intention in question.

This argument, if sound, would establish the truth of (P1'), and hence (P1), in contradiction with WIP. It suggests that WIP should not be applied to *deterrent intentions*, i.e., those conditional intentions whose existence is based on the agent's desire to thereby deter others from actualizing the antecedent condition of the intention. Such intentions are rather strange. They are, by nature, self-stultifying: if a deterrent intention fulfills the agent's purpose, it ensures that the intended (and possibly evil) act is not performed, by preventing the circumstances of performance from arising. The unique nature of such intentions can be further explicated by noting the distinction between intending to do something, and desiring (or intending) to intend to do it. Normally, an agent will form the intention to do something because he either desires doing that thing as an end in itself, or as a means to other ends. In such cases, little importance attaches to the distinction between intending and desiring to intend. But, in the case of deterrent intentions, the ground of the desire to form the intention is entirely distinct from any desire to carry it out. Thus, what may be inferred about the agent who seeks to form such an intention is this. He desires *having the intention* as a means of deterrence. Also, he is willing, in order to prevent the offense, to accept a certain *risk* that, in the end, he will apply the sanction. But this is entirely consistent with his having a strong desire not to apply the sanction, and no desire at all to apply it. Thus, while the object of his deterrent intention might be an evil act, it does not follow that, in desiring to adopt that intention, he desires to do evil, either as an end or as a means.

WIP ties the morality of an intention exclusively to the moral qualities of its object (i.e., the intended act). This is not unreasonable since, typically, the only significant effects of intentions are the acts of the

---

[8] A qualification is necessary. Although having the intention involves only a small risk of applying the threatened sanction to innocent people, it follows, from points made in section IV, that forming the intention might also involve risks of performing *other* inherently evil acts. Hence, what really follows is that forming the intention is right in those SDSs in which the composite risk is small. This limitation in the scope of (P1') is to be henceforth understood. It does not affect (P1), (P2), or (P3), since each is governed by an existential quantifier.

agent (and the consequences of these acts) which flow from these intentions. However, in certain cases, intentions may have *autonomous effects* that are independent of the intended act's actually being performed. In particular, intentions to act may influence the conduct of other agents. When an intention has important autonomous effects, these effects must be incorporated into any adequate moral analysis of it. The first paradox arises because the autonomous effects of the relevant deterrent intention are dominant in the moral analysis of an SDS, but the extremely plausible WIP ignores such effects.[9]

III

(P1') implies that a rational moral agent in an SDS should want to form the conditional intention to apply the sanction if the offense is committed, in order to deter the offense. But will he be able to do so? Paradoxically, he will not be. He is a captive in the prison of his own virtue, able to form the requisite intention only by bending the bars of his cell out of shape. Consider the preliminary formulation of this new paradox:

> (P2') In an SDS, a rational and morally good agent cannot (as a matter of logic) have (or form) the intention to apply the sanction if the offense is committed.[10]

The argument for (P2') is as follows. An agent in an SDS recognizes that there would be conclusive moral reasons not to apply the sanction if the offense were committed. If he does not regard these admittedly conclusive moral reasons as conclusive reasons for him not to apply the sanction, then he is not moral. Suppose, on the other hand, that he does regard himself as having conclusive reasons not to apply the sanction if the offense is committed. If, nonetheless, he is disposed to apply it, because the reasons for applying it motivate him more strongly than do the conclusive reasons not to apply it, then he is irrational.

But couldn't our rational moral agent recognize, in accordance with (P1'), that he ought to form the intention to apply the sanction? And couldn't he then simply grit his teeth and pledge to himself that he will apply the sanction if the offense is committed? No doubt he could, and

---

[9]In *Nuclear Weapons*, Kenny and others use WIP to argue that nuclear deterrence is immoral because it involves having the conditional intention to kill innocent people. The considerations advanced in this section suggest that this argument, at best, is inconclusive, since it presents only one side of a moral paradox, and, at worst, is mistaken, since it applies WIP in just the sort of situation in which its applicability is most questionable.

[10]'Rational and morally good' in this and later statements of the second and third paradoxes, means rational and moral in the given situation. A person who usually is rational and moral, but fails to be in the situation in question, could, of course, have the intention to apply the sanction. (P2') is quite similar to a paradox concerning utilitarianism and deterrence developed by D. H. Hodgson in *Consequences of Utilitarianism* (Oxford: Clarendon Press, 1967), chap. 4.

this would amount to trying to form the intention to apply the sanction. But the question remains whether he can succeed in forming that intention, by this or any other process, while remaining rational and moral. And it appears he cannot. There are, first of all, psychological difficulties. Being rational, how can he dispose himself to do something that he knows he would have conclusive reasons not to do, when and if the time comes to do it? Perhaps, though, some exceptional people can produce in themselves dispositions to act merely by pledging to act. But even if one could, in an SDS, produce a disposition to apply the sanction in this manner, such a disposition would not count as a *rational intention* to apply the sanction. This is because, as recent writers on intentions have suggested, it is part of the concept of rationally intending to do something, that the disposition to do the intended act be caused (or justified) in an appropriate way by the agent's view of reasons for doing the act.[11] And the disposition in question does not stand in such a relation to the agent's reason for action.

It might be objected to this that people sometimes intend to do things (and do them) for no reason at all, without being irrational. This is true, and indicates that the connections between the concepts of intending and reasons for action are not so simple as the above formula implies. But it is also true that intending to do something for no reason at all, in the face of recognized significant reasons not to do it, would be irrational. Similarly, a disposition to act in the face of the acknowledged preponderance of reasons, whether called an "intention" or not, could not qualify as rational. It may be claimed that such a disposition, in an SDS, is rational in the sense that the agent knows it would further his aims to form (and have) it. This is not to deny the second paradox, but simply to express one of its paradoxical features. For the point of (P2') is that the very disposition that *is* rational in the sense just mentioned, is at the same time irrational in an equally important sense. It is a disposition to act in conflict with the agent's own view of the balance of reasons for action.

We can achieve some insight into this by noting that an intention that is deliberately formed, resides at the intersection of two distinguishable actions. It is the beginning of the act that is its object and is the end of the act that is its formation. As such, it may be assessed as rational (or moral) or not, according to whether either of two different acts promotes the agent's (or morality's) ends. Generally, the assessments will agree. But, as Schelling and others have noted, it may sometimes promote one's aims *not* to be disposed to act to promote one's aims should certain contingencies arise. For example, a small country may deter invasion by a larger country if it is disposed to resist any invasion, even

---

[11]See, e.g., S. Hampshire and H. L. A. Hart, "Decision, Intention and Certainty," *Mind*, LXVII.1, 265 (January 1958): 1–12; and G. E. M. Anscombe, *Intention* (Ithaca, N.Y.: Cornell, 1966).

when resistance would be suicidal. In such situations, the assessment of the rationality (or morality) of the agent's intentions will depend upon whether these intentions are treated as components of their object-acts or their formation-acts. If treated as both, conflicts can occur. It is usual and proper to assess the practical rationality of an agent, at a given time, according to the degree of correspondence between his intentions and the reasons he has for performing the acts that are the objects of those intentions. As a result, puzzles such as (P2') emerge when, for purposes of moral analysis, an agent's intentions are viewed partly as components of their formation-acts.

Let us return to the main path of our discussion by briefly summarizing the argument for (P2'). A morally good agent regards conclusive moral reasons for action as conclusive reasons for action *simpliciter*. But the intentions of a rational agent are not out of line with his assessment of the reasons for and against acting. Consequently, a rational moral agent cannot intend to do something that he recognizes there are conclusive moral reasons not to do. Nor can he intend conditionally to do what he recognizes he would have conclusive reasons not to do were that condition to be fulfilled. Therefore, in an SDS, where one has conclusive moral reasons not to apply the sanction, an originally rational and moral agent cannot have the intention to apply it without ceasing to be fully rational or moral; nor can he form the intention (as this entails having it).

We have observed that forming an intention is a process that may generally be regarded as an action. Thus, the second paradox can be reformulated as:

> (P2) There are situations (namely SDSs) in which it would be right for agents to perform certain actions (namely forming the intention to apply the sanction) and in which it is possible for some agents to perform such actions, but impossible for rational and morally good agents to perform them.

(P2), with the exception of the middle clause, is derived from the conjunction of (P1') and (P2') by existential generalization. The truth of the middle clause follows from consideration of the vengeful agent, who desires to punish those who commit seriously harmful and unjust offenses, no matter what the cost to others.

(P2) is paradoxical because it says that there are situations in which rationality and virtue preclude the possibility of right action. And this contravenes our usual assumption about the close logical ties between the concepts of right action and agent goodness. Consider the following claim. *Doing something is right if and only if a morally good man would do the same thing in a given situation.* Call this the Right-Good Principle. One suspects that, aside from qualifications concerning the good man's possible imperfections or factual ignorance, most people regard this principle, which directly contradicts (P2), as being virtually analytic. Yet the plight of the good man described in the second paradox does not arise out of an insufficiency of either knowledge or goodness. (P2) says there are conceivable situations in which virtue and knowledge combine with rationality to preclude right action, in which virtue is an obstacle to doing the right thing. If (P2) is true, our views about the close logical connection between right action and agent goodness, as embodied in the Right-Good Principle, require modifications of a sort not previously envisioned.

IV

A rational moral agent in an SDS faces a cruel dilemma. His reasons for intending to apply the sanction if the offense is committed are, according to (P1'), conclusive. But they outrun his reasons for doing it. Wishing to do what is right, he wants to form the intention. However, unless he can substantially alter the basic facts of the situation or his beliefs about those facts, he can do so only by making himself less morally good; that is, by becoming a person who attaches grossly mistaken weights to certain reasons for and against action (e.g., one who prefers retribution to the protection of the vital interests of innocent people).[12] We have arrived at a third paradox:

> (P3) In certain situations, it would be morally right for a rational and morally good agent to deliberately (attempt to) corrupt himself.[13]

(P3) may be viewed in light of a point about the credibility of threats which has been made by conflict theorists. Suppose a defender is worried about the credibility of his deterrent threat, because he thinks the wrongdoer (rightly) regards him as unwilling to apply the threatened sanction. He may make the threat more credible by passing control of the sanction to some *retaliation-agent*. Conflict theorists consider two sorts of retaliation-agents: people known to be highly motivated to punish the offense in question, and machines programmed to retaliate automatically if the offense occurs. What I wish to note is that future selves of the defender himself are a third class of retaliation-agents. If the other kinds are unavailable, a defender may have to

---

[12]Alternatively, the agent could undertake to make himself into an *irrational* person whose intentions are quite out of line with his reasons for action. However, trying to become irrational, in these circumstances, is less likely to succeed than trying to change one's moral beliefs, and, furthermore, might itself constitute self-corruption. Hence, this point does not affect the paradox stated below.

[13]As Donald Regan has suggested to me, (P3) can be derived directly from our normative assumption: imagine a villain credibly threatening to kill very many hostages unless a certain good man corrupts himself. I prefer the indirect route to (P3) given in the text, because (P1) and (P2) are interesting in their own right and because viewing the three paradoxes together makes it easier to see what produces them.

create an agent of this third sort (i.e., an altered self willing to apply the sanction), in order to deter the offense. In cases in which applying the sanction would be wrong, this could require self-corruption.

How would a rational and moral agent in an SDS, who seeks to have the intention to apply the sanction, go about corrupting himself so that he may have it? He cannot form the intention simply by pledging to apply the sanction; for, according to the second paradox, his rationality and morality preclude this. Instead, he must seek to initiate a causal process (e.g., a reeducation program) that he hopes will result in his beliefs, attitudes, and values changing in such a way that he can and will have the intention to apply the sanction should the offense be committed. Initiating such a process involves taking a rather odd, though not uncommon attitude toward oneself: viewing oneself as an object to be molded in certain respects by outside influences rather than by inner choices. This is, for example, the attitude of the lazy but ambitious student who enrolls in a fine college, hoping that some of the habits and values of his highly motivated fellow students will "rub off" on him.

We can now better understand the notion of "risking doing X" which was introduced in section I. For convenience, let "X" be "killing." Deliberately risking killing is different from risking deliberately killing. One does the former when one rushes an ill person to the hospital in one's car at unsafe speed, having noted the danger of causing a fatal accident. One has deliberately accepted the risk of killing by accident. One (knowingly) risks deliberately killing, on the other hand, when one undertakes a course of action that one knows may, by various causal processes, lead to one's later performing a deliberate killing. The mild-mannered youth who joins a violent street gang is an example. Similarly, the agent in an SDS, who undertakes a plan of self-corruption in order to develop the requisite deterrent intention, knowingly risks deliberately performing the wrongful act of applying the sanction.

The above description of what is required of the rational moral agent in an SDS, leads to a natural objection to the argument that supports (P3). According to this objection, an attempt at self-corruption by a rational moral agent is very likely to fail. Hence, bluffing would surely be a more promising strategy for deterrence than trying to form retaliatory intentions by self-corruption. Three replies may be given to this objection. First, it is certainly *conceivable* that, in a particular SDS, undertaking a process of self-corruption would be more likely to result in effective deterrence than would bluffing. Second, and more important, bluffing and attempting to form retaliatory intentions by self-corruption will generally not be mutually exclusive alternatives. An agent in an SDS may attempt to form the retaliatory intention while bluffing, and plan to continue bluffing as a "fall-back" strategy, should he fail. If the offense to be prevented is disastrous enough, the additional expected utility generated by following such a combined strategy (as opposed to simply bluffing) will be very large, even if his attempts to form the intention are unlikely to succeed. Hence, (P3) would still follow from our normative assumption. Finally, consider the rational and *partly corrupt* agent in an SDS who already has the intention to retaliate. (The nations participating in the balance of terror may be examples.) The relevant question about him is whether he ought to act to become less corrupt, with the result that he would lose the intention to retaliate. The present objection does not apply in this case, since the agent already has the requisite corrupt features. Yet, essentially the same argument that produces (P3) leads, when this case is considered, to a slightly different, but equally puzzling, version of our third paradox:

> (P3*) In certain situations, it would be morally wrong for a rational and partly corrupt agent to (attempt to) reform himself and eliminate his corruption.

A rather different objection to (P3) is the claim that its central notion is incoherent. This claim is made, apparently, by Thomas Nagel, who writes:

> The notion that one might sacrifice one's moral integrity justifiably, in the service of a sufficiently worthy end, is an incoherent notion. For if one were justified in making such a sacrifice (or even morally required to make it), then one would not be sacrificing one's moral integrity by adopting that course: one would be preserving it (132/3).

Now the notion of a justified sacrifice of moral virtue (integrity) would be incoherent, as Nagel suggests, if one could sacrifice one's virtue only by doing something wrong. For the same act cannot be both morally justified and morally wrong. But one may also be said to sacrifice one's virtue when one deliberately initiates a causal process that one expects to result, and does result, in one's later becoming a less virtuous person. And, as the analysis of SDSs embodied in (P1′) and (P2′) implies, one may, in certain cases, be justified in initiating such a process (or even be obligated to initiate it). Hence, it would be a mistake to deny (P3) on the grounds advanced in Nagel's argument.

There is, though, a good reason for *wanting* to reject (P3). It conflicts with some of our firmest beliefs about virtue and duty. We regard the promotion and preservation of one's own virtue as a vital responsibility of each moral agent, and self-corruption as among the vilest of enterprises. Further, we do not view the duty to promote one's virtue as simply one duty among others, to be weighed and balanced against the rest, but rather as a special duty that encompasses the other moral duties. Thus, we assent to the Virtue Preservation Principle: *It is wrong to deliberately lose (or reduce the degree of) one's moral virtue.* To many, this principle seems fundamental to our very conception of morality.[14] Hence the suggestion that duty could require the abandonment of virtue seems quite unacceptable. The fact that this suggestion can be supported by strong arguments produces a paradox.

This paradox is reflected in the ambivalent attitudes that merge when we attempt to evaluate three hypothetical agents who respond to the demands of SDSs in various ways. The first agent refuses to try to corrupt himself and allows the disastrous offense to occur. We respect the love of virtue he displays, but are inclined to suspect him of too great a devotion to his own purity relative to his concern for the well-being of others. The second agent does corrupt himself to prevent disaster in an SDS. Though we do not approve of his new corrupt aspects, we admire the person that he *was* for his willingness to sacrifice what he loved—part of his own virtue—in the service of others. At the same time, the fact that he succeeded in corrupting himself may make us wonder whether he was entirely virtuous in the first place. Corruption, we feel, does not come easily to a good man. The third agent reluctantly but sincerely tries his best to corrupt himself to prevent disaster, but fails. He may be admired both for his willingness to make such a sacrifice and for having virtue so deeply engrained in his character that his attempts at self-corruption do not succeed. It is perhaps characteristic of the paradoxical nature of the envisioned situation, that we are inclined to admire most the only one of these three agents who fails in the course of action he undertakes.

V

It is natural to think of the evaluation of agents, and of actions, as being two sides of the same moral coin. The moral paradoxes of deterrence suggest they are more like two separate coins that can be fused together only by significantly deforming one or the other. In this concluding section, I shall briefly explain this.

Our shared assortment of moral beliefs may be viewed as consisting of three relatively distinct groups: beliefs about the evaluation of actions, beliefs about the evaluation of agents and their states (e.g.,

---

[14]Its supporters might, of course, allow exceptions to the principle in cases in which only the agent's feelings, and not his acts or dispositions to act, are corrupted. (For example, a doctor "corrupts himself" by suppressing normal sympathy for patients in unavoidable pain, in order to treat them more effectively.) Further, advocates of the doctrine of double-effect might consider self-corruption permissible when it is a "side effect" of action rather than a means to an end. For example, they might approve of a social worker's joining a gang to reform it, even though he expects to assimilate some of the gang's distorted values. Note, however, that neither of these possible exceptions to the Virtue Preservation Principle (brought to my attention by Robert Adams) applies to the agent in an SDS who corrupts his *intentions* as a chosen *means* of preventing an offense.

motives, intentions, and character traits), and beliefs about the relationship between the two. An important part of this last group of beliefs is represented by the three bridge principles introduced above: the Wrongful Intentions, Right-Good, and Virtue Preservation principles. Given an agreed-upon set of bridge principles, one could go about constructing a moral system meant to express coherently our moral beliefs in either of two ways: by developing principles that express our beliefs about act evaluation and then using the bridge principles to derive principles of agent evaluation — or vice versa. If our bridge principles are sound and our beliefs about agent and act evaluation are mutually consistent, the resulting systems would, in theory, be the same. If, however, there are underlying incompatibilities between the principles we use to evaluate acts and agents, there may be significant differences between moral systems that are *act-oriented* and those which are *agent-oriented*. And these differences may manifest themselves as paradoxes which exert pressure upon the bridge principles that attempt to link the divergent systems, and the divergent aspects of each system, together.

It seems natural to us to evaluate acts at least partly in terms of their consequences. Hence, act-oriented moral systems tend to involve significant utilitarian elements. The principle of act evaluation usually employed in utilitarian systems is: in a given situation, one ought to perform the most useful act, that which will (or is expected to) produce the most utility. What will maximize utility depends upon the facts of the particular situation. Hence, as various philosophers have pointed out, the above principle could conceivably recommend one's (i) acting from nonutilitarian motives, (ii) advocating some nonutilitarian moral theory, or even (iii) becoming a genuine adherent of some nonutilitarian theory.[15] Related quandaries arise when one considers, from an act-utilitarian viewpoint, the deterrent intention of a defender in an SDS. Here is an intention whose object-act is anti-utilitarian and whose formation-act is a utilitarian duty that cannot be performed by a rational utilitarian.

A utilitarian might seek relief from these quandaries in either of two ways. First, he could defend some form of rule-utilitarianism. But then he would face a problem. Shall he include, among the rules of his system, our normative assumption that requires the performance of the most useful act, whenever an enormous amount of utility is at stake (and certain other conditions are satisfied)? If he does, the moral paradoxes of deterrence will appear within his system. If he does not, it would seem that his system fails to attach the importance to the conse-

[15]See Hodgson, *Consequences.* Also, Adams, "Motive Utilitarianism," this JOURNAL, LXXIII, 14 (Aug. 12, 1976): 467–81; and Bernard Williams, "A Critique of Utilitarianism," in J. J. C. Smart and Williams, *Utilitarianism: For and Against* (New York: Cambridge, 1973), sec. 6.

quences of particular momentous acts that any reasonable moral, much less utilitarian, system should. An alternative reaction would be to stick by the utilitarian principle of act evaluation, and simply accept (P1)–(P3), and related oddities, as true. Taking this line would require the abandonment of the plausible and familiar bridge principles that contradict (P1)–(P3). But this need not bother the act-utilitarian, who perceives his task as the modification, as well as codification, of our moral beliefs.

Agent-oriented (as opposed to act-oriented) moral systems rest on the premise that what primarily matters for morality are the internal states of a person: his character traits, his intentions, and the condition of his will. The doctrines about intentions and virtue expressed in our three bridge principles are generally incorporated into such systems. The paradoxes of deterrence may pose serious problems for some agent-oriented systems. It may be, for example, that an adequate analysis of the moral virtues of justice, selflessness, and benevolence, would imply that the truly virtuous man would feel obligated to make whatever personal sacrifice is necessary to prevent a catastrophe. If so, the moral paradoxes of deterrence would arise within agent-oriented systems committed to these virtues.

There are, however, agent-oriented systems that would not be affected by our paradoxes. One such system could be called Extreme Kantianism. According to this view, the only things having moral significance are such features of a person as his character and the state of his will. The Extreme Kantian accepts Kant's dictum that morality requires treating oneself and others as ends rather than means. He interprets this to imply strict duties to preserve one's virtue and not to deliberately impose serious harms or risks on innocent people. Thus, the Extreme Kantian would simply reject (P1)–(P3) without qualm.

Although act-utilitarians and Extreme Kantians can view the paradoxes of deterrence without concern, one doubts that the rest of us can. The adherents of these extreme conceptions of morality are untroubled by the paradoxes because their viewpoints are too one-sided to represent our moral beliefs accurately. Each of them is closely attentive to certain standard principles of agent *or* act evaluation, but seems too little concerned with traditional principles of the other sort. For a system of morality to reflect our firmest and deepest convictions adequately, it must represent a middle ground between these extremes by seeking to accommodate the valid insights of both act-oriented and agent-oriented perspectives. The normative assumption set out in section I was chosen as a representative principle that might be incorporated into such a system. It treats utilitarian considerations as relevant and potentially decisive, while allowing for the importance of other factors. Though consistent with the absolute prohibition of certain sorts of acts, it treats the distinction between harms and risks as significant and rules out absolute prohibitions on the latter as unreasonable. It is an extremely plausible middle-ground principle; but, disturbingly, it leads to paradoxes.

That these paradoxes reflect conflicts between commonly accepted principles of agent and act evaluation, is further indicated by the following observation. Consider what initially appears a natural way of viewing the evaluation of acts and agents as coordinated parts of a single moral system. According to this view, reasons for action determine the moral status of acts, agents, and intentions. A right act is an act that accords with the preponderance of moral reasons for action. To have the right intention is to be disposed to perform the act supported by the preponderance of such reasons, because of those reasons. The virtuous agent is the rational agent who has the proper substantive values, i.e., the person whose intentions and actions accord with the preponderance of moral reasons for action. Given these considerations, it appears that it should always be possible for an agent to go along intending, and acting, in accordance with the preponderance of moral reasons; thus ensuring both his own virtue and the rightness of his intentions and actions. Unfortunately, this conception of harmonious coordination between virtue, right intention, and right action, is shown to be untenable by the paradoxes of deterrence. For they demonstrate that, in any system that takes consequences plausibly into account, situations can arise in which the rational use of moral principles leads to certain paradoxical recommendations: that the principles used, and part of the agent's virtue, be abandoned, and that wrongful intentions be formed.

One could seek to avoid these paradoxes by moving in the direction of Extreme Kantianism and rejecting our normative assumption. But to do so would be to overlook the plausible core of act-utilitarianism. This is the claim that, in the moral evaluation of acts, how those acts affect human happiness often is important — the more so as more happiness is at stake — and sometimes is decisive. Conversely, one could move toward accommodation with act-utilitarianism. This would involve qualifying, so that they do not apply in SDSs, the traditional moral doctrines that contradict (P1)–(P3). And, in fact, viewed in isolation, the considerations adduced in section II indicate that the Wrongful Intentions Principle ought to be so qualified. However, the claims of (P2) and (P3): that virtue may preclude right action and that morality may require self-corruption, are not so easily accepted. These notions remain unpalatable even when one considers the arguments that support them.

Thus, tinkering with our normative assumption or with traditional moral doctrines would indeed enable us to avoid the paradoxes, at least in their present form. But this would require rejecting certain significant and deeply entrenched beliefs concerning the evaluation either of agents or of actions. Hence, such tinkering would not go far toward solving the fundamental problem of which the paradoxes are symptoms: the apparent incompatibility of the moral principles we use to evaluate acts and agents. Perhaps this problem can be solved. Perhaps the coins of agent and act evaluation can be successfully fused. But it is not apparent how this is to be done. And I, for one, do not presently see an entirely satisfactory way out of the perplexities that the paradoxes engender.

PART SIX
DIRECT AND OBLIQUE STRATEGIES

HOW SHOULD A utilitarian try to increase happiness? The simplest view is that the decision between alternative possible actions should be made by estimating the likely consequences for happiness of each of them. This view, act-utilitarianism, has attracted much criticism.

Some of the criticisms have already been noted. It is said that consequences cannot be precisely predicted, and happiness cannot be precisely measured. It is also sometimes suggested that the act utilitarian will have to spend too much of life calculating before each act. It has also been said that when acts are chosen on the basis of their particular consequences, appallingly wicked things will sometimes be done. Some of these objections are practical, and some are deontological. Many utilitarians have been troubled by them and have sought to meet them. They have two possible strategies. One is to deny that act-utilitarianism *is* unworkable or immoral. The other is to produce a modified form of utilitarianism designed to meet the objections.

The objection about the impracticability of act-utilitarianism has been given a new twist by D. H. Hodgson. He argues not that act-utilitarianism is merely hard to put into practice, but that it is logically self-defeating. His case is that some essential features of social life, such as communication, depend on expectations that act-utilitarians cannot generate. If his ingenious argument is correct, the adoption of act-utilitarianism would itself be a utilitarian disaster. His argument should be read together with Peter Singer's reply, which claims that the objection fails through underrating the resources available to utilitarians.

The objection that, even if act-utilitarian calculation can be done, it

193

gives the wrong answers, has also been given a new twist in contemporary discussion. This has taken two forms. It is objected that act-utilitarianism demands too much of us and that in some contexts it demands too little of us.

How can act-utilitarianism demand too much of us? One suggestion is that it does so by leaving us no leisure. Suppose I am sitting in the square outside my house, enjoying the sun and talking to friends. Is it likely that this is the best contribution to happiness I can make? Would it not have better consequences if I spent this afternoon earning money to send to victims of famine in Ethiopia? Perhaps I could save several lives by doing so. How can this enjoyable conversation possibly outweigh the deaths of several people? But this utilitarian line of thought can arise whenever I am relaxing, bringing a constant demand that I do something more useful. To take act-utilitarianism seriously seems to be stifling, leaving no space in which to relax and to live our own lives.

One reply to this is that we too readily assume that such a demanding doctrine must be wrong. We live in a world with enormous misery and horror in it. Those of us lucky in where we were born are psychologically protected by distance from the plight of those without food or without clean drinking water. If a starving family came and sat down beside my friends and me in the square, we would have to stop the conversation and do something for them. Is it so clear a point against a morality that it breaks down the protective barriers between such demands and ourselves?

An alternative response is to work out a modified form of utilitarianism, which makes less horrifying demands on us. Samuel Scheffler proposes a version containing "agent-centered permissions." Such a view differs from deontological views in allowing that it is always acceptable to do what brings about the best consequences, but denies that it is always obligatory to do so.

The claim that act-utilitarianism demands too little of us is also made. Very often it appears that my doing something makes no significant difference to the outcome. In an election my vote is extremely unlikely to determine the outcome. And other people are unlikely to be influenced by whether or not I vote. So, if there are things I would enjoy doing more than voting, it is hard to make a utilitarian case in favour of going to vote. If I can cheat the bus company by not paying my fare, the difference to the bus company is negligible. They will not go bankrupt or have to cut back on the number of buses they run because of losing one fare from me. It may seem again that, judged by consequences, there is little case against cheating. Or, again, there is the argument that, "if I don't do it, someone else will." Suppose I am a chemist and I am offered a job working on a new technique that will enable napalm to be cheaply and so more widely produced. Surely I should not do this? Yet, judged by consequences, the case may go the other way. I may know that if I don't take the job, someone else will. So my refusal will not hold back the project at all. Suppose I very much need the money, and since I am not famous, my example either way will have hardly any influence. In this case, as in those of voting and cheating the bus company, there is an intuitive feeling that act-utilitarianism sets an alarmingly low standard of conduct.

In some cases of this type, act-utilitarianism comes closer to our intuitions that these bald descriptions suggest. In the case of working on the napalm project, there are subtle psychological effects on me of taking the job, which may over time have disastrous consequences for me and for the way I behave in future. And there are ways of turning a refusal into part of a campaign against the project.

More importantly, we often ignore the way in which apparently insignificant contributions, repeated by many different individuals, can together make a real difference. In the case of cheating the bus company, it is tempting to suppose that what I do makes *no* difference. But this is wrong. The apparently pedantic distinction between no difference and a minute difference turns out to be important.

Consider the implications of treating a minute difference as no difference. Suppose a village contains 100 unarmed tribesmen. As they eat their lunch, 100 hungry armed bandits descend on the village. Each bandit at gunpoint takes one tribesman's lunch and eats it. The bandits then go off, each having done a noticeable amount of harm to each tribesman. Next week, the bandits are tempted to do the same thing again, but this time they start to worry about the morality of such a raid. But one of them, who thinks a minute difference is the same as no difference, is able to reassure them. They then raid the village, tie up the tribesmen, and look at their lunch. As expected each tribesman's bowl contains 100 baked beans. The pleasure from one baked bean is too small to be noticed. Instead of each bandit eating a single plateful as last week, each takes one bean from each plate. They leave after eating all the beans, pleased to have done no harm, as each has done only an undetectably small harm to each person, which can be treated as zero.

When the cumulative impact of imperceptibly small contributions is understood, the act-utilitarian will less often choose kinds of action (or inaction) that seem antisocial. But, even when all such effects are included, there may still be cases where the "antisocial" choice has best consequences. At this point, the utilitarian can either accept the unpalatable implication, or else abandon or modify the theory.

One modification of this sort is the co-operative utilitarianism proposed by Donald H. Regan. This sees morality as a communal rather than an individual affair. It requires identifying those who will co-operate in bringing about good consequences, and then engaging with them in a consciously common effort. Act-utilitarians will also carry out this process, so the fundamental difference is perhaps one of viewpoint.

The psychological perspective is a shared one, rather than an individualistic one. But there is a residual question of how far the actions chosen will differ from those of the act-utilitarian.

Perhaps the most popular modification is to move from act to rule-utilitarianism. Instead of judging each act in terms of its consequences, we should think of the set of rules that will have best consequences, and judge acts by those rules. (There are different versions of rule-utilitarianism. Some favour the rules already part of the conventional morality of a society. Some favour the set of rules that, if universally followed, would have best consequences. Some favour those that, if universally accepted, would have best consequences, allowing for some slippage between accepting a rule and actually following it in practice.)

The motives for adopting rule-utilitarianism are of two kinds. The first is the desire to find a version of utilitarianism that avoids giving some of the intuitively "wrong" answers that act-utilitarianism seems to give. The second is to avoid some of the practical problems of act-utilitarianism, such as the danger of time-wasting calculation and the likelihood that people will do the calculations in a biased or incompetent way. Henry Sidgwick thought that the best strategy for utilitarians was to keep utilitarianism as an "esoteric" morality: one confined to an elite few. Others should be encouraged to believe in conventional moral rules rather than in utilitarianism. The sophisticated utilitarian would sometimes be justified in breaking the rules, provided this was done in secrecy. But this view should itself not be publicized: "Thus the utilitarian conclusion, carefully stated, would seem to be this; that the opinion that secrecy may render an action right that would not otherwise be so should itself be kept comparatively secret; and similarly it seems expedient that the doctrine that esoteric morality is expedient should itself be kept esoteric." (Sidgwick wisely wrote this on page 490 of *The Methods of Ethics*.)

J. J. C. Smart brings out a problem for any form of rule-utilitarianism. The rules are chosen because following them will in general maximize happiness. But there may be cases where this is not so. Perhaps breaking the rule will sometimes have better consequences than keeping it, even when the possible bad precedent is taken into account. What is then the right thing to do? To keep the rule (whose only point is its beneficial consequences) may seem a piece of irrational "rule worship." But to break the rule seems to leave rule-utilitarianism indistinguishable from act-utilitarianism. The dilemma for rule-utilarianism seems to be that either it collapses into act-utilitarianism, or else it is only partly utilitarian.

Another modification to utilitarianism along similar lines is to use a generalized version of the utilitarian test. On this view, the question I should ask is not "what will the consequences be if I do this?" but rather "what would the consequences be if everyone did this?" This approach — the generalization test — has been devastatingly discussed by David Lyons, in his book *Forms and Limits of Utilitarianism*. When the test is applied, everything hangs on how the act is described. Lyons argues that utilitarians applying the test have to include in the description of the act all those features that affect the utility of the outcome. So in the napalm case, we have to ask, not the odd question "what would happen if everyone worked on napalm?" but some question more like "what would happen if all chemists who have these special skills, and were offered jobs developing napalm, accepted the jobs in those cases where, if they refused, someone else equally able would accept?" This question in turn is no doubt too simple. But the plausible claim made by Lyons is that the more complete the description becomes, the closer the test comes to giving the same answer as "what will happen if I do it?" As with rule-utilitarianism, this modification seems either not fully utilitarian, or else equivalent to act-utilitarianism.

The claim that utilitarianism gives intuitively "wrong" answers in various possible cases is given critical scrutiny by R. M. Hare. He says that these often "fantastic and unusual" cases are misused in arguments against utilitarianism. He distinguishes between two levels of moral thinking. Principles on Level One are those that people should be educated to accept and that should be applied in practice. Level Two principles are those that are ultimately defensible in leisurely and informed philosophical debate. The fully worked out Level Two principles should be used to choose workable Level One principles for immediate practical guidance. (On this view, Sidgwick's *Methods of Ethics* was advocating utilitarianism on Level Two, and derived from it conventional moral principles for use on Level One). On Hare's view, farfetched cases have their place in Level Two thinking, but not on Level One, where principles should be devised for situations likely to arise. He believes that the anti-utilitarian intuitions are derived from Level One thinking, where the utilitarian principle would not be helpful. But, he suggests, thinking on Level Two need not show such respect for intuitions resulting from Level One moral education.

One possible difficulty for this view is that raised by Smart for rule-utilitarianism. If I know that my own Level One principles have been chosen on the basis of Level Two utilitarianism, what should I do when it looks as if best consequences will come from breaking a Level One rule? Is there a danger that Level One thinking will either become rule-worship, or will constantly drift in the direction of act-utilitarianism?

Another oblique utilitarian strategy is the motive utilitarianism discussed by Robert Merrihew Adams. Perhaps what we need is neither calculation of the consequences of each act, nor rules, but a set of motives that will in general make people act in ways that have the best consequences. This is a very appealing approach, avoiding both excessive calculation and excessive rigidity. But there is again a dilemma parallel to that of the rule-utilitarian. What should I do when I see that the generally beneficial motive, on which I am about to act, will in this case bring about worse consequences than some alternative course?

With all these oblique strategies, there is a common pattern. Few are satisfied with all the implications of act-utilitarianism. The oblique approaches try to accommodate what the critics value. In doing so they broaden utilitarianism, but in doing so they blur the boundary between utilitarian and nonutilitarian morality. A sufficiently generous theory may do more justice to our values. Such a hybrid theory borrows from different traditions, and we may lose grip on whether it is utilitarian or not. But perhaps this does not matter. In moral theories, adequacy matters more than ancestry.

J. J. C. SMART*

Act-Utilitarianism and Rule-Utilitarianism

THE SYSTEM OF normative ethics which I am here concerned to defend is, as I have said earlier, *act*-utilitarianism. Act-utilitarianism is to be contrasted with rule-utilitarianism. Act-utilitarianism is the view that the rightness or wrongness of an action is to be judged by the consequences, good or bad, of the action itself. Rule-utilitarianism is the view that the rightness or wrongness of an action is to be judged by the goodness and badness of the consequences of a rule that everyone should perform the action in like circumstances. There are two sub-varieties of rule-utilitarianism according to whether one construes "rule" here as "actual rule" or "possible rule." With the former, one gets a view like that of S. E. Toulmin[1] and with the latter, one like Kant's.[2] That is, if it is permissible to interpret Kant's principle "Act only on that maxim through which you can at the same time will that it should become a universal law" as "Act only on that maxim which you as a humane and benevolent person would like to see established as a universal law." Of course Kant would resist this appeal to human feeling, but it seems necessary in order to interpret his doctrine in a plausible way. A subtle version of the Kantian type of rule-utilitarianism is given by R. F. Harrod in his "Utilitarianism Revised."[3]

*From J. J. C. Smart, "An Outline of a System of Utilitarian Ethics," in J. J. C. Smart and Bernard Williams, *Utilitarianism, For and Against*.
[1]*An Examination of the Place of Reason in Ethics* (Cambridge University Press, London, 1950).
[2]Immanuel Kant, *Groundwork of the Metaphysic of Morals*. Translated from the German in *The Moral Law*, by H. J. Paton (Hutchinson, London, 1948).
[3]*Mind* 45 (1936) 137–56.

I have argued elsewhere[4] the objections to rule-utilitarianism as compared with act-utilitarianism.[5] Briefly they boil down to the accusation of rule worship:[6] The rule-utilitarian presumably advocates his principle because he is ultimately concerned with human happiness: why then should he advocate abiding by a rule when he knows that it will not in the present case be most beneficial to abide by it? The reply that in most cases it is most beneficial to abide by the rule seems irrelevant. And so is the reply that it would be better that everybody should abide by the rule than that nobody should. This is to suppose that the only alternative to "everybody does A" is "no one does A." But clearly we have the possibility "some people do A and some don't." Hence to refuse to break a generally beneficial rule in those cases in which it is not most beneficial to obey it seems irrational and to be a case of rule worship.

The type of utilitarianism which I shall advocate will, then, be act-utilitarianism, not rule-utilitarianism.

David Lyons has recently argued that rule-utilitarianism (by which, I think, he means the sort of rule-utilitarianism which I have called the Kantian one) collapses into act-utilitarianism.[7] His reasons are briefly as follows. Suppose that an exception to a rule R produces the best possible consequences. Then this is evidence that the rule R should be modified so as to allow this exception. Thus we get a new rule of the form "do R except in circumstances of the sort C." That is, whatever would lead the act-utilitarian to break a rule would lead the Kantian rule-utilitarian to modify the rule. Thus an adequate rule-utilitarianism would be extensionally equivalent to act-utilitarianism.

Lyons is particularly interested in what he calls "threshold effects." A difficulty for rule-utilitarianism has often appeared to be that of rules like "do not walk on the grass" or "do not fail to vote at an election." In these cases it would seem that it is beneficial if some people, though not

---

[4]In my article "Extreme and Restricted Utilitarianism," *Philosophical Quarterly* 6 (1956) 344–54. This contains bad errors and a better version of the article will be found in Philippa Foot (ed.), *Theories of Ethics* (Oxford University Press, London, 1967), or Michael D. Bayles (ed.), *Contemporary Utilitarianism* (Doubleday, New York, 1968). In this article I used the terms "extreme" and "restricted" instead of Brandt's more felicitous "act" and "rule" which I now prefer.

[5]For another discussion of what in effect is the same problem see A. K. Stout's excellent paper, "But Suppose Everyone Did the Same," *Australasian Journal of Philosophy* 32 (1954) 1–29.

[6]On rule worship see I. M. Crombie, "Social Clockwork and Utilitarian Morality," in D. M. Mackinnon (ed.), *Christian Faith and Communist Faith* (Macmillan, London, 1953). See p. 109.

[7]David Lyons, *The Forms and Limits of Utilitarianism* (Oxford University Press, London, 1965). Rather similar considerations have been put forward by R. M. Hare, *Freedom and Reason* (Oxford University Press, London, 1963), pp. 131–6, and R. B. Brandt, "Toward a Credible Form of Utilitarianism," in H. N. Castañeda and G. Nakhnikian, *Morality and the Language of Conduct* (Wayne State University Press, Detroit, 1963), esp. pp. 119–23.

too many, break the rule. Lyons points out that we can distinguish the action of doing something (say, walking on the grass) after some largish number n other people have done it from the action of doing it when few or no people have done it. When these extra circumstances are written into the rule, Lyons holds that the rule will come to enjoin the same actions as would the act-utilitarian principle. However there seems to be one interesting sort of case which requires slightly different treatment. This is the sort of case in which not too many people must do action X, but each person must plan his action in ignorance of what the other person does. That is, what A does depends on what B does, and what B does depends on what A does.

I am inclined to think that an adequate rule-utilitarianism would not only be extensionally equivalent to the act-utilitarian principle (i.e. would enjoin the same set of actions as it) but would in fact consist of one rule only, the act-utilitarian one: "maximize probable benefit." This is because any rule which can be formulated must be able to deal with an indefinite number of unforeseen types of contingency. No rule, short of the act-utilitarian one, can therefore be safely regarded as extensionally equivalent to the act-utilitarian principle unless it is that very principle itself. I therefore suggest that Lyons' type of consideration can be taken even further, and that rule-utilitarianism of the Kantian sort must collapse into act-utilitarianism in an even stronger way: it must become a "one-rule" rule-utilitarianism which is identical to act-utilitarianism.

HENRY SIDGWICK*

༄༅

Esoteric Morality

༄༅

IT APPEARS TO me, [therefore,] that the cases in which practical doubts
are likely to arise, as to whether exceptions should be permitted from
ordinary rules on Utilitarian principles, will mostly be those [which I
discussed in the first paragraph of this section:] where the exceptions
are not claimed for a few individuals, on the mere ground of their
probable fewness, but either for persons generally under exceptional
circumstances, or for a class of persons defined by exceptional qualities
of intellect, temperament, or character. In such cases the Utilitarian
may have no doubt that in a community consisting generally of enlightened Utilitarians, these grounds for exceptional ethical treatment
would be regarded as valid; still he may, as I have said, doubt whether
the more refined and complicated rule which recognises such exceptions is adapted for the community in which he is actually living; and
whether the attempt to introduce it is not likely to do more harm by
weakening current morality than good by improving its quality. Supposing such a doubt to arise, either in a case of this kind, or in one of the
rare cases discussed in the preceding paragraph, it becomes necessary
that the Utilitarian should consider carefully the extent to which his
advice or example are likely to influence persons to whom they would
be dangerous: and it is evident that the result of this consideration may
depend largely on the degree of publicity which he gives to either
advice or example. Thus, on Utilitarian principles, it may be right to do

*From Henry Sidgwick: *The Methods of Ethics*, Book 4, Chapter 5.

and privately recommend, under certain circumstances, what it would not be right to advocate openly; it may be right to teach openly to one set of persons what it would be wrong to teach to others; it may be conceivably right to do, if it can be done with comparative secrecy, what it would be wrong to do in the face of the world; and even, if perfect secrecy can be reasonably expected, what it would be wrong to recommend by private advice or example. These conclusions are all of a paradoxical character:[1] there is no doubt that the moral consciousness of a plain man broadly repudiates the general notion of an esoteric morality, differing from that popularly taught; and it would be commonly agreed that an action which would be bad if done openly is not rendered good by secrecy. We may observe, however, that there are strong utilitarian reasons for maintaining generally this latter common opinion; for it is obviously advantageous, generally speaking, that acts which it is expedient to repress by social disapprobation should become known, as otherwise the disapprobation cannot operate; so that it seems inexpedient to support by any moral encouragement the natural disposition of men in general to conceal their wrong doings; besides that the concealment would in most cases have importantly injurious effects on the agent's habits of veracity. Thus the Utilitarian conclusion, carefully stated, would seem to be this; that the opinion that secrecy may render an action right which would not otherwise be so should itself be kept comparatively secret; and similarly it seems expedient that the doctrine that esoteric morality is expedient should itself be kept esoteric. Or if this concealment be difficult to maintain, it may be desirable that Common Sense should repudiate the doctrines which it is expedient to confine to an enlightened few. And thus a Utilitarian may reasonably desire, on Utilitarian principles, that some of his conclusions should be rejected by mankind generally; or even that the vulgar should keep aloof from his system as a whole, in so far as the inevitable indefiniteness and complexity of its calculations render it likely to lead to bad results in their hands.

---

[1]In particular cases, however, they seem to be admitted by Common Sense to a certain extent. For example, it would be commonly thought wrong to express in public speeches disturbing religious or political opinions which may be legitimately published in books.

D. H. HODGSON*

Is Act-Utilitarianism Self-Defeating?

IN THIS CHAPTER is advanced a utilitarian argument against act-utilitarianism which is not based on the possibility of the misapplication of the
system. This argument shows that even correct application of act-utilitarianism, either by everyone in a community, or by individuals in a
non-act-utilitarian society like our own, would not necessarily have
better consequences, and would probably have worse consequences,
than would acceptance of specific conventional moral rules and personal rules.

1. *Act-Utilitarianism Universally Accepted*

First, let us consider a society in which everyone accepts the act-utilitarian principle as his only personal rule, and attempts always to act in
accordance with it. We assume that everyone is highly rational, sufficiently so to understand the implications of the use of act-utilitarianism
(including those to be demonstrated in this section). We assume too
that the universal use of act-utilitarianism and universal rationality is
common knowledge, in the sense that everyone knows of it, and everyone knows that everyone knows, and so on. We leave open the possibility that everyone might always succeed in acting in accordance with his
personal rule. We assume that there are no conventional moral rules in

*From D. H. Hodgson: *Consequences of Utilitarianism*, Chapter 2.

this society: everyone knows that everyone else attempts with high rationality to act in accordance with act-utilitarianism, and so no one is concerned to criticize the conduct of others or to make demands of them.

On the basis of these assumptions (which should represent the act-utilitarian's ideal), I show that there would be problems and possible disutilities in regard to promising and telling the truth. Our assumptions have not excluded the possibility that everyone in this society could know rules (like those in existing societies) defining and structuring activities such as promising and truth-telling, and could purport to engage in these activities. However, there would be no conventional moral rules requiring conformity, by persons purporting to engage in the activities, to such of the defining rules as require certain things to be done (such as keeping promises and telling the truth). The position would be similar to that, mentioned earlier, of the twenty-two act-utilitarians purporting to play cricket. As in that case, the question in our postulated society would be whether or not the act-utilitarian principle would require conformity to the defining rules. The following alternatives might seem possible.

(A) If the act-utilitarian principle would generally require such conformity to the defining rules, then such conformity would generally be expected by our rational act-utilitarians: in this case, there would be point in purporting to engage in the activities, the activities would presumably be engaged in by our act-utilitarians, and the defining rules would generally be complied with.

(B) If the act-utilitarian principle would not require conformity to the defining rules, conformity would not be expected: in this case, there would be no point in purporting to engage in the activities, and the activities would presumably not be engaged in.

This then, is the matter in issue: which of these two alternative situations (A) and (B) would hold in our postulated society?

We consider promising first. In our act-utilitarian society, promising would be pointless unless a promisee sometimes expected an act which had been promised *more* than he would have expected the act if it had not been promised, but (say) merely mentioned as a possibility. And we may suppose that one would never thus expect a promise to be kept if it were known that there could be no good reason for so expecting.

Now in a non-act-utilitarian society, there are usually several good reasons for expecting a promise to be kept. In most cases, it is required by a conventional moral rule, a rule which many persons also accept as a personal rule; most promises are kept; some promisors are known to be trustworthy; and (as we shall see) to keep a promise usually has best consequences. However, some of these reasons might not apply in our act-utilitarian society. There are no conventional moral rules, and everyone's only personal rule is the act-utilitarian principle. The question whether or not most promises would be kept is of course a question at issue here. And similarly, trustworthiness in relation to promises would be possible only if the former of the alternative situations, that is, situation (A), held in our postulated society: so this too is in issue. This leaves only the last of the above reasons for expecting a promise to be kept, the possibility that to keep a promise would usually have best consequences.

In our act-utilitarian society, we may therefore suppose, there would be good reason for a promisee to expect that a promise would be kept if and only if (in the promisor's belief) to keep it would have best consequences. And there would be good reason for one to expect the act which has been promised *more* than one would have expected it had it not been promised but merely mentioned as a possibility, if and only if (in the promisor's belief) doing the act would have better consequences, as compared with failure to do it, than it would have had if he had not promised to do it.

Now, in a non-act-utilitarian society, an act which a person has promised to do usually has better consequences, as compared with failure to do it, than it would have had if he had not promised to do it. This is so for three reasons. First, because of the conventional moral rule as to promise-keeping, failure to keep a promise may result in criticism of and loss of respect for the promisor, making it harder for him to play a useful part in society. Second, failure to keep a promise may damage this useful conventional moral rule in one or more of the three ways discussed in the next chapter, that is, by example, by making others less willing to conform, and/or by undermining confidence in the observance of the rule. Third, a promisee usually expects an act which has been promised more than he would have expected the act if it had not been promised, and may make arrangements in reliance upon it; so that if the promise is not kept, he will usually be disappointed, and further bad consequences may result because of arrangements made in reliance upon the promise.

In our act-utilitarian society, however, there are no conventional moral rules, so the first two reasons are eliminated, leaving only the third. Therefore, an act which has been promised could have greater (comparative) utility than it would have had if it had not been promised, only if the promisee expects the act promised more than he would have done if it had not been promised. But we have established that the promisee would have good reason for such greater expectation only if (in the promisor's belief) the promised act would have such greater utility.

So, a promised act could have greater (comparative) utility (than it would have had if it had not been promised) only if the promisee has a greater expectation that it would be done (than he would have had if it had not been promised); but there would be a good reason for such greater expectation only if (in the promisor's belief) the act would have such greater utility. Being highly rational, the promisor would know that the greater expectation was a condition precedent for the greater utility; and so would not believe that the act would have greater utility unless he believed that the promisee had greater expectation. Also being highly rational, the promisee would know this, and so would not have greater expectation unless he believed that the promisor believed that he had greater expectation. And this, of course, the promisor would know.

Now, the promisor could reason that if the promisee had greater expectation, the act might have greater utility, and that if he *supposed* that the promisee had greater expectation and concluded that the act would have greater utility, then there would be good reason for the promisee's greater expectation. But such bootstrap-tugging would not help. For (as both promisor and promisee would know) a person could equally reason thus in regard to another's expectation of an act merely mentioned as a possibility by the former, as compared with his expectation of the act if it had been promised, and so reach exactly the opposite conclusion. Therefore, it would seem that making a promise to do an act, as compared with merely mentioning the act as a possibility, would make no difference at all either to the comparative utility of the promised act or to the degree to which it would be expected. We may conclude, therefore, that in our act-utilitarian society, promising would be pointless.

Now we come to telling the truth; and our discussion follows the same lines as in regard to keeping promises. In our act-utilitarian society, it would be pointless to attempt to communicate information to another (as distinct from merely raising the question whether or not something was the case) unless a person sometimes took information communicated to him as more likely to be true than false (or vice versa), so that his beliefs would be affected by the communication. And we may suppose that one would never so take information if it were known that there could be no good reason for doing so.

In a non-act-utilitarian society, there are usually several good reasons for taking information as more likely to be true than false. In most cases, truth-telling is required by a conventional moral rule, a rule which many persons accept as a personal rule; more often than not, the truth is told; some persons are known to be trustworthy; one can often know if a person is telling a lie; it is usually easier to tell the truth; and (as we shall see) to tell the truth usually has best consequences. As in the case of promises, some of these reasons might not apply in our act-utilitarian society. There are no conventional moral rules, and everyone's only personal rule is the act-utilitarian principle. The question whether or not the truth would usually be told is a question at issue here. Similarly, trustworthiness would be possible only if the former of the alternative situations outlined above, that is, situation (A), held good in the society: so this too is in issue. The signs that a lie is being told, such as guilt and lack of conviction, could only be significant if the act-utilitarian principle generally required the truth to be told, and persons did purport to communicate information. The *difficulty* of telling a lie in a non-act-utilitarian society arises mainly because of the need to tell a "*good*" lie, in order to avoid both detection and the bad consequences of someone's being misled. In our postulated society, unless the act-utilitarian principle required the truth to be told, there would be no need to prevent detection, and no question of anyone's being misled; and so the lie would not have to be a "good" one. A minimal degree of inventiveness might perhaps still be required to tell a lie; but we may assume that our rational act-utilitarians would have this, and that if any disvalue were involved in the effort required to use this inventiveness, it would be balanced by the satisfaction of exercising the skill. So again we are left only with the possibility that to tell the truth would usually have best consequences.

We may thus suppose that in our act-utilitarian society, there would be good reason for taking information communicated to one as being true rather than false if and only if (in the informant's belief) it would have "very best" consequences to tell the truth. By this I mean the following. A tells B that X is Y. There is good reason for B to believe him if and only if the following hold good: if X were Y, it would (in A's belief) have best consequences for A to tell him so, while if X were not Y, it would (in A's belief) not have best consequences for A to tell him that X was Y.

In a non-act-utilitarian society, these conditions would usually hold. For a conventional moral rule requires the truth to be told, and failure to tell the truth may result in criticism and loss of respect, and may also damage this useful conventional moral rule. Further, a person is likely to believe what he has been told, and this may have bad consequences if it is untrue. This is so because he may make arrangements in reliance upon the information, which would have bad consequences if it is untrue; and even if he does not, he is likely to resent being deceived, so that bad consequences could follow from discovery of the truth.

In an act-utilitarian society, there are no conventional moral rules, and so reasons dependent upon this are ruled out. The other reasons are dependent upon a person's believing what he is told, upon his taking the information communicated as true rather than false: unless he would do this, it could not have very best consequences to tell him the truth. But we have established that he would have good reason for taking information as true rather than false only if (in the informant's belief) it would have very best consequences to tell him the truth.

Being highly rational, the informant would know that the taking of the information as true rather than false was a condition precedent for telling the truth to have very best consequences; and so would not believe that it would have very best consequences unless he believed that the other would take the information as true rather than false. Also being highly rational, the other would know this, and would not so take the information unless he believed that the informant believed he would so take the information. And this, of course, the informant would know. He could reason that if the other would take his information as true rather than false, it might have very best consequences to tell the truth, and that if he supposed that the other would so take his information and concluded that it would have very best consequences to tell the truth, then there would be good reason for the other so to take the information. But (as both would know), the informant could equally reason that if he supposed that the other would take his information as false and concluded that it would have very best consequences not to tell the truth, then there would be good reason for the other to take the information as false.

We conclude, therefore, that in our act-utilitarian society, no one could take information communicated to him as more likely to be true than false (or vice versa); and that therefore it would be pointless to attempt to communicate information to another.

Thus, in regard to both promise-keeping and truth-telling, the *expectations* upon which the comparatively good consequences of such acts depend could not be promoted in our postulated society; and so such acts would not be performed by the act-utilitarian members of this society. Therefore, the good consequences which such acts would have, if there were these expectations, could not be promoted.

Because the making of promises and the communication of information would be pointless in our act-utilitarian society, so that these practices would not be engaged in, there could be no human relationships as we know them. It seems likely that whatever criteria of value one accepted, this bad situation would outweigh any good consequences which would result from the universal and rational (even correct) application of act-utilitarianism. As compared with almost any society that has ever existed, this "society" would be at a disadvantage, because so much that is of value, on any criteria, is bound up with human relationships. It is important to see that this is quite consistent even with an assumption that everyone would apply act-utilitarianism correctly, and that every act done in the society would have better consequences than any possible alternative. For this means only that the consequences would be the best possible *in the circumstances*; and since the circumstances (universal acceptance and rational application of act-utilitarianism, and common knowledge of this) preclude human relationships, the best possible consequences in these circumstances could be worse than consequences which are not the best possible in other more favourable circumstances.

Of course, if these circumstances could be changed for the better by anyone's actions, then these actions would be justified by act-utilitarianism. But the changing of these circumstances means either the rejection of act-utilitarianism by some at least of the members of the society, or the promotion of irrationality or ignorance in this respect among some members of the society. We may surely dismiss the latter alternative, and consider only the former, the rejection of act-utilitarianism by some members of the society. We shall not go into the question of what proportion of people in a society would have to be non-act-utilitarians, and what proportion would have to be *believed* to be non-act-utilitarians, before there could be effective conventional moral rules requiring truth-telling and promise-keeping. Nor shall we consider the utility of being an act-utilitarian when this minimum is just filled: in the next section we shall deal with a similar question, the utility of an individual's accepting act-utilitarianism in a predominantly non-act-utilitarian society. Here it is sufficient to point out that the only reasonable way to avoid the disutilities which we have been discussing involves the rejection of act-utilitarianism by some persons in the society. The fact that this rejection may be justified by act-utilitarianism itself does not affect the argument at all. If this rejection were so justified, it would mean simply that universal and correct application of act-utilitarianism could not persist, because it would involve rejection of act-utilitarianism by at least some persons.

Thus, a utilitarian argument against act-utilitarianism, without assumptions of misapplication, is not absurd. More realistically, perhaps, our argument shows that the fact that persons promise and communicate with each other *presupposes* either ignorance or irrationality in, or some actions done on non-act-utilitarian criteria by, at least some of these persons. So advocacy of act-utilitarianism, as providing a criterion of rightness of actions to be used by all persons in a society, involves either advocacy of no communication of information between such persons, or advocacy of the ignorance or irrationality which would be necessary to allow communication in an act-utilitarian society.

An act-utilitarian usually emphasizes that steps taken to form certain habits can themselves be useful acts. If it would be of great disutility that one could never expect or rely upon the truth being told or promises being kept, would it not have good consequences for persons to take steps to form the habits of telling the truth and keeping promises, so that these acts might come to be expected, and so could have good consequences, and so could all the more be expected and relied upon? Such steps could have good consequences, but, although perhaps justified by act-utilitarianism, they would amount to a partial rejection of act-utilitarianism and so would be inconsistent with our assumptions. These steps would amount to a partial rejection of act-utilitarianism, because the persons would be forming habits to do acts known not to be justified according to act-utilitarianism; and they could form these habits only if they resolved to refrain from applying act-utilitarianism in relation to these acts.

PETER SINGER*

Is Act-Utilitarianism Self-Defeating?

Act-Utilitarianism

HODGSON'S FORMULATION OF the principle of act-utilitarianism, which I shall accept for the purposes of discussion, is as follows:

> An act is right if and only if it would have best consequences, that is, consequences at least as good as those of any alternative act open to the agent [p. 1].

Hodgson, for convenience, uses "best" to mean "best or equal best," and I shall do the same.

Hodgson's arguments concern keeping promises and telling the truth. To take promise-keeping first: when we ask why we would be more concerned to do something we have promised we would do, than to do an act which we just happen to have mentioned we might do, the standard act-utilitarian reply is that the person to whom we made the promise normally has expectations of the promised act being performed, which he would not have if the act had merely been mentioned as a possibility. It is, ultimately, because of these expectations that the performance of the promised act will have greater utility than the performance of the act which was mentioned as a possibility. But, Hodgson asks, would this be true in an act-utilitarian society of the kind specified? His answer is that it would not, because in such a society the promisee will know that the promise made to him will not be kept

*From Peter Singer, "Is Act-Utilitarianism Self-Defeating?" *Philosophical Review*, 1972. All references are to D. H. Hodgson, *Consequences of Utilitarianism* (Oxford, 1967).

unless keeping it has best consequences. The fact that the act was promised will not lead to its performance having greater utility than it would have had, had it not been promised, unless the promisee will, because of the promise, have a greater expectation of its being performed than he would otherwise have had. The promisee will have good reason for this greater expectation only if he believes that the promisor believes that the act will be expected by him, the promisee, with greater expectation than it would have been, had it not been promised, but merely mentioned. The promisor will know this, and the promisee will know that he knows, and so on. A spiral has been set up which cannot be cut across. Any attempt to build up a basis for a greater expectation of the promised act is, Hodgson says, mere boot-strap-tugging. The expectation can have no rational basis, and hence there is no greater utility in doing something one has promised to do than there is in doing something one has merely mentioned one might do. So promising would be pointless in an act-utilitarian society.

A parallel argument applies to telling the truth. Imagine that A tells B: "X is Y." In an act-utilitarian society, B would have good reason to believe A only under the following conditions. If X were Y, it would, in A's belief, be best to tell B; if X were not Y it would, in A's belief, not be best to tell B that X is Y. These conditions will hold generally only if B is likely to take the information conveyed as true, for only then will the utilitarian benefits which come from the conveying of true information —such as the possibility of making arrangements based on the information—be possible. But as B's taking the information to be true rather than false is a condition precedent of A's having good reason to tell B the truth, the situation is precisely similar to that of promise-keeping.

Hodgson concludes that for these reasons a society in which everyone acted according to act-utilitarianism would be at a grave disadvantage compared to a society in which people acted on moral rules. For without promise-keeping and the communication of information there would be no human relationships as we know them. Hodgson emphasizes that this conclusion applies even if everyone applies act-utilitarianism correctly in the circumstances in which they are, but these circumstances—universal acceptance of act-utilitarianism and highly rational application of it—are in fact highly unfavorable to the production of good consequences.

One question that might be asked about Hodgson's ingenious arguments is whether he has himself considered sufficiently carefully all the effects which the circumstances of the society he has described would have. It will be recalled that Hodgson specified that in this society everyone adopts the principle of act-utilitarianism as his only personal rule, and attempts always to act in accordance with it. Under these circumstances, people would not act from the motives which most commonly lead people to make false promises and to tell lies — motives like self-interest, malevolence, pride, and so on. Nor would there be any need to make false promises or tell lies from utilitarian motives, in the sort of circumstances of which critics of utilitarianism are so fond: there would be no need to make consoling promises to dying people who wish their estates to be distributed in some way contrary to utility, since dying people would not wish this; no need, either, to tell a lie to save a man from his would-be murderer. Hodgson fails to see that there is any problem here. He writes of act-utilitarians breaking promises or telling lies without suggesting how doing so would bring about best consequences. His argument is based not on the existence of a reason for lying or breaking a promise, but on the absence of a sufficient reason for telling the truth or keeping a promise. This is significant, as we can see if we try to construct an example.

Let us imagine a case in which A has the choice of telling B the truth or a lie. A and B, we shall say, are working together in an office. (In constructing an example, it is impossible to avoid begging the question at issue to some extent. If Hodgson is right in saying that in an act-utilitarian society no communication would be possible, then offices and the other elements of this example would not be possible either. If this is considered a weakness, we might avoid the difficulty by assuming that, an instant before the events of my example take place, everyone in an until-then-normal society is miraculously converted to act-utilitarianism.) On this particular day, B intends to work overtime. His only means of transport home is by bus. If he misses the bus, he will have to walk, which will make him very tired, waste time, and lead to his wife's worrying about him. In this situation, of which both A and B are aware, B asks A: "What time does the last bus go?" A knows the answer. Is it not in accordance with act-utilitarianism for A to tell B the correct time? Hodgson would reply that it would have better consequences for A to tell B the truth only if B were likely to take the information as true, and B would know that A would have no reason to tell the truth unless A believed that he, B, was likely to take the information as true, and so on. But consider the matter from A's point of view. He has the choice of telling B the correct time, a fictitious time, or saying nothing. There is no possibility, barring extraordinary accidents, of any beneficial consequences arising from any course of action except telling B the correct time; but there is a fifty-fifty chance that telling B the correct time will lead to the beneficial consequences of B going to the bus stop at the right time. For even if there is no good reason for B to believe that A will tell him the truth, there is also no good reason for him to believe that A will tell him a lie, and so there is an even chance that B will take the information A gives him to be true. It is of course possible that if A tells B a fictitious time, B will treat this false information as false, but this cannot ensure, or even make it likely, that B will go to the bus stop

at the right time. The point here is just that there is only one way for
A's statement to be true, but many ways for it to be false. Because of
this, A has a reason for telling B the truth.

Once there is some reason for A to tell the truth, there is more than
enough reason for him to do so. For B, being highly rational, will have
thought of the considerations just pointed to, and will be aware that
there is a reason for A to tell him the truth, and A will know this, and so
on. So we get the Hogdson spiral working in the other direction, and A
will have the normal utilitarian reason for telling the truth — that is,
that B will take the information to be true and make arrangements
based on its truth.

It might be objected that I have constructed an especially favorable
case. In a real-life situation, would it not be possible that a lie would
have best consequences? In the example, for instance, might it not be
the case that A believes that great good will come if B works an hour
longer than he would if he left to catch the last bus? If this is possible,
would not A be right, on act-utilitarian grounds, to tell B that the last
bus left an hour later than it really does leave?

This objection forgets that both A and B take act-utilitarianism as
their personal rule and always try to act on it. So if it is the case that the
good of B working an extra hour outweighs the disutility of his having
to walk home, all that is necessary to ensure that he does the extra work
is that A explain this to him, thereby avoiding at least some of the
disutility that would come from A telling B that the bus comes later
than it really does — B will not have to wait unnecessarily, and he can
telephone his wife so that she will not worry. So A still has no good
reason for lying.

A different objection to my example might be that it depends on a
question being asked to which there is only one true answer, and more
than one false answer. Does our conclusion apply to other situations as
well? In reply to this, one could say that it would seem to be possible to
ask even ordinary questions, which would normally require a simple
yes/no answer, in such a way as to make two false answers possible. If
an office worker wished to know whether or not to reply to a letter, he
could ask: "Shall I reply to this letter, file it, or make a paper dart out of
it?" In this way the person addressed has a better chance of producing
best consequences by saying what he really thinks best. Admittedly, if
this were really necessary, act-utilitarianism would cause inconvenience, but it would not be disastrous, and it is certainly not clear that
this inconvenience would outweigh the benefits of everyone's adopting
act-utilitarianism.

In any case, there are other grounds for believing that in a society of
act-utilitarians there would be sufficient reason for telling the truth in
normal situations. Let us consider an example in which information is
volunteered. I am walking along the street when A comes up to me and

says: "There is a very good film on at the local cinema this week." How am I to take this remark? Is it possible that A wants me to go to the cinema for some reason, even though the film is very bad? Perhaps the cinema will have to close if it does not get good audiences this week, and the disutility of this outweighs the disutility of people being bored by the film. But this explanation will not do, for, as in the previous example, A could explain these facts to me, and I could buy a ticket without wasting my time by actually sitting through the film. Nevertheless, Hodgson might say, I cannot assume that A was telling me the truth. He may have been trying to warn me away from a very bad film, believing that I would take what he had told me to be false. This is not feasible either. Why would A have bothered to speak at all, since I am just as likely to take his remark to be true as to be false? Hodgson may claim that this is just his point. No one would have any reason to speak, and communication would cease. Before we accept this, however, consider the situation from the point of view of the recipient of the information. Since by going through the business of inverting what A says to me — thinking to myself, "He says the film is good, but he may be telling a lie, so the film may be bad" — I am no more likely to arrive at the truth than if I take what A says at face value, why should I bother to invert it? Am I not just a fraction more likely to take it at face value? If I am, A, being highly rational, will know this, and will know that he is more likely to produce best consequences if he tells the truth, while I, being highly rational, will know this, and so expect A to tell the truth . . . and so we get the spiral unspiraling once again, and we have all the reason we need for telling the truth.

Analogously with the argument just made, we could also ask why A should not save himself the bother of inventing a lie by telling the truth, thus making it fractionally more likely that he would tell the truth, and reversing the spiral once again. Hodgson attempts to forestall this objection by saying that any disvalue involved in the need to invent a lie would be balanced by the satisfaction of exercising the skill of lying (p. 43). Hodgson apparently has not noticed that the point is equally effective if made in regard to the recipient of the information, and his reply, which is not particularly convincing in the case of the person making the statement, would be quite implausible if made in respect of the recipient.

Hodgson does at one point suggest that even if it were possible to arouse expectations in the recipient that the information is true, it would not be possible to place much reliance on it, because it would still be better to tell a lie if the consequences on the whole would be better — and since the recipient would know this, he would not have very strong expectations (p. 50). This again seems to overlook the fact that if everyone were an act-utilitarian most of the reasons, selfish and unselfish, which we would otherwise have for lying would not exist.

Hence I believe that once the expectations can be aroused, at least as much reliance could be placed on them as is possible in our society at present, outside the circle of those we know to be sincere.

I have questioned only Hodgson's argument about truth-telling, but similar points could be made about his argument in respect of keeping promises. If there is little reason for making false statements, then there is little reason for making false statements of intention. But a promise implies, in some sense, a statement of intention, and whatever the promise adds to the statement of intention would not seem to affect the validity of the application of the previous argument about statements in general to the statements of intention implied by promises. In fact, it seems to me that a statement of firm intention to do an act, coupled with a recommendation to the hearer to make arrangements based on the expectation that the intention be carried out, is just as useful as, if it is not equivalent to, a promise. If, because of unforeseen events, the "promisor" is in doubt as to whether doing as he said he intended to do will have the best consequences, he must, as an act-utilitarian, take into account the expectations raised and arrangements which may have been made as a result of his statement of intention. This, of course, is as much as an act-utilitarian would ever want to say in defense of the institution of promising.

Quite apart from these objections to Hodgson's central argument, there is a more obvious one, which he does consider but not, in my opinion, refute. It is independent of the arguments I have put so far, and for the purposes of discussing it, we may assume that what I have said up to now has been mistaken.

The obvious objection is that if the situation were as Hodgson describes it, it would be justifiable on act-utilitarian grounds to take steps to form a social practice of telling the truth and making and keeping firm statements of intention (which I shall, for convenience, continue to call "promises"). Any steps toward the formation of these practices would have the good consequences of making desirable activities possible. Since telling the truth and keeping promises could help in the formation of these practices, while lying and breaking promises could not, this would given an additional reason for telling the truth and keeping promises. The spiraling effect would come into operation. This would ensure the rapid development of the practices. The informer or promisor would then have the dual reasons of preserving the useful practice and fulfilling expectations.

Hodgson seems to be aware of this kind of objection to his arguments. Yet his reply to it is puzzling:

> Such steps could have good consequences, but, although perhaps justified by act-utilitarianism, they would amount to a partial rejection of act-utilitarianism and so would be inconsistent with our assumptions.

> These steps would amount to a partial rejection of act-utilitarianism, because the persons would be forming habits to do acts known not to be justified according to act-utilitarianism; and they could form these habits only if they resolved to refrain from applying act-utilitarianism in relation to these acts [p. 48].

I am puzzled by the statement that acts could be justified by act-utilitarianism, and yet amount to a partial rejection of act-utilitarianism. This looks like a contradiction. Perhaps Hodgson means that while the taking of steps to get the habit, or practice, established is justified by act-utilitarianism, the practice itself is one of refraining from the calculation of consequences in respect of the particular acts, so that acts done in accordance with the practice may not be justified by act-utilitarianism. There are two points that may be made in reply to this. First, if acts may be justified because they help to get a practice established, surely they may also be justified because they help to preserve a useful, established practice. Second, Hodgson's admission that the acts which establish the practice may be justified by act-utilitarianism undermines the arguments he made earlier; for once the practice is established the point about lack of expectation, that promises will be kept and information given true, will not apply. Where there is a practice there are expectations, and the standard act-utilitarian justifications of keeping promises and telling the truth will operate.

It may be that in talking of "forming habits to do acts known not to be justified according to act-utilitarianism" Hodgson has in mind the formation of habits or practices of *always* telling the truth, and *always* keeping promises, no matter what the consequences. This would certainly be inconsistent with act-utilitarianism, but it would also be unnecessary. The benefits of communication and reliability may be gained without having such absolutist practices. All that is necessary is that there be habits of telling the truth and keeping promises unless there is a clear disutility in doing so which outweighs the benefits of preserving the useful practices and fulfilling the expectations aroused. It is, after all, an advantage of act-utilitarianism that it does not force us to reveal the hiding places of innocent men to their would-be murderers, or leave accident victims groaning by the roadside in order to avoid being late for an appointment we have promised to keep.

It might be more plausible to argue that it is the initial acts, before the practice has been established, and the expectations aroused, that would be contrary to act-utilitarianism. Hodgson does not argue this in the context of the passage we have been discussing, but in a subsequent discussion of the justification of a decision by a judge to punish an offender, Hodgson argues that although an unbroken record of punishment might deter potential offenders, such an unbroken record can never, on act-utilitarian grounds, get started. Hodgson's argument is that no single case can be a necessary or sufficient condition for such an unbroken record, because if we did not punish in any particular case, we could still have an unbroken record from the *next* case onward which would deter just as well [p. 93]. This argument seems to be based on the assumption that the only consequences of an act which may be taken into account, in deciding whether that act is justified by the act-utilitarian principle, are those for which the act is a necessary or sufficient condition. (This assumption has, incidentally, been the basis of claims by other writers that act-utilitarianism cannot explain why we ought to vote at elections, or obey power restrictions, when failure to do so will not bring about the defeat of our candidate or a general power breakdown.) Although some act-utilitarian writers may have assumed that only consequences for which the act is a necessary or sufficient condition should be taken into account, there is no good reason for an act-utilitarian to do so. An act may contribute to a result without being either a necessary or sufficient condition of it, and if it does contribute, the act-utilitarian should take this contribution into account. The contribution that my vote makes toward the result I judge to be best in an election is a relevant consideration in deciding whether to vote, although it is, almost certainly, neither a necessary nor a sufficient condition of that result; for if this were not so, the act-utilitarian view would leave us with a result which was unconnected with the actions of any of the voters, since what is true of my vote is equally true of every individual vote. In the punishment case, the first act of punishing may be justified, on act-utilitarian grounds, by its probable contribution to an unbroken record of punishment which will have a deterrent effect. In the cases we were considering originally, an act of telling the truth or keeping a promise will normally have greater utility than would its opposite, because it has a reasonable chance of contributing to the beneficial consequences of setting up a desirable practice. Our act-utilitarians, being highly rational, would understand this, and so contribute to the establishing of the practice themselves, as well as expecting other act-utilitarians to do so. The expectations so generated would increase the utility of conforming to the practice, which would therefore become established very quickly.

It seems to me, then, that Hodgson fails to establish the challenging central thesis of his book; and as I have said, the remainder of the work is based on the arguments we have just been discussing. This does not mean that the later sections are without interest, once these arguments have been rejected. On the contrary, there is much here that is stimulating for anyone interested in rule-utilitarianism or the justification of legal decisions — particularly the latter topic, which takes up almost exactly half of the book's total length.

I should also say, perhaps, that in dissenting from Hodgson's conclusions I have not been concerned to deny that there are no problems at all, of the sort Hodgson raises, in being an act-utilitarian. There may be occasions when a person is handicapped by being known to be an act-utilitarian—for example, a doctor, who assures a seriously ill patient, depressed and fearful that he will die, that his condition is hopeful, is less likely to be believed if he is known to be an act-utilitarian than if he is known to believe that lying is always wrong. These occasions would, I think, be few enough and unimportant enough for the balance of advantage to favor act-utilitarianism. My concern has been to show that act-utilitarianism does not have the catastrophic consequences which Hodgson argues it would have.

DONALD H. REGAN*

⮜⧄⮞

Utilitarianism and Co-operation

⮜⧄⮞

WHAT CU [Co-operative Utilitarianism] requires each agent to do is the following: He must hold himself ready to take part in a co-operative effort. He must identify others who are willing and able to do their part. (The "able" here does not refer to physical ability, since no agent's "part" could be something he was physically unable to do. It refers to psychological ability — freedom from last-minute backsliding, conative disruptions, or whatever — which might or might not be thought to be already covered by the agent's "willingness," depending on how we interpret that.) He must ascertain the behaviour or dispositions to behave of the *non-co-operators* who have been identified thus far (that is, the agents who are *not* willing and able to do their part), and he must ascertain the best pattern of behaviour for the co-operators in the circumstances. He must then decide whether anyone he currently regards as a co-operator has made any mistake so far. If any putative co-operator has made a mistake, then all who have made mistakes are eliminated from the class of putative co-operators, and the process of identifying the best behaviour for the (reduced) class of co-operators is repeated. And so on, until it is discovered that no putative co-operator has made a mistake. At this point the inquiry shifts to the question of whether the putative co-operators are all terminating their investigations into each others' decision-making. If any putative co-operator is not terminating his investigation here but is going on to another round

*From Donald H. Regan: *Utilitarianism and Co-operation*, Chapters 10 and 12.

220

of checking on his fellow co-operators, then the agent in question goes on also, to be sure of catching any last minute errors the others might make. Only when the agent in question discovers that the putative co-operators are all stopping does he stop and do his part in the current best plan.

The Community of Co-operators

I am a moral agent, and I have moral decisions to make, but I am not alone. I share that condition, both liberating and burdensome, with many other persons. The existence of a multiplicity of moral agents suggests that the business of behaving morally ought to be viewable as a community enterprise. If we believe in consequentialism, then we ought to view the business of producing good consequences as a community enterprise. CU brings this feature of the moral life much more clearly to the fore than any other consequentialist theory.

To put the same point another way, a central problem with which any consequentialist theory must deal is the problem of how each agent is to view the behaviour of other agents. Act-utilitarianism tells each agent in effect to take the behaviour of all others as given. Rule-utilitarianism and utilitarian generalization, in their pure forms, tell each agent in effect to ignore others' behaviour entirely. Only CU embodies an approach to others' behaviour which emphasizes constantly that, whoever the agents are who are willing to try to produce the best consequences possible, they are engaged in a common project.

Let us consider a bit more closely just why the various traditional theories are unsatisfactory in their treatment of others' behaviour. Act-utilitarianism requires of each individual that he do the best thing available to him, given what everyone else is doing. So far as act-utilitarianism is concerned, others' behaviour (or dispositions to behave) affects obligations in precisely the same way as brute natural phenomena. Of course, in deciding what consequences to promote, the act-utilitarian takes others' interests into account. But we are not concerned at this point with how the act-utilitarian regards others' interests. We are concerned with how he regards their behaviour.

There is no reference in the act-utilitarian principle itself to the need for co-operation or to the fact that producing good consequences is a task which many moral agents share. To be sure, act-utilitarianism requires each agent to engage, when he has the opportunity, in behaviour which will improve others' behaviour or which will increase the likelihood of desirable co-ordination. Each agent should try to influence others to better behaviour, to enter into useful agreements, and so on. But there is still a fundamental dichotomy between the agent's own behaviour and everyone else's. The point of view embodied in the act-utilitarian's ultimate criterion of right behaviour is the point of view of one agent alone. It is not the point of view of an agent who is participating in a joint effort.

Rule-utilitarianism slights the communal nature of the moral enterprise in a different way. If rules are justified as a means of co-ordination, then obviously there is explicit reference within the rule-utilitarian's theory to the fact that producing good consequences is a shared task. But the rules are not usually regarded as merely instrumental, as useful tools in the joint enterprise which should be set aside when more effective tools come to hand. Instead, the rules take on an importance of their own. They become the only criterion for the rightness of individual acts. In the final analysis, the rule-utilitarian is directed by his theory to ignore other agents' actual behaviour. He must consider how other agents *might* behave in formulating the best overall pattern of behaviour; but he need not pay any attention to how others behave in fact. The rules take on all the burden of producing co-ordination, and the agent is separated by the rules from other agents who are part of the common enterprise. The agent is encouraged to indulge in a sort of Pontius Pilatism, taking the view that as long as he keeps his own hands clean, the other agents as well as the overall consequences can take care of themselves.

There is an analogy which may illuminate the sense in which a system of rules tends to come between agents who are endeavouring to behave morally. Most persons have, at some point in their lives, played on an athletic team, or danced in an ensemble, or played in an orchestra, or sung in a chorus. The point I have in mind could be made in connection with any of these, but since I am a singer, I consider the chorus. A chorus can make a fairly decent sound, and even sing moderately expressively, if the individual singers are adequate, if each individual knows his part, and if each hews to his part to the best of his ability, more or less ignoring everyone else. But unless the individual singers have achieved only a low level of competence, the chorus will not do its best this way, nor will the experience be very satisfying to the individuals who make up the chorus. If the chorus is really to work as a chorus, it is necessary for each individual to listen to all the others, to tune to them, to breathe with them, to swell and diminish with them, and so on. The unity that is required for really successful choral work cannot be guaranteed even by everyone's paying attention to a conductor, although that helps. Everybody just has to listen to everybody else and feel himself part of a community. "Rules," in the form of individual parts, are not enough, and preoccupation with the rules interferes both with the achievement of the joint goal and with the individual satisfaction from taking part.

SAMUEL SCHEFFLER*

Agent-Centered Prerogatives

THESE "HYBRID" CONCEPTIONS, as I refer to them, depart from consequentialism through their incorporation of something I call an "agent-
centred prerogative," which has the effect of denying that one is
always required to produce the best overall states of affairs, and which
is thus in some form a feature of fully agent-centred conceptions as
well.[1] At the same time, however, hybrid conceptions are akin to
consequentialist conceptions in their rejection of agent-centred restrictions; that is, in their acceptance of the idea that it is always permissible
to do what would produce the best overall state of affairs. In other
words, hybrid conceptions are like fully agent-centred conceptions and
unlike consequentialist conceptions in maintaining that one need not
always do what would produce the best outcome; but they are like
consequentialist conceptions and unlike fully agent-centred conceptions in accepting the plausible-sounding idea that one *may* always do
what would produce the best outcome.

It seems to me that there are different ways in which a moral conception can take account of the independence of the personal point of
view. Sophisticated consequentialist conceptions do it one way, moral

*From Samuel Scheffler: *The Rejection of Consequentialism*, Chapters 1 and 3.
[1]That is, since fully agent-centred conceptions do, as I have said, deny that one is
required to do what would have the best overall outcome on all of those occasions when
the agent-centred restrictions do not forbid it, they in effect include an agent-centred
prerogative of some form, although not necessarily of the very same form as I describe in
Chapter Two of this book, and although the term "agent-centred prerogative" is of
course my own.

conceptions that incorporate an agent-centred prerogative do it another way. Neither type of view ignores this feature of persons. Sophisticated consequentialist conceptions take account of it by requiring, roughly, that each agent at all times act in a way that will serve to maximize the number of people who are successfully pursuing their projects and plans. I will call this "the maximization strategy." The guiding intuitions behind this strategy are two. The first is that if the independence of the personal point of view is an important fact for morality, that is because it fundamentally affects the character of human fulfilment and hence the constitution of the individual good. The second is that, given this conception of the importance of the fact of personal independence, a moral theory gives most weight to that fact if it seeks to maximize the number of individuals who actually achieve fulfilment from their points of view, by incorporating (a) some distribution-sensitive conception of the overall good which reflects the desirability of as many people as possible pursuing their plans as successfully as possible, and (b) a conception of the right which requires production of the best available states of affairs.

By incorporating an agent-centred prerogative, hybrid theories take account of the independence of the personal point of view in a different way. In order to appreciate the motivation for this alternative approach, let us reconsider some aspects of the maximization strategy. As we have seen, this strategy takes account of the person's nature as a being with a point of view by taking account from an impersonal standpoint of the significance to agents of personal commitments and projects, and of the hardships associated with abandoning such commitments and projects. If it turns out, despite the hardship to some given agent, that it would be best from the impersonal standpoint for him to abandon his projects, then he must do so, for the hardship to him has already been taken account of. Yet, as has been noted, having a personal point of view typically involves caring about one's projects and commitments out of proportion to their relative weight in the overall, impersonal sum. And so although the hardship to this agent may have been "taken account of" from an impersonal standpoint, that is unlikely to exhaust his own feeling about the matter. But provided that this feeling has itself been assigned a "cost" which has been fed into the impersonal calculus, it has no further moral relevance as far as the maximization strategy is concerned. This highlights a notable feature of the strategy: its insistence that the *moral* significance of a personal point of view, with its accompanying commitments and concerns, is entirely exhausted by the weight that point of view carries in the impersonal calculus, *even for the person who has the point of view*. Thus while sophisticated consequentialism does take account of the fact that persons have sources of energy and concern which are independent of the impersonal perspective, it does so in such a way as to deny that these points of view are *morally* independent. That is, it denies that personal projects and commitments can have any moral weight for an agent — any role in determining what the agent may do — independently of the weight those projects and commitments have in the impersonal calculus. Although sophisticated consequentialism takes account of the natural independence of the personal point of view, it, like other consequentialist theories, refuses to grant *moral* independence to this point of view.

A moral conception that incorporates an agent-centred prerogative, by contrast, takes account of the natural independence of the personal point of view precisely by granting it moral independence: by permitting agents to devote energy and attention to their projects and commitments out of proportion to the value from an impersonal standpoint of their doing so. I will call this "the liberation strategy," The guiding intuitions behind this strategy are two. The first is that if the independence of the personal point of view is an important fact for morality, that is not just because of its role in determining the nature of human fulfilment, but also, simply, because of what it tells us about the character of personal agency and motivation: people do not typically view the world from the impersonal perspective, nor do their actions typically flow from the kinds of concerns a being who actually did inhabit the impersonal standpoint might have. The second intuition is that, given *this* conception of the importance of the natural fact of personal independence, a moral view gives sufficient weight to that fact only if it *reflects* it, by freeing people from the demand that their actions and motives always be optimal from the impersonal perspective, and by allowing them to devote attention to their projects and concerns to a greater extent than impersonal optimality by itself would allow.[2]

Here, then, are two different ways in which moral theories can respond to the independence of the personal point of view. The two strategies appear to be incompatible: maximization precludes liberation, and liberation precludes maximization. Each strategy is said by its (imagined) adherents to give more weight than the other to the fact of independence. How can the conflict between these competing claims be resolved? Two possibilities suggest themselves.

First, of course, and most straightforwardly, one might try to resolve the conflict by showing that one of the claims is correct and the other incorrect: that one of the strategies simply does give more weight than the other to the independence of the personal point of view. Thus, for example, someone might say: liberation really does give more weight to

---

[2]The liberation strategy, incidentally, seems to me to capture most of what is worth capturing in Nozick's reminder that, with respect to each individual, 'his is the only life he has' (*Anarchy, State, and Utopia*, p. 33). Nozick himself believes that this reminder also points to a motivation for agent-centred restrictions. His argument seems to me unpersuasive, but I will not consider it until Chapter Four.

personal independence than does maximization, for the liberation strategy, by reflecting the natural independence of the personal point of view, gives weight to the fact of personal independence *per se*, while the maximization of strategy, by seeking to increase fulfilment, only gives weight to the *effects* of independence.

The difficulties with arguments of this type are evident: to speak of a moral theory giving a certain amount of weight to some fact is to use a figure of speech, and one that is misleading to the extent that it suggests the possibility of precise measurement. It is simply not clear what standard one is supposed to use in comparing the 'weights' given to some fact by different moral conceptions. So it is not clear how one is to judge whether arguments of this type succeed or fail. Still, it may be possible to provide a clear standard for the relevant comparative judgements. But before deciding whether this is a task worth undertaking, let us consider the other possibility for resolving the conflict under discussion.

Rather than trying to show that one strategy really does give more weight than the other to the independence of the personal point of view, one might suggest that they are simply two different ways of giving weight to personal independence, with the choice between them properly dependent on one's ultimate moral attitudes, and not on any supposedly neutral determination of the magnitudes of the respective weights. The two strategies, as we have seen, are guided by different conceptions of the importance of personal independence. And each is a plausible strategy for acknowledging personal independence, in the following sense: each conceives of independence as an especially important fact under *some* (accurate) description, and embodies an evidently rational method for taking account of the fact so described. The maximization strategy regards independence as important primarily for the influence it exerts on the character of human fulfilment and hence the constitution of the individual good, and responds by seeking to maximize the number of individuals who succeed in achieving their good so understood. The liberation strategy, though compatible with a recognition of the effects of independence on the character of human fulfilment,[3] also emphasizes the importance of the natural independence of the personal point of view simply as a fact about human agency. It responds by insisting that the norms *governing* human agency must grant *moral* independence to every personal point of view, whatever account of personal fulfilment those norms rely on. Thus, one might suggest, the relative appeal of these two strategies will depend on one's ultimate moral attitudes, for there is no obvious or

---

[3]Recall that the distributive hybrid, for example, regards an individual's good as consisting in the pursuit of a rational plan of life.

straight-forward sense in which the relative merits of the strategies are objectively decidable.

Which of these two ways of resolving the conflict seems the more promising? It is important to emphasize that my goal is to identify the principled rationale underlying an agent-centred prerogative, and so my interest in deciding which way to resolve the conflict is not intrinsic. I am concerned to make this decision only if it is necessary to do so in order to reach that goal. Thus it is natural to begin by asking whether the two different methods for resolving the conflict would yield significantly different accounts of the rationale for the prerogative. Suppose, first, that one *could* show that the liberation strategy gives more weight than the maximization strategy to the independence of the personal point of view. Then one could say that whether or not consequentialism systematically undermines integrity, there is in any case a principled motivation for departing from consequentialism to the extent of accepting an agent-centred prerogative: namely, to give more weight than consequentialism does to the nature of a person as a being with a naturally independent point of view.

Now suppose instead that the liberation and maximization strategies were thought of as embodying two plausible ways of taking account of personal independence, with the choice between them a matter of one's ultimate moral attitudes. In this case, one could still say that there was a rationale for an agent-centred prerogative: namely, that it embodies a rational strategy for taking account of the nature of a person as a being with an independent point of view, given one construal of the importance of that aspect of persons. To be sure, the principled motivation that would have been identified, given this second way of resolving the conflict, would not constitute a conclusive demonstration that moral conceptions that include an agent-centred prerogative are superior to consequentialist conceptions. Since the prerogative would have been motivated by showing that it gives rational expression to a certain ultimate moral attitude, it would appear to be legitimate for someone who lacked the attitude in question to reject the prerogative. Indeed, the sophisticated consequentialist might even propose as a rationale for *his* theory that *it* embodies a rational strategy for taking account of the nature of a person as a being with an independent point of view, given another construal of the importance of that aspect of persons. But remember than my project is not to give a conclusive proof of the superiority of hybrid conceptions, or to show that it is *only* hybrid conceptions whose salient structural feature has a plausible underlying motivation. The project is rather to conduct a comparative examination of two types of moral conceptions that depart from consequentialism: hybrid conceptions and fully agent-centred conceptions. In the case of hybrid conceptions, I am trying to show that not only is their salient structural feature responsive to certain intuitive objections to consequentialism, but that this feature also has an underlying principled rationale: it gives rational expression to some plausible attitude towards persons. Although I agree that agent-centred restrictions are similarly responsive to a variety of intuitive objections to consequentialism, I want to go on to explore the question whether there is a comparable underlying motivation for them. My project, in other words, is to explore the question whether agent-centred restrictions are as well-motivated as an agent-centred prerogative is. And for the purposes of this project, it appears that even if the conflict under consideration were resolved in the second way, a motivation of the requisite type for an agent-centred prerogative would still have been identified. For even given a resolution of this sort, it would have been demonstrated that such a prerogative does indeed embody a rational strategy for taking account of one significant feature of the person.

It may thus begin to seem that it is not essential to decide which way to resolve the conflict. For whether the liberation strategy gives more weight than the maximization strategy to the natural independence of the personal point of view, or whether instead the liberation strategy just constitutes one rational response to this aspect of persons, either way there appears to be a motivation for an agent-centred prerogative of just the right sort.

Someone might suppose, however, that the rationale for a prerogative would be much stronger if one could resolve the conflict in the first way, showing that the liberation strategy really does give more weight to personal independence than the maximization strategy. Then, it might be thought, we really would have a conclusive demonstration that hybrid theories are superior to consequentialist theories. But it would be a mistake to think this. Even if 'sophisticated consequentialists' were forced to agree that they had been wrong in claiming that their theory gives more weight than hybrid theories to personal independence, it is not at all obvious that they would then have to concede the inferiority of their theory. They might instead reason as follows: "It has already been agreed that the maximization strategy embodies an evidently rational procedure for acknowledging personal independence, given our construal of the importance of that feature of persons. Now, even if it can be said that this strategy gives less weight to independence than the liberation strategy does, in some absolute sense, that does not show that the maximization strategy is *not* a rational method for acknowledging independence, after all. For it does not show either that our construal of the importance of independence is untenable, or that the relation between that construal and the maximization strategy is any less close than it initially appeared to be. What it does show instead is that, given our interpretation of the importance of independence, a strategy that gives it less weight is the strategy it is rational to prefer." The apparent availability to the sophisticated con-

sequentialist of this response confirms the suspicion that it is not necessary to decide how to resolve the dispute under consideration. No
matter which way the dispute is resolved, there is in any case a rationale for an agent-centred prerogative of just the right sort. And no
matter which way the dispute is resolved, the identification of the
rationale does not constitute a conclusive demonstration of the absolute
superiority of hybrid theories or the absolute inferiority of consequentialist theories.

It is thus possible, at long last, to state the rationale for an agent-
centred prerogative in its final form. Whether or not there is some
absolute sense in which hybrid theories incorporating an agent-centred
prerogative give more weight than consequentialist theories to the
natural independence of the personal point of view, the prerogative is,
at the very least, a structural feature whose incorporation into a moral
conception embodies a rational strategy for taking account of personal
independence, given one construal of the importance of that aspect of
persons.

R. M. HARE*

Levels of Moral Thinking

IT IS SOMETIMES said to be a fault in utilitarianism that it makes us give weight to bad desires (such as the desire of a sadist to torture his victim) solely in proportion to their intensity; received opinion, it is claimed, gives no weight at all, or even a negative weight, to such desires. But received opinion has grown up to deal with cases likely to be encountered; and we are most *un*likely, even if we give sadistic desires weight in accordance with their intensity, to encounter a case in which utility will be maximised by letting the sadist have his way. For first, the suffering of the victim will normally be more intense than the pleasure of the sadist. And, secondly, sadists can often be given substitute pleasures or even actually cured. And, thirdly, the side-effects of allowing the sadist to have what he wants are enormous. So it will be clear, when I have explained in more detail why fantastic cases in which those disutilities do not occur cannot legitimately be used in this kind of argument, why it is perfectly all right to allow weight to bad desires.

We have now, therefore, to make an important distinction between two kinds or "levels" of moral thinking. It has some affinities with a distinction made by Rawls in his article "Two Concepts of Rules"[1] (in which he was by way of defending utilitarianism), though it is not the same; it also owes something to Sir David Ross,[2] and indeed to others. I call it the difference between level-1 and level-2 thinking, or between

*From R. M. Hare, "Ethical Theory and Utilitarianism," in H. D. Lewis (ed.): *Contemporary British Philosophy*, Fourth Series.

[1]*Ph. Rev.*, 64 (1955).

[2]*The Right and the Good* (Oxford, 1930), pp. 19ff.

the principles employed at these two levels.[3] Level-1 principles are for use in practical moral thinking, especially under conditions of stress. They have to be general enough to be impartable by education (including self-education), and to be "of ready application in the emergency,"[4] but are not to be confused with rules of thumb (whose breach excites no compunction). Level-2 principles are what would be arrived at by leisured moral thought in completely adequate knowledge of the facts, as the right answer in a specific case. They are universal but can be as specific (the opposite of "general," not of "universal"[5]) as needs be. Level-1 principles are inculcated in moral education; but the selection of the level-1 principles for this purpose should be guided by leisured thought, resulting in level-2 principles for specific considered situations, the object being to have those level-1 principles whose general acceptance will lead to actions in accord with the best level-2 principles in most situations that are actually encountered. Fantastic and highly unusual situations, therefore, need not be considered for this purpose.

I have set out this distinction in detail elsewhere; here we only need to go into some particular points which are relevant. The thinking that I have been talking about so far in this paper, until the preceding paragraph, and indeed in most of my philosophical writings until recently, is level-2. It results in a kind of act-utilitarianism which, because of the universalisability of moral judgements, is practically equivalent to a rule-utilitarianism whose rules are allowed to be of any required degree of specificity. Such thinking is appropriate only to "a cool hour," in which there is time for unlimited investigation of the facts, and there is no temptation to special pleading. It can use hypothetical cases, even fantastic ones. In principle it can, given superhuman knowledge of the facts, yield answers as to what should be done in any cases one cares to describe.

The commonest trick of the opponents of utilitarianism is to take examples of such thinking, usually addressed to fantastic cases, and confront them with what the ordinary man would think. It makes the utilitarian look like a moral monster. The anti-utilitarians have usually confined their own thought about moral reasoning (with fairly infrequent lapses which often go unnoticed) to what I am calling level 1, the level of everyday moral thinking on ordinary, often stressful, occasions in which information is sparse. So they find it natural to take the side of the ordinary man in a supposed fight with the utilitarian whose views lead him to say, if put at the disconcertingly unfamiliar standpoint of

---

[3]See my review of Rawls, cited in note 4, p. 153; "Principles," *Proc. Arist. Soc.*, 72 (1972–3); "Rules of War and Moral Reasoning," cited in note 1; *FR*, pp. 43–5.

[4]Burke; see *FR*, p. 45.

[5]See "Principles," cited in note 16.

the archangel Gabriel, such extraordinary things about these carefully contrived examples.

To argue in this way is entirely to neglect the importance for moral philosophy of a study of moral education. Let us suppose that a fully-informed archangelic act-utilitarian is thinking about how to bring up his children. He will obviously not bring them up to practise on every occasion on which they are confronted with a moral question the kind of archangelic thinking that he himself is capable of; if they are ordinary children, he knows that they will get it wrong. They will not have the time, or the information, or the self-mastery to avoid self-deception prompted by self-interest; this is the real, as opposed to the imagined, veil of ignorance which determines our moral principles.

So he will do two things. First, he will try to implant in them a set of good general principles. I advisedly use the word "implant"; these are not rules of thumb, but principles which they will not be able to break without the greatest repugnance, and whose breach by others will arouse in them the highest indignation. These will be the principles they will use in their ordinary level-1 moral thinking, especially in situations of stress. Secondly, since he is not always going to be with them, and since they will have to educate *their* children, and indeed continue to educate themselves, he will teach them, as far as they are able, to do the kind of thinking that he has been doing himself. This thinking will have three functions. First of all, it will be used when the good general principles conflict in particular cases. If the principles have been well chosen, this will happen rarely; but it will happen. Secondly, there will be cases (even rarer) in which, though there is no conflict between general principles, there is something highly unusual about the case which prompts the question whether the general principles are really fitted to deal with it. But thirdly, and much the most important, this level-2 thinking will be used to *select* the general principles to be taught both to this and to succeeding generations. The general principles may change, and should change (because the environment changes). And note that, if the educator were not (as we have supposed him to be) archangelic, we could not even assume that the best level-1 principles were imparted in the first place; perhaps they might be improved.

How will the selection be done? By using level-2 thinking to consider cases, both actual and hypothetical, which crucially illustrate, and help to adjudicate, disputes between rival general principles. But, because the general principles are being selected for use in actual situations, there will have to be a careful proportioning of the weight to be put upon a particular case to the probability of its actually occurring in the lives of the people who are to use the principles. So the fantastic cases that are so beloved of anti-utilitarians will have very little employment in this kind of thinking (except as a diversion for philosophers or to illustrate purely logical points, which is sometimes necessary). Fantastic unlikely cases will never be used to turn the scales as between rival general principles for practical use. The result will be a set of general principles, constantly evolving, but on the whole stable, such that their use in moral education, including self-education, and their consequent acceptance by the society at large, will lead to the nearest possible approximation to the prescriptions of archangelic thinking. They will be the set of principles with the highest acceptance-utility. They are likely to include principles of justice.

It is now necessary to introduce some further distinctions, all of which, fortunately, have already been made elsewhere, and can therefore be merely summarised. The first, alluded to already, is that between specific rule-utilitarianism (which is practically equivalent to universalistic act-utilitarianism) and general rule-utilitarianism.[7] Both are compatible with act-utilitarianism if their roles are carefully distinguished. Specific rule-utilitarianism is appropriate to level-2 thinking, general rule-utilitarianism to level-1 thinking; and therefore the rules of specific rule-utilitarianism can be of unlimited specificity, but those of general rule-utilitarianism have to be general enough for their role. The thinking of our archangel will thus be of a specific rule-utilitarian sort; and the thinking of the ordinary people whom he has educated will be for the most part of a general rule-utilitarian sort, though they will supplement this, when they have to and when they dare, with such archangelic thinking as they are capable of.

The second distinction is that between what Professor Smart[8] calls (morally) "right" actions and (morally) "rational" actions. Although Smart's way of putting the distinction is not quite adequate, as he himself recognises, I shall, as he does, adopt it for the sake of brevity. Both here, and in connexion with the "acceptance-utility" mentioned above, somewhat more sophisticated calculations of probability are required than might at first be thought. But for simplicity let us say that an action is rational if it is the action most likely to be right, even if, when all the facts are known, as they were not when it was done, it turns out not to have been right. In such a society as we have described, the (morally) rational action will nearly always be that in accordance with the good general principles of level 1, because they have been selected precisely in order to make this the case. Such actions may not always turn out to have been (morally) right in Smart's sense when the cards are turned face upwards; but the agent is not to be blamed for this.

It is a difficult question, just how simple and general these level-1 principles ought to be. If we are speaking of the principles to be

[7]See "Principles," cited in note 16.
[8]Smart and Williams, op. cit., pp. 46f.

inculcated throughout the society, the answer will obviously vary with the extent to which the members of it are sophisticated and morally self-disciplined enough to grasp and apply relatively complex principles without running into the dangers we have mentioned. We might distinguish sub-groups within the society, and individuals within these sub-groups, and even the same individual at different stages, according to their ability to handle complex principles. Most people's level-1 principles become somewhat more complex as they gain experience of handling different situations, and they may well become so complex as to defy verbal formulation; but the value of the old simple maxims may also come to be appreciated. In any case, level-1 principles can never, because of the exigencies of their role, become as complex as level-2 principles are allowed to be.

A third distinction is that between good actions and the right action.[9] The latter is the action in accordance with level-2 principles arrived at by exhaustive, fully-informed and clear thinking about specific cases. A good action is what a good man would do, even if not right. In general this is the same as the morally rational action, but there may be complications, in that the motivation of the man has to be taken into account. The good (i.e. the morally well-educated) man, while he is sometimes able and willing to question and even to amend the principles he has been taught, will have acquired in his upbringing a set of motives and dispositions such that breaking these principles goes very much against the grain for him. The very goodness of his character will make him sometimes do actions which do not conform to archangelic prescriptions. This may be for one of at least two reasons. The first is that when he did them he was not fully informed and perhaps knew it, and knew also his own moral and intellectual weaknesses, and therefore (humbly and correctly) thought it morally rational to abide by his level-1 principles, and thus did something which turned out in the event not to be morally right. The second is that, although he could have known that the morally rational action was on this unusual occasion one in breach of his ingrained principles (it required him, say, to let down his closest friend), he found it so much against the grain that he just could not bring himself to do it. In the first case what he did was both rational and a morally good action. In the second case it was morally good but misguided—a wrong and indeed irrational act done from the best of motives. And no doubt there are other possibilities.

The situation I have been describing is a somewhat stylised model of our own, except that we had no archangel to educate us, but rely on the deliverances, not even of philosopher kings, but of Aristotelian *phronimoi* of very varying degrees of excellence. What will happen if a lot of moral philosophers are let loose on this situation? Level-1 thinking

---

[9]See my *The Language of Morals*, p. 186.

forms the greater part of the moral thinking of good men, and perhaps the whole of the moral thinking of good men who have nothing of the philosopher in them, including some of our philosophical colleagues. Such are the intuitionists, to whom their good ingrained principles seem to be sources of unquestionable knowledge. Others of a more enquiring bent will ask why they should accept these intuitions, and, getting no satisfactory answer, will come to the conclusion that the received principles have no ground at all and that the only way to decide what you ought to do is to reason it out on each occasion. Such people will at best become a crude kind of act-utilitarians. Between these two sets of philosophers there will be the sort of ludicrous battles that we have been witnessing so much of. The philosopher who understands the situation better will see that both are right about a great deal and that they really ought to make up their quarrel. They are talking about different levels of thought, both of which are necessary on appropriate occasions.

ROBERT MERRIHEW ADAMS*

Motive Utilitarianism

PHILOSOPHERS HAVE WRITTEN much about the morality of traits of character, much more about the morality of actions, and much less about the
morality of motives. [By "motives" here I mean principally wants and
desires, considered as giving rise, or tending to give rise to actions. A
desire, if strong, stable, and for a fairly general object (e.g., the desire
to get as much money as possible), may perhaps constitute a trait of
character; but motives are not in general the same, and may not be as
persistent, as traits of character.] Utilitarian theories form a good place
to begin an investigation of the relation between the ethics of motives
and the ethics of actions, because they have a clear structure and
provide us with familiar and comprehensible, if not always plausible,
grounds of argument. I believe that a study of possible treatments of
motives in utilitarianism will also shed light on some of the difficulties
surrounding the attempt to make the maximization of utility the guiding interest of ethical theory.

I

What would be the motives of a person morally perfect by utilitarian
standards? It is natural to suppose that he or she would be completely

*The largest part of my work on this paper was supported by a fellowship from the
National Endowment for the Humanities. I am indebted to several, and especially to
Gregory Kavka, Jan Narveson, and Derek Parfit, for helpful discussion and comments on
earlier versions.
From Robert Merrihew Adams, "Motive Utilitarianism," *Journal of Philosophy*, 1976.

controlled, if not exclusively moved, by the desire to maximize utility. Isn't this ideal of singlemindedly optimific motivation demanded by the principle of utility, if the principle, as Bentham puts it, "states the greatest happiness of all those whose interest is in question, as being the right and proper, and only right and proper and universally desirable, end of human action"?[1]

But there is a good utilitarian objection to such singlemindedness: it is not in general conducive to human happiness. As Sidgwick says, "Happiness [general as well as individual] is likely to be better attained if the extent to which we set ourselves consciously to aim at it be carefully restricted."[2] Suggestions of a utilitarian theory about motivation that accommodates this objection can be found in both Bentham and Sidgwick.

The test of utility is used in different theories to evaluate different objects. It is applied to acts in act utilitarianism and to roles, practices, and types of action in the various forms of rule utilitarianism. In the view about motives stated in the first paragraph above, the test is not applied at all: nothing is evaluated for its utility, but perfect motivation is identified with an all-controlling desire to maximize utility. The test of utility could be applied in various ways in the evaluation of motives.

It could be applied directly to the motives themselves, and is so applied by Bentham, when he says,

> If they [motives] are good or bad, it is only on account of their effects: good, on account of their tendency to produce pleasure, or avert pain: bad, on account of their tendency to produce pain, or avert pleasure (*Introduction*, 102).

Alternatively, we could apply the test directly to objects of desire and only indirectly to the desires, saying that the best motives are desires for the objects that have most utility. Sidgwick seems to take this line when he says,

> While yet if we ask for a final criterion of the comparative value of the different objects of men's enthusiastic pursuit, and of the limits within which each may legitimately engross the attention of mankind, we shall none the less conceive it to depend upon the degree in which they respectively conduce to Happiness (*Methods*, 406).

Or we could apply the test of utility to the acts to which motives give rise (or are likely to give rise) and, thence, indirectly to the motives; the best motives would be those productive of utility-maximizing acts.[3]

[1]Jeremy Bentham, *An Introduction to the Principles of Morals and Legislation* (New York: Hafner, 1961) (referred to hereafter as *Introduction*, with page number), p. 1n.

[2]Henry Sidgwick, *The Methods of Ethics*, seventh edition (New York: Dover, 1966) (referred to hereafter as *Methods*, with page number), p. 405.

[3]This too may find some support in Sidgwick.Cf. *Methods*, 493, on the praise of motives conceived to prompt to felicific conduct.

Another approach, also endorsed by Bentham, is to evaluate motives by the intentions to which they give rise: "A motive is good, when the intention it gives birth to is a good one; bad, when the intention is a bad one" (*Introduction*, 120). The value of an intention to do an act, he regards as depending, in turn, on whether "the consequences of the act, had they proved what to the agent they seemed likely to be, *would* have been of a beneficial nature" or the opposite (*Introduction*, 93). This approach seems inconsistent with Bentham's insistence that the test of utility must be applied to everything that is to be evaluated — that

> Strictly speaking, nothing can be said to be good or bad, but either in itself; which is the case only with pain or pleasure: or on account of its effects; which is the case only with things that are the causes or preventives of pain and pleasure (*Introduction*, 87; cf. 102).

Bentham would presumably defend the evaluating of intentions by the utility of expected consequences of the intended act rather than the utility of the intentions themselves in the same way that he defends a similar method of evaluating dispositions. That is, he would appeal to the assumption "that in the ordinary course of things the consequences of actions commonly turn out conformable to intentions" (*Introduction*, 133), so that there is no practical difference between the utility of the intention and the utility of the expected consequences of the intended action. This assumption is plausible as regards the short-term consequences of our actions, though even there it yields at best a very rough equivalence between utility of intentions and utility of expected consequences. It is wildly and implausibly optimistic as regards our ability to foresee the long-term consequences of our actions.[4]

Bentham similarly regards the evaluating of motives by the value of intentions arising from them as consistent with (or even practically equivalent to) a direct application of the test of utility to motives, on the ground that the intention resulting from a motive is responsible for "the most material part of [the motive's] effects" (*Introduction*, 120). His position will still be inconsistent, however, unless he maintains (falsely, I believe) that the resulting intentions to act are responsible for *all* the relevant effects of having a motive.

If the moral point of view, the point of view from which moral evaluations are made, is dominated by concern for the maximization of human happiness, then it seems we must revert to the thesis that the test of utility is to be applied directly to everything, including motives. This is the conclusion toward which the following argument from Sidgwick tends:

---

[4]Also, as Gregory Kavka has pointed out to me, the utility of *having* an intention (e.g., to retaliate if attacked) may be quite different from the utility (actual or expected) of *acting* on it. I shall be making a similar point about motives, below.

Finally, the doctrine that Universal Happiness is the ultimate *standard* must not be understood to imply that Universal Benevolence is the only right or always best *motive* of action. For . . . if experience shows that the general happiness will be more satisfactorily attained if men frequently act from other motives than pure universal philanthropy, it is obvious that these other motives are reasonably to be preferred on Utilitarian principles (*Methods*, 413).

Accordingly, the theory that will be my principal subject here is that one pattern of motivation is morally better than another to the extent that the former has more utility than the latter. The morally perfect person, on this view, would have the most useful desires, and have them in exactly the most useful strengths; he or she would have the most useful among the patterns of motivation that are causally possible for human beings.[5] Let us call this doctrine *motive utilitarianism*.

II

It is distinct, both theoretically and practically, from act utilitarianism. It can be better, by motive-utilitarian standards, to have a pattern of motivation that will lead one to act wrongly, by act-utilitarian standards, than to have a motivation that would lead to right action. Even if there is no difference in external circumstances, the motivational pattern that leads to more useful actions is not necessarily the more useful of two motivational patterns, on the whole. For the consequences of any acts one is thereby led to perform are not always the only utility-bearing consequences of being influenced, to a given degree, by a motive.[6]

This can be seen in the following fictitious case. Jack is a lover of art who is visiting the cathedral at Chartres for the first time. He is greatly excited by it, enjoying it enormously, and acquiring memories which will give him pleasure for years to come. He is so excited that he is spending much more time at Chartres than he had planned, looking at the cathedral from as many interior and exterior angles, and examining as many of its details, as he can. In fact, he is spending too much time there, from a utilitarian point of view. He had planned to spend only the morning, but he is spending the whole day; and this is going to cause him considerable inconvenience and unpleasantness. He will miss

---

[5] It is difficult to say what is meant by the question, whether a certain pattern of motivation is causally possible for human beings, and how one would answer it. I shall sidestep these issues here, for I shall be making comparative evaluations of motives assumed to be possible, rather than trying to determine the most useful of all causally possible motivations.

[6] I am here denying, as applied to motives, what Bernard Williams rather obscurely calls the "act-adequacy premise" ["A Critique of Utilitarianism", in J. J. C. Smart and Willams, *Utilitarianism, For and Against* (New York: Cambridge, 1975), pp. 119–130].

his dinner, do several hours of night driving, which he hates, and have trouble finding a place to sleep. On the whole, he will count the day well spent, but some of the time spent in the cathedral will not produce as much utility as would have been produced by departing that much earlier. At the moment, for example, Jack is studying the sixteenth to eighteenth century sculpture on the stone choir screen. He is enjoying this less than other parts of the cathedral, and will not remember it very well. It is not completely unrewarding, but he would have more happiness on balance if he passed by these carvings and saved the time for an earlier departure. Jack knows all this, although it is knowledge to which he is not paying much attention. He brushes it aside and goes on looking at the choir screen because he is more strongly interested in seeing, as nearly as possible, everything in the cathedral than in maximizing utility. This action of his is therefore wrong by act-utilitarian standards, and in some measure intentionally so. And this is not the only such case. In the course of the day he knowingly does, for the same reason, several other things that have the same sort of act-utilitarian wrongness.

On the other hand, Jack would not have omitted these things unless he had been less interested in seeing everything in the cathedral than in maximizing utility. And it is plausible to suppose that if his motivation had been different in that respect, he would have enjoyed the cathedral much less. It may very well be that his caring more about seeing the cathedral than about maximizing utility has augmented utility, through enhancing his enjoyment, by more than it has diminished utility through leading him to spend too much time at Chartres. In this case his motivation is right by motive-utilitarian standards, even though it causes him to do several things that are wrong by act-utilitarian standards.

Perhaps it will be objected that the motive utilitarian should say that Jack ought indeed to have been as interested in the cathedral as he was, but ought to have been even more interested in maximizing utility. Thus he would have had as much enjoyment from the more rewarding parts of the cathedral, according to the objector, but would not have spent too much time on the less rewarding parts. The weak point in this objection is the assumption that Jack's enjoyment of the things he would still have seen would not be diminished in these circumstances. I think, and I take it that Sidgwick thought too,[7] that a great concern to squeeze out the last drop of utility is likely to be a great impediment to the enjoyment of life. Therefore it seems plausible to suppose that from a motive-utilitarian point of view Jack ought not only to have been as

---

[7]I believe this is the most natural reading of Sidgwick, but it may be barely possible to construe him as meaning only that the perpetual *consciousness* of such a concern would be an impediment. See *Methods*, 48f.

strongly interested in seeing the cathedral as he was, but also to have been as weakly interested in maximizing utility as he was.

In describing this case I have been treating the maximization of utility as a unitary end which Jack might have pursued for its own sake. Perhaps it will be suggested that, although an all-controlling desire for that end would have diminished utility by dulling Jack's enjoyment, he could have had undimmed enjoyment without wrong action if he had had the maximization of utility as an *inclusive end*—that is, if he had been moved by desire for more particular ends for their own sakes, but in exact proportion to their utility.[8] But this suggestion is not plausible. While he is in the cathedral Jack's desire to see everything in it is stronger, and his desire for the benefits of an early departure is weaker, than would be proportionate to the utility of those ends. And a stronger desire for an early departure would probably have interfered with his enjoyment just as much as a stronger desire for utility maximization as such. We are likely in general to enjoy life more if we are often more interested in the object of an enthusiastic pursuit, and less concerned about other ends, than would be proportionate to their utility. It follows that failing (to some extent) to have utility maximization as an inclusive end is often right by motive-utilitarian standards, and may be supposed to be so in Jack's case.

In order to justify the view that motive utilitarianism implies something practically equivalent to act utilitarianism one would have to show that the benefits that justify Jack's motivation by motive-utilitarian standards also justify his spending time on the choir screen by act-utilitarian standards. But they do not. For they are not consequences of his spending time there, but independent consequences of something that caused, or manifested itself in, his spending time there. It is not that deciding to devote only a cursory inspection to the choir screen would have put him in the wrong frame of mind for enjoying the visit. It is rather that, being in the right frame of mind for enjoying the visit, he could not bring himself to leave the choir screen as quickly as would have maximized utility

III

The act utilitarian may try to domesticate motive utilitarianism, arguing (A) that motive utilitarianism is merely a theorem of act utilitarianism, and denying (B) that behavior like Jack's inspection of the choir screen,

---

[8]The terminology of "dominant" and "inclusive" ends was developed by W. F. R. Hardie, "The Final Good in Aristotle's Ethics," *Philosophy*, XL, 154 (October 1965): 277–295; Rawls makes use of it. J. S. Mill seems to treat the maximization of utility as an inclusive end in *Utilitarianism*, ch. 4, §§ 5–8.

if resulting from obedience to the dictates of motive utilitarianism, can properly be called wrong action.

(A) Since act utilitarianism implies that one ought to do whatever has most utility, it implies that, other things equal, one ought to foster and promote in oneself those motives which have most utility. And that, it may be claimed, is precisely what motive utilitarianism teaches.

(B) Jack was once, let us suppose, an excessively conscientious act utilitarian. Recognizing the duty of cultivating more useful motives in himself, he took a course of capriciousness training, with the result that he now stands, careless of utility, before the choir screen. It would be unfair, it may be argued, to regard what Jack is now doing as a wrong action by utilitarian standards. Rather, we must see it as only an inescapable part of a larger, right action, which began with his enrolling for capriciousness training — just as we do not say that a person rightly jumped from a burning building, saving his life, but wrongly struck the ground, breaking his leg. It is unreasonable, on this view, to separate, for moral evaluation, actions that are causally inseparable.

Both of these arguments are to be rejected. The second (B) involves deep issues about the individuation of actions and the relation between causal determination and moral responsibility. It seems clear enough, however, that Jack's staying at the choir screen in separable from his earlier efforts at character reform in a way that striking the ground is not separable from jumping out of a building. Once you have jumped, it is no longer in your power to refrain from striking the ground, even if you want to. If you are sane and well informed about the situation, you have only one choice to make: to jump or not to jump. There is no further choice about hitting the ground, and therefore it is inappropriate to separate the impact from the leap, as an object of moral evaluation. But even after Jack has taken capriciousness training, it is still in his power to leave the choir screen if he wants to; it is just that he does not want to. His choice to stay and examine it is a new choice, which he did not make, years ago, when he decided to reform. He did decide then to become such that he would sometimes make nonutilitarian choices, but it may not even have occurred to him then that he would ever be in Chartres. It seems perfectly appropriate to ask whether the choice that he now makes is morally right or wrong.

It is plausible, indeed, to say that Jack is not acting wrongly in acting on the motivation that he has rightly cultivated in himself. But I think that is because it is plausible to depart from act utilitarianism at least so far as to allow the rightness or wrongness of Jack's action in this case to depend partly on the goodness or badness of his motive, and not solely on the utility of the act. It is noteworthy in this connection that it would be no less plausible to acquit Jack of wrongdoing if he had always been as easygoing as he now is about small increments of utility, even though there would not in that case be any larger action of character reform, of which Jack's present scrutiny of the choir screen could be regarded as an inescapable part.

A similar irrelevant emphasis on doing something about one's own motivational patterns also infects the attempt (A) to derive motive utilitarianism from act utilitarianism. Motive utilitarianism is not a theorem of act utilitarianism, for the simple reason that motive utilitarianism is not about what motives one ought to foster and promote, or *try* to have, but about what motives one ought to *have*. There is a preconception to be overcome here which threatens to frustrate from the outset the development of any independent ethics of motives. I refer to the assumption that "What should I (try to) do?" is *the* ethical question, and that we are engaged in substantive *ethical* thinking only insofar as we are considering *action*-guiding principles.[9] If we hold this assumption, we are almost bound to read "What motives should I have?" as "What motives should I try to develop and maintain in myself?"

There are other questions, however, that are as fundamental to ethics as "What should I do?" It is characteristic of moral as opposed to pragmatic thinking that, for example, the question, "Have I lived well?" is of interest for its own sake. In pragmatic self-appraisal that question is of interest only insofar as the answer may guide me toward future successes. If I am personally concerned, in more than this instrumental way, and not just in curiosity about whether I have lived well, my concern is not purely pragmatic, but involves at least a sense of style, if not of morality.

If the question is "Have I lived well?" the motives I have *had* are relevant, and not just the motives I have *tried* to have. If I tried to have the right motive, but nonetheless had the wrong one — if I tried to love righteousness and my neighbors, but failed and did my duty out of fear of hellfire for the most part — then I did not live as well as I would have lived if I had *had* the right motive.

Suppose, similarly, that Martha is an overscrupulous utilitarian, completely dominated by the desire to maximize utility. She has acted rightly, by act-utilitarian standards, just as often as she could. Among her right actions (or attempts at right action) are many *attempts* to become strongly interested in particular objects — more strongly, indeed, than is proportionate to their utility. For she realizes that she and her acquaintances would be happier if she had such interests. But all these attempts have failed.

Mary, on the other hand, has not had to work on herself to develop such nonutilitarian interests, but has always had them; and, largely because of them, her motivational patterns have had more utility, on

---

[9]Cf. Jan Narveson, *Morality and Utility* (Baltimore, Md.: John Hopkins, 1967), p. 105: "Let us begin by recalling the primary function of ethical principles: to tell us what to do, i.e., to guide action. Whatever else an ethical principle is supposed to do, it must do that, otherwise it could not (logically) be an ethical principle at all."

the whole, than Martha's. The motive utilitarian will take this as a reason (not necessarily decisive) for saying that Martha has *lived less well* than Mary. This censure of Martha's motives is not derivable from act utilitarianism, for her actions have been the best that were causally possible for her. (If you are tempted to say that Martha's conscientiousness if better than Mary's more useful motives, you are experiencing a reluctance to apply the test of utility to motives.)

IV

I have argued that right action, by act-utilitarian standards, and right motivation, by motive-utilitarian standards, are incompatable in some cases. It does not immediately follow, but it may further be argued, that act utilitarianism and motive utilitarianism are incompatible theories.

One argument for this conclusion is suggested, in effect, by Bernard Williams. He does not formulate or discuss motive utilitarianism, but he holds that it is inconsistent of J. J. C. Smart, following Sidgwick, "to present direct [i.e., act] utilitarianism as a doctrine merely about justification and not about motivation." Williams's argument is,

> There is no distinctive place for *direct* utilitarianism unless it is, within fairly narrow limits, a doctrine about how one should decide what to do. This is because its distinctive doctrine is about what acts are right, and, especially for utilitarians, the only distinctive interest or point of the question what acts are right, relates to the situation of deciding to do them (*op. cit.*, 128).

The doctrine about motives that Williams believes to be implied by act utilitarianism is presumably the doctrine, discarded at the beginning of my present essay, that one ought always to be controlled by the desire or purpose of maximizing utility. And this doctrine, if conjoined with plausible empirical beliefs illustrated in section II above, is inconsistent with motive utilitarianism.

There are two questionable points in Williams's argument. One is the claim that for utilitarians the only use of the question, What acts are right? is for guidance in deciding what to do. He defends this claim, arguing that "utilitarians in fact are not very keen on people blaming themselves, which they see as an unproductive activity," and that they therefore will not be interested in the question, "Did he (or I) do the right thing?" (124). I am not convinced by this defense. Blame is a self-administered negative reinforcement which may perhaps cause desirable modifications of future behavior. The retrospective question about the evaluation of one's action is a question in which one can hardly help taking an interest if one has a conscience; one who desires to act well will naturally desire to *have* acted well. And the desire to act well, at least in weighty matters, will surely be approved on motive-utilitarian grounds.

But suppose, for the sake of argument, we grant Williams that the point of act-utilitarian judgments, when they have a point, is to guide us in deciding what to do. His argument still rests on the assumption that the act utilitarian is committed to the view that it is generally useful to ask what acts are right, and that one ought always or almost always to be interested in the question. Why should the act utilitarian be committed to this view? If he is also a motive utilitarian, he will have reason to say that, although it is indeed useful to be guided by utilitarian judgments in actions of great consequence, it is sometimes better to be relatively uninterested in considerations of utility (and so of morality). "For everything there is a season and a time for every matter under heaven: . . . a time to kill, and a time to heal; a time to break down, and a time to build up," said the Preacher (Ecclesiastes 3:1, 3 RSV). The act-and-motive utilitarian adds, "There is time to be moral, and a time to be amoral." (The act-and-motive utilitarian is one who holds both act and motive utilitarianism as *theories*. He does not, for he cannot, always satisfy the demands of both theories in his acts and motives.)

Perhaps it will be objected that this reply to Williams overlooks the utility of conscientiousness. Conscience is, in part, a motive: the desire to act or live in accordance with moral principles. If the moral principles are mainly sound, it is so useful a motive that it is important, from a motive-utilitarian standpoint, not to undermine it. This consideration might make a motive utilitarian reluctant to approve the idea of "a time to be amoral," lest such "moral holidays" weaken a predominantly useful conscience.

The question facing the act-and-motive utilitarian at this point is, what sort of conscience has greatest utility. We have seen reason to believe that an act-utilitarian conscience that is scrupulous about small increments of utility would have bad effects on human happiness, smothering many innocent enjoyments in a wet blanket of excessive earnestness. A more useful sort of conscience is probably available to the act-and-motive utilitarian. It would incorporate a vigorous desire to *live well*, in terms of the over-all utility of his life, but not necessarily to *act rightly* on every occasion. Having such a conscience, he would be strongly concerned (1) not to act in ways gravely detrimental to utility, and (2) not to be in a bad motivational state. If he performs a mildly unutilitarian action as an inevitable consequence of the most useful motivation that he can have, on the other hand, he is still living as well as possible, by his over-all utilitarian standards; and there is no reason why such action should undermine his determination to live well. A conscience of this sort seems as possible, and at least as likely to be stable, as a conscience that insists on maximizing utility in every action.

Thus the act-and-motive utilitarian has good motive-utilitarian reasons for believing that he should sometimes be, in relation to his act-utilitarian principles, amoral.

V

But this conclusion may be taken, quite apart from Williams's argument, as grounds for thinking that act utilitarianism and motive utilitarianism are incompatible in the sense that holding the latter ought reasonably to prevent us from holding the former as a *moral* theory. The incompatibility has to do with moral seriousness. The problem is not just that one cannot *succeed* in living up to the ideals of both theories simultaneously. It is rather that the motive utilitarian is led to the conclusion that it is morally better on many occasions to be so motivated that one will not even *try* to do what one ought, by act-utilitarian standards, to do. If the act-and-motive utilitarian accepts this conclusion, however, we must wonder whether all his act-utilitarian judgments about what one ought to do are really judgments of *moral* obligation. For it is commonly made a criterion for a theory's being a theory of *moral* obligation, that it claim a special seriousness for its judgments of obligation. By this criterion, act utilitarianism cannot really be a theory of moral obligation (as it purports to be) if it is conjoined with the view that some of its dictates should be taken as lightly as motive utilitarianism would lead us to think they should be taken.

This argument depends on the triviality of any reasonable human interest in some of the obligations that act utilitarianism would lay on us. And the triviality is due to the totalitarian character of act utilitarianism, to its insistence that, as Sidgwick puts it, "it is *always* wrong for a man knowingly to do *anything* other than what he believes to be most conducive to Universal Happiness" (*Methods*, 492, italics mine).

Without this triviality a conflict between the ethics of actions and the ethics of motives need not destroy the seriousness of either. Maybe *no* plausible comprehensive ethical theory can avoid all such conflicts. Are there *some* circumstances in which it is best, for example, in the true morality of motives, to be unable to bring oneself to sacrifice the happiness of a friend when an important duty obliges one, in the true morality of actions, to do so? I don't know. But if there are, the interests involved, on both sides, are far from trivial, and the seriousness of both moralities can be maintained. If one fails to perform the important duty, one ought, seriously, to feel guilty; but one could not do one's duty in such a case without having a motivation of which one ought, seriously, to be ashamed. The situation presents a tragic inevitability of moral disgrace.

There are, accordingly, two ways in which the utilitarian might deal with the argument if he has been trying to combine act and motive utilitarianism and accepts the view I have urged on him about the kind of conscience it would be most useful to have. (A) He could simply acknowledge that he is operating with a modified conception of moral obligation, under which a special seriousness attaches to some but not all moral obligations.[10] He would claim that his use of "morally ought" nonetheless has enough similarity, in other respects, to the traditional use, to be a reasonable extension of it.

(B) The other, to my mind more attractive, way is to modify the act-utilitarian principle, eliminating trivial obligations, and limiting the realm of duty to actions that would be of concern to a conscience of the most useful sort. Under such a limitation it would not be regarded as morally wrong, in general, to fail to maximize utility by a *small* margin. One's relatively uninfluential practical choices would be subject to moral judgment only indirectly, through the motive-utilitarian judgment on the motives on which one acted (and perhaps a character-utilitarian judgment on the traits of character manifested by the action). Some acts, however, such as shoplifting in a dime store or telling inconsequential lies, would still be regarded as wrong even if only slightly detrimental in the particular case, because it is clear that they would be opposed by the most useful sort of conscience. I leave unanswered here the question whether a conscience of the most useful kind would be offended by some acts that maximize utility—particularly by some utility-maximizing violations of such rules as those against stealing and lying. If the answer is affirmative, the position we are considering would have approximately the same practical consequences as are commonly expected from rule utilitarianism. This position—that we have a *moral duty* to do an act, if and only if it would be demanded of us by the most useful kind of conscience we could have—may be called "conscience utilitarianism," and is a very natural position for a motive utilitarian to take in the ethics of actions.

The moral point of view—the point of view from which moral judgments are made—cannot safely be defined as a point of view in which the test of utility is applied directly to all objects of moral evaluation. For it is doubtful that the most useful motives, and the most useful sort of conscience, are related to the most useful acts in the way that the motives, and especially the kind of conscience, regarded as right must be related to the acts regarded as right in anything that is to count as a morality. And therefore it is doubtful that direct application of the test of utility to everything results in a system that counts as a morality.

---

[10]It may be thought that Sidgwick has already begun this modification, by holding that good actions ought not to be praised, nor bad ones blamed, except insofar as it is useful to praise and blame them. See *Methods*, 428 f., 493.

VI

Considered on its own merits, as a theory in the ethics of motives, which may or may not be combined with some other type of utilitarianism in the ethics of actions, how plausible is motive utilitarianism? That is a question which we can hardly begin to explore in a brief paper, because of the variety of forms that the theory might assume, and the difficulty of stating some of them. The exploration might start with a distinction between individualistic and universalistic motive utilitarianism, analogous to the distinction between and act and rule utilitarianism.

Individualistic motive utilitarianism holds that a person's motivation on any given occasion is better, the greater the utility of *his* having it on *that* occasion. This seemed to Bentham, on the whole, the least unsatisfactory view about the moral worth of motives:

> The only way, it should seem, in which a motive can with safety and propriety be styled good or bad, is with reference to its effects *in each individual instance* (*Introduction*, 120, italics mine).

This doctrine seems liable to counterexamples similar to those which are commonly urged against act utilitarianism. An industrialist's greed, a general's bloodthirstiness, may on some occasions have better consequences on the whole than kinder motives would, and even predictably so. But we want to say that they remain worse motives.

Universalistic motive utilitarianism is supposed to let us say this, but is difficult to formulate. If we try to state it as the thesis that motives are better, the greater the utility of *everybody's* having them on *all* occasions, we implausibly ignore the utility of diversity in motives. A more satisfactory view might be that a motivation is better, the greater the average probable utility of *anyone's* having it on *any* occasion. This formulation gives rise to questions about averaging: do we weigh equally the utility of a motive on all the occasions when it could conceivably occur, or do we have some formula for weighing more heavily the occasions when it is more likely to occur? There are also difficult issues about the relevant description of the motive. One and the same concrete individual motive might be described correctly as a desire to protect Henry Franklin, a desire to protect (an individual whom one knows to be) one's spouse, a desire to protect (an individual whom one knows to be) the chief executive of one's government, and a desire to protect (an individual whom one knows to be) a betrayer of the public trust; these motive types surely have very different average utilities. If one makes the relevant description of the motive too full, of course, one risks making universalistic motive utilitarianism equivalent to individualistic.[11] If the description is not full enough, it will be hard

---

[11]By a process similar to that by which David Lyons, in his *Forms and Limits of Utilitarianism* (New York: Oxford, 1965), has tried to show that rule utilitarianism is equivalent to act utilitarianism.

to get any determination of average utility at all. Bentham's principal effort, in his discussion of the ethics of motives, is to show, by a tiresome profusion of examples, that the application of the test of utility to sorts of motive yields no results, because "there is no sort of motive but may give birth to any sort of action" (*Introduction*, 128); his argument depends on the use of very thin descriptions of sorts of motive.

The doctrine that a type of motive is better, the greater the utility of commending or fostering it in a system of moral education, might seem to be another version of universalistic motive utilitarianism, but is not a form of motive utilitarianism at all. For in it the test of utility is directly applied not to motives or types of motive, but to systems of moral education.

I am not convinced (nor even inclined to believe) that any purely utilitarian theory about the worth of motives is correct. But motive-utilitarian considerations will have some place in any sound theory of the ethics of motives, because utility, or conduciveness to human happiness (or more generally, to the good), is certainly a great advantage in motives (as in other things), even if it is not a morally decisive advantage.

BIBLIOGRAPHY

Part I: History and General Works

1. CLASSICAL UTILITARIANISM

David Hume. *Treatise of Human Nature*, Book III, London, 1740.
————. *Enquiry Concerning the Principles of Morals*, London, 1751.
Jeremy Bentham. *Introduction to the Principles of Morals and Legislation*, London, 1789.
John Stuart Mill. *Bentham, London and Westminster Review*, 1838.
————. *On Liberty*, London, 1859.
————. *Utilitarianism*, London, 1863.
————. *Autobiography*, London, 1873.
Henry Sidgwick. *The Methods of Ethics*, London, 1874.

2. CLASSICAL CRITICS

Karl Marx. *Capital*, Volume I, Chapter 24, section 5, 1867.
Fyodor Dostoyevsky. *Crime and Punishment*, 1866.
Friedrich Nietzsche. *On the Genealogy of Morals*, Preface and First Essay, 1887.
Charles Dickens. *Hard Times*, London, 1854.
John Grote. *An Examination of the Utilitarian Philosophy*, Cambridge, 1870.
F. H. Bradley. *Ethical Studies*, Chapter 3, Oxford, 1876.
G. E. Moore. *Principia Ethica*, Chapter 3, Cambridge, 1903.

3. HISTORICAL STUDIES

Leslie Stephen. *The English Utilitarians*, 3 volumes, London, 1900.
Elie Halevy. *The Growth of Philosophic Radicalism*, translated by M. Morris, London, 1928.

John Plamenatz. *The English Utilitarians*, Oxford, 1949.
Karl Britton. *John Stuart Mill*, London, 1953.
R. P. Anschutz. *The Philosophy of John Stuart Mill*, London, 1953.
Alasdair MacIntyre. *A Short History of Ethics*, New York, 1966.
————. *After Virtue, A Study in Moral Theory*, Chapter 6, London, 1981.
J. B. Schneewind (ed.). *Mill, A Collection of Critical Essays*, London, 1968.
Alan Ryan. *John Stuart Mill*, New York, 1970.
Anthony Quinton. *Utilitarian Ethics*, London, 1973.
J. B. Schneewind. *Sidgwick's Ethics and Victorian Moral Philosophy*, Oxford, 1977.

4. General Works on Utilitarianism

A. J. Ayer. "The Principle of Utility," in A. J. Ayer: *Philosophical Essays*, London, 1954.
Jan Narveson. *Morality and Utility*, Baltimore, 1967.
J. J. C. Smart. "Utilitarianism," *The Encyclopedia of Philosophy*, Vol. 8, pp. 206–212.
Michael D. Bayles (ed.) *Contemporary Utilitarianism*, New York, 1968.
J. J. C. Smart and Bernard Williams. *Utilitarianism, For and Against*, Cambridge, 1973.
Amartya Sen and Bernard Williams (eds.). *Utilitarianism and Beyond*, Cambridge, 1982.

Part II: Issues

1. Foundations

John Stuart Mill. *Utilitarianism*, Chapter 4, 1863.
Henry Sidgwick. *The Methods of Ethics*, Book, Chapters 2 and 3, London, 1874.
G. E. Moore. *Principia Ethica*, Chapter 3, Cambridge, 1903.
Mary Warnock. *Ethics Since 1900*, Oxford, 1960, Chapter 1.
Alan Ryan. *John Stuart Mill*, Chapter 11, New York, 1970.
John C. Harsanyi. *Morality and the Theory of Rational Behavior, Social Research*, 1977.
R. M. Hare. *Freedom and Reason*, Parts II and III, Oxford, 1963.
————. "Ethical Theory and Utilitarianism," in H. D. Lewis (ed.), *Contemporary British Philosophy*, London, 1976.
————. *Moral Thinking, Its Levels, Method and Point*, Part II, Oxford, 1981.
T. M. Scanlon. "Contractualism and Utilitarianism," in Amartya Sen and Bernard Williams (eds.), *Utilitarianism and Beyond*, Cambridge, 1982.
Bernard Williams. *Ethics and the Limits of Philosophy*, Chapter 5, London, 1985.

2. Happiness

Aldous Huxley. *Brave New World*, London, 1932.
C. C. W. Taylor. "Pleasure," *Analysis Supplement*, 1963.
Anthony Kenny. "Happiness," *Proceedings of the Aristotelian Society*, 1965–1966.
D. L. Perry. *The Concept of Pleasure*, The Hague, 1967.
Jean Austin. "Pleasure and Happiness," *Philosophy*, 1968.

J. L. Cowan. *Pleasure and Pain*, New York, 1968.
J. C. B. Gosling. *Pleasure and Desire*, Oxford, 1969.
Robert Nozick. *Anarchy, State and Utopia*, New York, Chapter 3, 1974.
Amartya Sen. *Rational Fools: A Critique of the Behavioral Foundations of Economic Theory, Philosophy and Public Affairs*, 1977.
Richard Brandt. *A Theory of the Good and the Right*, Oxford, 1979.
Amartya Sen. "Plural Utility," *Proceedings of the Aristotelian Society*, 1981.
Jon Elster. *Sour Grapes; Studies in the Subversion of Rationality*, Chapter 3, Cambridge and Paris, 1983.
Derek Parfit. *Reasons and Persons*, Appendix I: What Makes Someone's Life Go Best, Oxford, 1984.
James Griffin. *Wellbeing, Its Meaning, Measurement and Moral Importance*, Parts I and II, Oxford, 1986.
Richard Warner. *Freedom, Enjoyment and Happiness*, Ithaca, 1987.

3. PERSONS, JUSTICE AND RIGHTS

Nicholas Rescher. *Distributive Justice, A Constructive Critique of the Utilitarian Theory of Distribution*, Chapters 1 and 2, Indianapolis, 1965.
H. J. McCloskey. "Utilitarian and Retributive Punishment, *Journal of Philosophy*, 1967
John Rawls. *A Theory of Justice*, sections 5 and 27 to 30, Harvard, 1971.
Derek Parfit. *Reasons and Persons*, Chapter 15, Oxford, 1984.
Bernard Williams. "Persons, Character and Morality," in Bernard Williams, *Moral Luck*, Cambridge, 1981.
Robert Nozick. *Anarchy, State and Utopia*, Chapter 7 and 8, New York, 1974.
Ronald Dworkin. "Reverse Discrimination," in *Taking Rights Seriously*, London, 1977.
H. L. A. Hart. "Between Utility and Rights," in Alan Ryan (ed.), *The Idea of Freedom, Essays in Honour of Isaiah Berlin*, Oxford, 1979.
Ronald Dworkin. "Is There a Right to Pornography?," *Oxford Journal of Legal Studies*, 1981.
T. M. Scanlon. "Preference and Urgency," *Journal of Philosophy*, 1975.
"Rights, Goals, and Fairness," in Stuart Hampshire (ed.), *Public and Private Morality*, Cambridge, 1978.
J. J. C. Smart. "Utilitarianism and Justice," *Journal of Chinese Philosophy*, 1978.
Amartya Sen. "Utilitarianism and Welfarism," *Journal of Philosophy*, 1979.
————. "Rights and Agency," *Philosophy and Public Affairs*, 1982.
R. G. Frey (ed.). *Utility and Rights*, Minneapolis, 1984.
James Griffin. *Wellbeing, Its Meaning, Measurement and Moral Importance*, Part III, Oxford, 1986.

4. LIFE AND DEATH

(a) UTILITARIANISM AND THE MORALITY OF KILLING

Richard G. Henson. "Utilitarianism and the Wrongness of Killing," *Philosophical Review*, 1971.
R. Steven Talmage. "Utilitarianism and the Morality of Killing, Philosophy, 1972.
Marvin Kohl. *The Morality of Killing*, London, 1974.
H. J. McCloskey. "The Right to Life," *Mind*, 1975.
John Harris. "The Survival Lottery," *Philosophy*, 1975.

Philip E. Devine. *The Ethics of Homicide*, Ithaca, 1978.
Peter Singer. *Animal Liberation, Towards an End to Man's Inhumanity to Animals*, London, 1976.
Wayne Sumner. *Abortion and Moral Theory*, Princeton, 1981.
Michael Tooley. *Abortion and Infanticide*, Oxford, 1983.
John Harris. *The Value of Life, An Introduction to Medical Ethics*, London, 1985.
James Rachels. *The End of Life, Euthanasia and Morality*, Oxford, 1986.

(b) CREATING PEOPLE

Henry Sidgwick. *The Methods of Ethics*, Book 4, Chapter one, London, 1974.
Jan Narveson. "Utilitarianism and New Generations," *Mind*, 1967.
———. "Moral Problems of Population," *The Monist*, 1973.
M. D. Bayles (ed.). *Ethics and Population*, Cambridge, Mass., 1976.
R. I. Sikora and Brian Barry (eds.). *Obligations to Future Generations*, Philadelphia, 1978.
Onora O'Neill and William Ruddick (eds.). *Having Children, Philosophical and Legal Reflections on Parenthood*, New York, 1979.
Jefferson McMahan. "Problems of Population Theory," *Ethics*, 1981.
G. Kavka. "*The Paradox of Future Individuals*," *Philosophy and Public Affairs*, 1982.
Derek Parfit. "Future Generations: Further Problems" *Philosophy and Public Affairs*, 1982.
T. M. Hurka. "Value and Population Size," *Ethics*, 1983.
Derek Parfit: *Reasons and Persons*, Chapters 16–19, Oxford, 1984.

5. CONSEQUENCES AND CHARACTER

(a) CONSEQUENTIALISM: GENERAL

G. E. M. Anscombe. "Modern Moral Philosophy," *Philosophy*, 1958.
Lars Bergstrom. *The Alternatives and Consequences of Actions, An Essay on Certain Fundamental Notions in Teleological Ethics*, Stockholm, 1966.
Judith Jarvis Thomson. "Killing, Letting Die and the Trolley Problem," *The Monist*, 1975.
Alan Donagan. *The Theory of Morality*, Chapter 6, Chicago, 1977.
Samuel Scheffler. *The Rejection of Consequentialism*, Oxford, 1982.
Michael Slote. *Commonsense Morality and Consequentialism*, London, 1985.
Philippa Foot. "Utilitarianism and the Virtues," *Mind*, 1985.
Stephen L. Darwall. "Agent-centered Restrictions from the Inside Out," *Philosophical Studies*, 1986.
Samuel Scheffler (ed.). *Consequentialism and Its Critics*, Oxford, 1988.

(b) CONSEQUENCES, CHARACTER AND INTEGRITY

A. Solzhenitsyn. *The First Circle*, New York, 1969.
———. "*One Word of Truth . . .*" London, 1972.
Bernard Williams. *A Critique of Utilitarianism*, in J.J.C. Smart and Bernard Williams, *Utilitarianism, For and Against*, Cambridge, 1973.
G. Kavka. "Some Paradoxes of Deterrence," *Journal of Philosophy*, 1978.
Stuart Hampshire, "Morality and Pessimism," in Stuart Hampshire, *Public and Private Morality*, Cambridge, 1978.
Nancy Davis. "Utilitarianism and Responsibility," *Ratio*, 1980.
Bernard Williams. "Utilitarianism and Moral Self-Indulgence," in Bernard Williams, *Moral Luck*, Cambridge, 1981.

R. M. Hare. *Moral Thinking, Its Levels, Methods and Point*, Chapters 2 and 3, Oxford, 1981.
Peter Railton. "Alienation, Consequentialism and the Demands of Morality," Philosophy and Public Affairs, 1984.
Conrad D. Johnson. "The Authority of the Moral Agent," *Journal of Philosophy*, 1985.
Bernard Williams. *Ethics and the Limits of Philosophy*, Chapter 5, London, 1985.

(c) Does Consequentialism Demand Too Much?

Peter Singer. "Famine, Affluence and Morality," *Philosophy and Public Affairs*, 1972.
Carolyn Morillo. "Doing, Refraining and the Strenuousness of Morality," *American Philosophical Quarterly*, 1977.
Samuel Scheffler. *The Rejection of Consequentialism*, Oxford, 1982.
James Fishkin. *The Limits of Obligation*, New Haven, 1982.
Susan Wolf. "Moral Saints," *Journal of Philosophy*, 1982.
Robert M. Adams. "Saints," *Journal of Philosophy*, 1984.
David O. Brink. "Utilitarian Morality and the Personal Point of View," *Journal of Philosophy*, 1986.
Thomas Nagel. *The View from Nowhere*, New York, 1986.
Shelly Kagan. *The Limits of Morality*, Oxford, 1989.

6. Direct and Oblique Strategies

Henry Sidgwick. *The Methods of Ethics*, Book IV, Chapter 5, London, 1874.
John Rawls. *Two Concepts of Rules, Philosophical Review*, 1955.
Thomas Schelling. *The Strategy of Conflict*. Cambridge, Mass., 1960.
Colin Strang. "What if Everyone Did That?," in Judith Jarvis Thomson and Gerald Dworkin (eds.), *Ethics*, New York, 1968.
David Lyons. *The Forms and Limits of Utilitarianism*, Oxford, 1965.
Joel Feinberg. "The Forms and Limits of Utilitarianism", *Philosophical Review*, 1967.
D. H. Hodgson. *Consequences of Utilitarianism*, Oxford, 1967.
Gertrude Ezorsky. "A Defense of Rule Utilitarianism Against David Lyons Who Insists on Tieing it to Act Utilitarianism, Plus a Brand New Way of Checking Out General Utilitarian Properties," *Journal of Philosophy*, 1968.
J. H. Sobel. "Utilitarianism, Simple and General," *Inquiry*, 1970.
Peter Singer. "Is Act Utilitarianism Self-Defeating?," *Philosophical Review*, 1972.
Rolf Sartorius. *Individual Conduct and Social Norms, A Utilitarian Account of Social Union and the Rule of Law*, Encino, 1975.
Michael Stocker. "The Schizophrenia of Modern Ethical Theories," *Journal of Philosophy*, 1976.
Robert M. Adams. "Motive Utilitarianism," *Journal of Philosophy*, 1976.
Richard Wollheim. "John Stuart Mill and Isaiah Berlin: The Ends of Life and the Preliminaries of Morality," in Alan Ryan (ed.): *The Idea of Freedom, Essays in Honour of Isaiah Berlin*, Oxford, 1979.
Donald Regan. *Utilitarianism and Cooperation*, Oxford, 1980.
R. M. Hare. *Moral Thinking, Its Levels, Method and Point*, Chapter 3, Oxford, 1981.
T. M. Scanlon. "Levels of Moral Thinking," in Douglas Seanor and N. Fotion (eds.), *Hare and Critics, Essays on "Moral Thinking"*, Oxford, 1988.